Written by Joe Harris

Art by **Matthew Dow Smith** and **Andrew Currie**

Colors by **Jordie Bellaire** and **Sebastian Cheng**

Letters by **Chris Mowry** and **Dezi Sienty**

Series Edits by **Denton J. Tipton**

Executive Producer: **Chris Carter**

Cover Art by **Menton3**

Collection Edits by **Justin Eisinger** and **Alonzo Simon**

Collection Design by **Ron Estevez**

Publisher: **Ted Adams**

The X-Files created by **Chris Carter**

Special thanks to **Joshua Izzo** and **Nicole Spiegel** at Twentieth Century Fox, and **Gabe Rotter** at Ten Thirteen Productions.

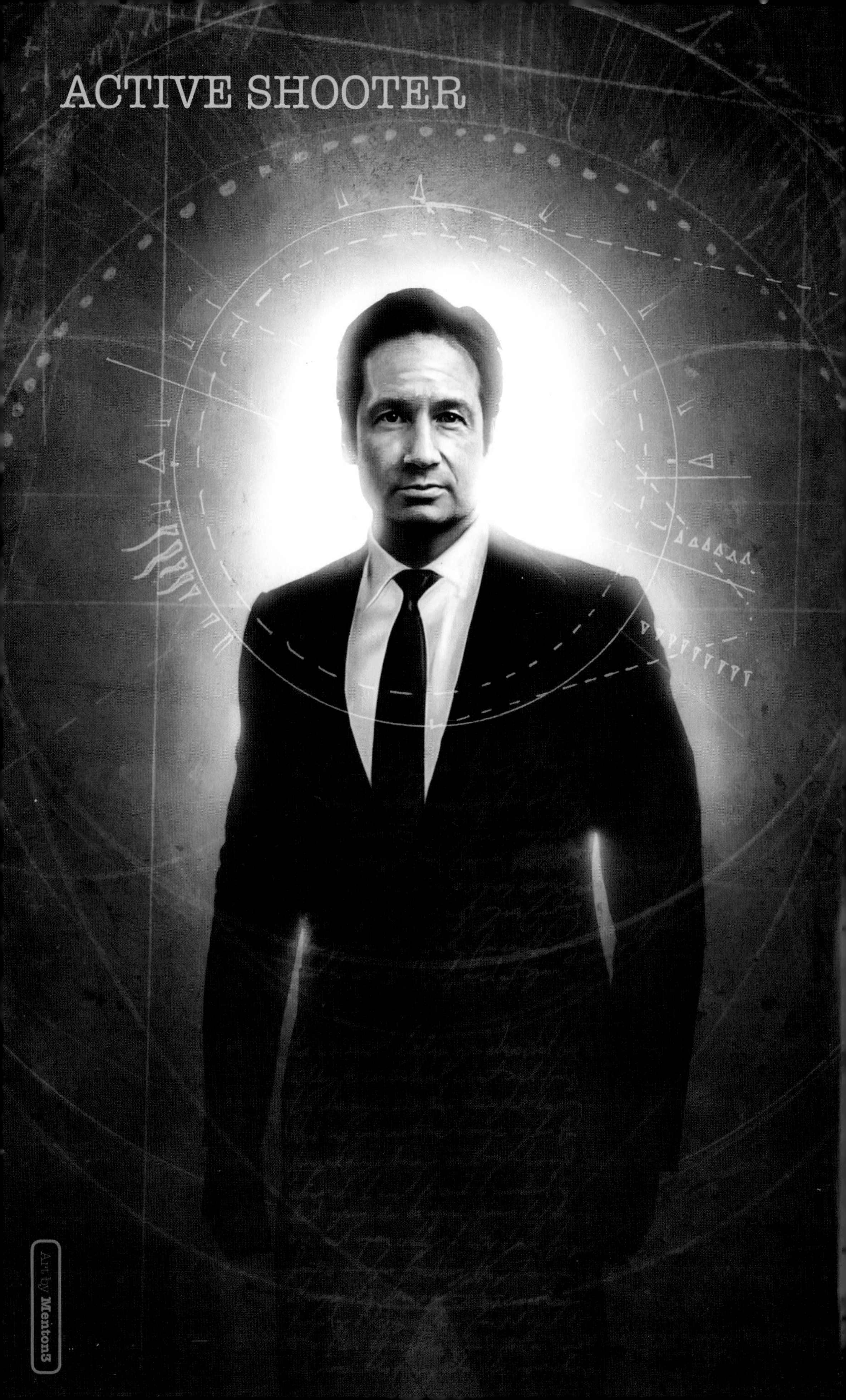
ACTIVE SHOOTER
Art by Menton3

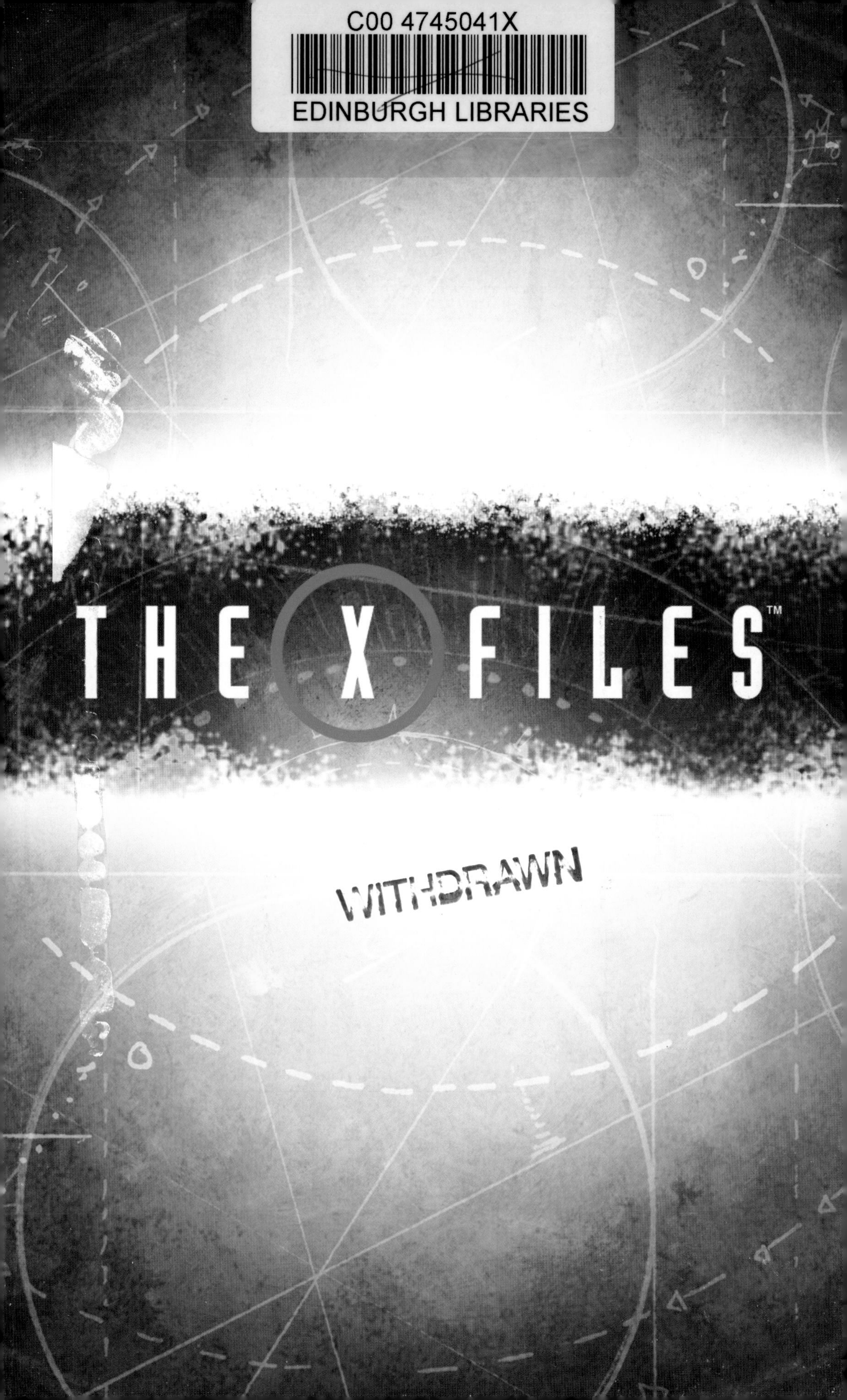
THE X FILES™

Become our fan on Facebook **facebook.com/idwpublishing**
Follow us on Twitter **@idwpublishing**
Subscribe to us on YouTube **youtube.com/idwpublishing**
See what's new on Tumblr **tumblr.idwpublishing.com**
Check us out on Instagram **instagram.com/idwpublsing**

ISBN: 978-1-63140-783-3   19 18 17 16   1 2 3 4

Originally published as THE X-FILES issues #1–5.

Ted Adams, CEO & Publisher
Greg Goldstein, President & COO
Robbie Robbins, EVP/Sr. Graphic Artist
Chris Ryall, Chief Creative Officer/Editor-in-Chief
Laurie Windrow, Senior Vice President of Sales & Marketing
Matthew Ruzicka, CPA, Chief Financial Officer
Dirk Wood, VP of Marketing
Lorelei Bunjes, VP of Digital Services
Jeff Webber, VP of Licensing, Digital and Subsidiary Rights
Jerry Bennington, VP of New Product Development

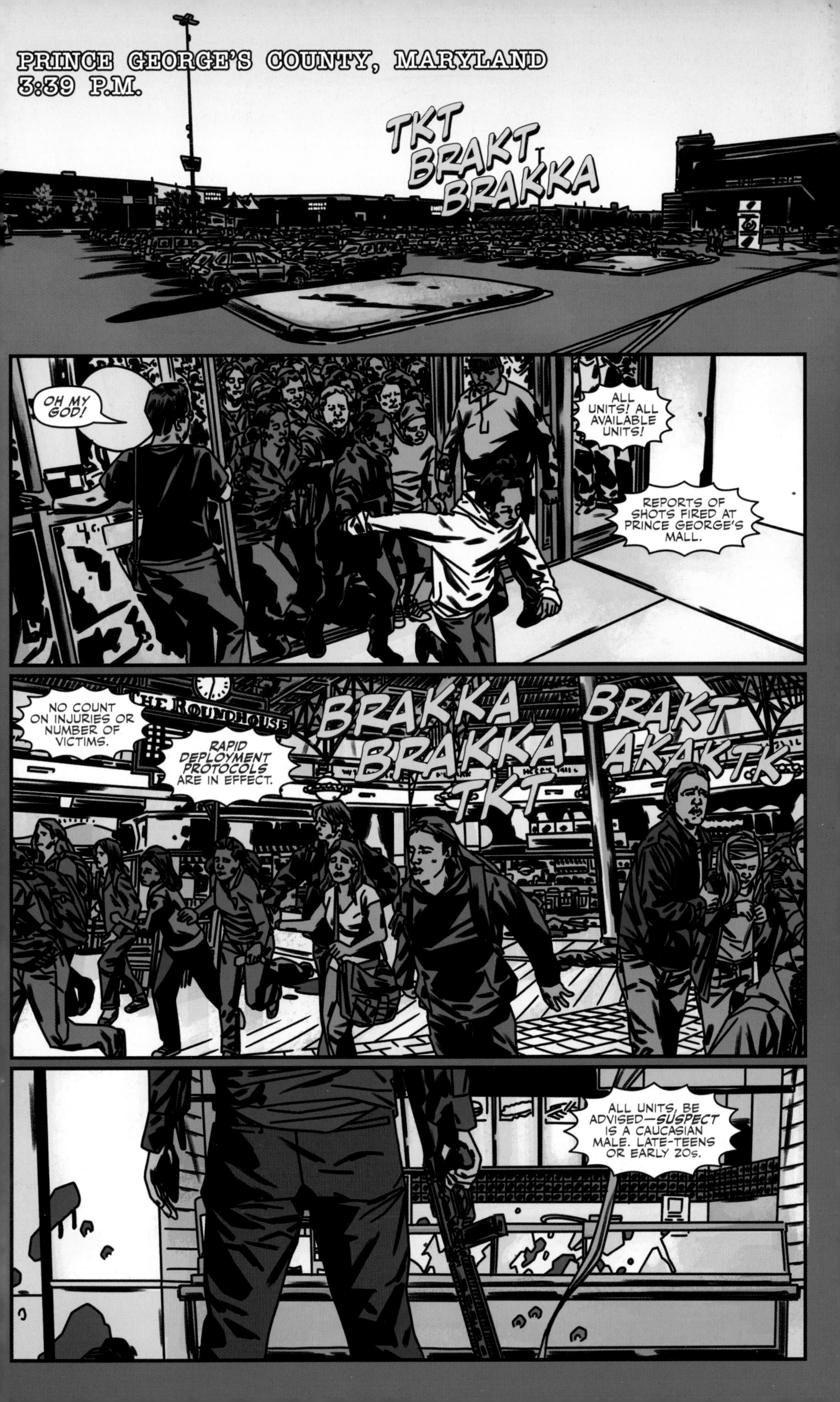
PRINCE GEORGE'S COUNTY, MARYLAND
3:39 P.M.
TKT BRAKT BRAKKA
OH MY GOD!
ALL UNITS! ALL AVAILABLE UNITS!
REPORTS OF SHOTS FIRED AT PRINCE GEORGE'S MALL.
NO COUNT ON INJURIES OR NUMBER OF VICTIMS.
THE ROUNDHOUSE
RAPID DEPLOYMENT PROTOCOLS ARE IN EFFECT.
BRAKKA BRAKT BRAKKA AKAKTK TKT
ALL UNITS, BE ADVISED—SUSPECT IS A CAUCASIAN MALE. LATE-TEENS OR EARLY 20s.

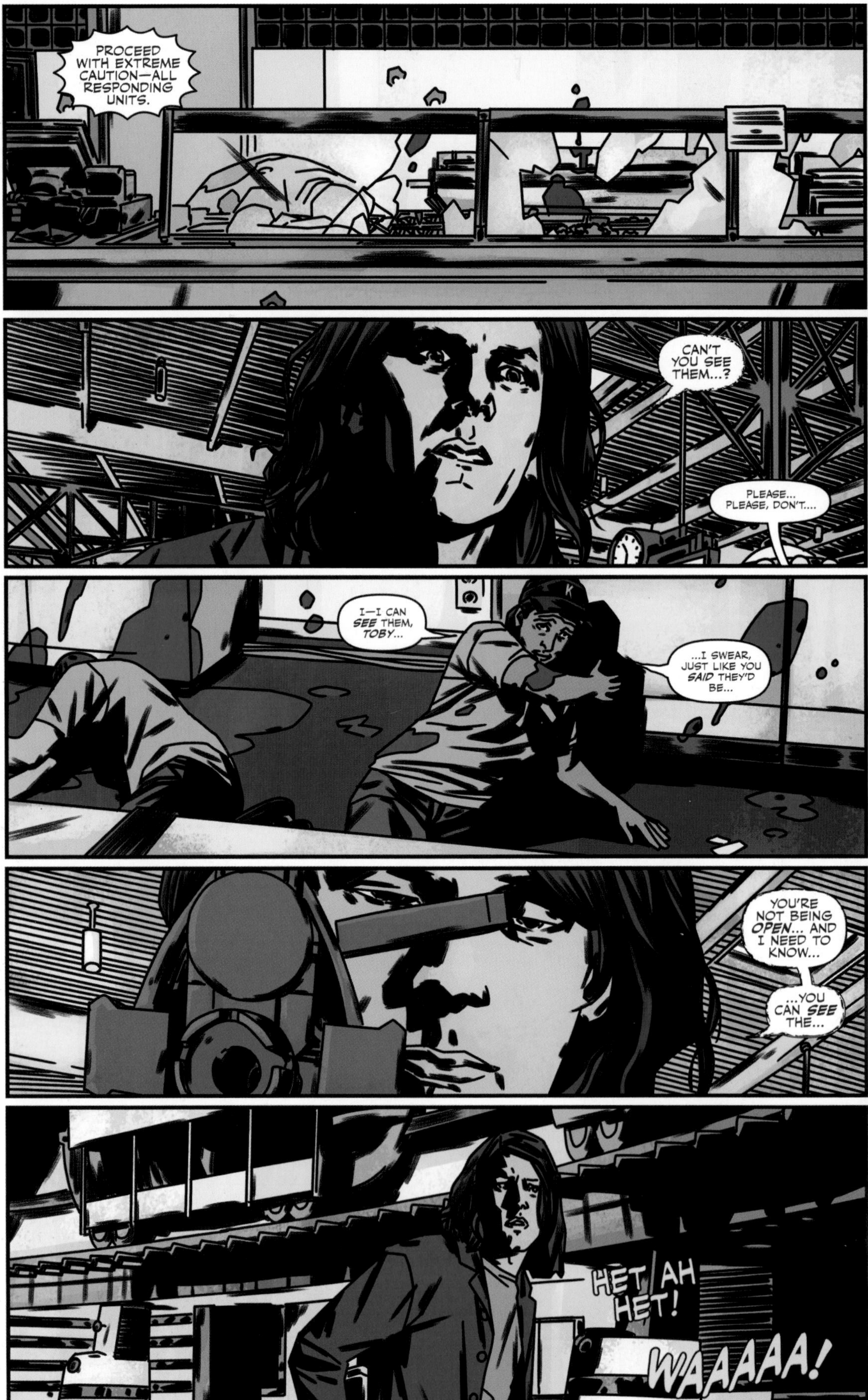
PROCEED WITH EXTREME CAUTION—ALL RESPONDING UNITS.
CAN'T YOU SEE THEM...?
PLEASE... PLEASE, DON'T....
I—I CAN SEE THEM, TOBY...
...I SWEAR, JUST LIKE YOU SAID THEY'D BE...
YOU'RE NOT BEING OPEN... AND I NEED TO KNOW...
...YOU CAN SEE THE...
HET AH HET!
WAAAAA!

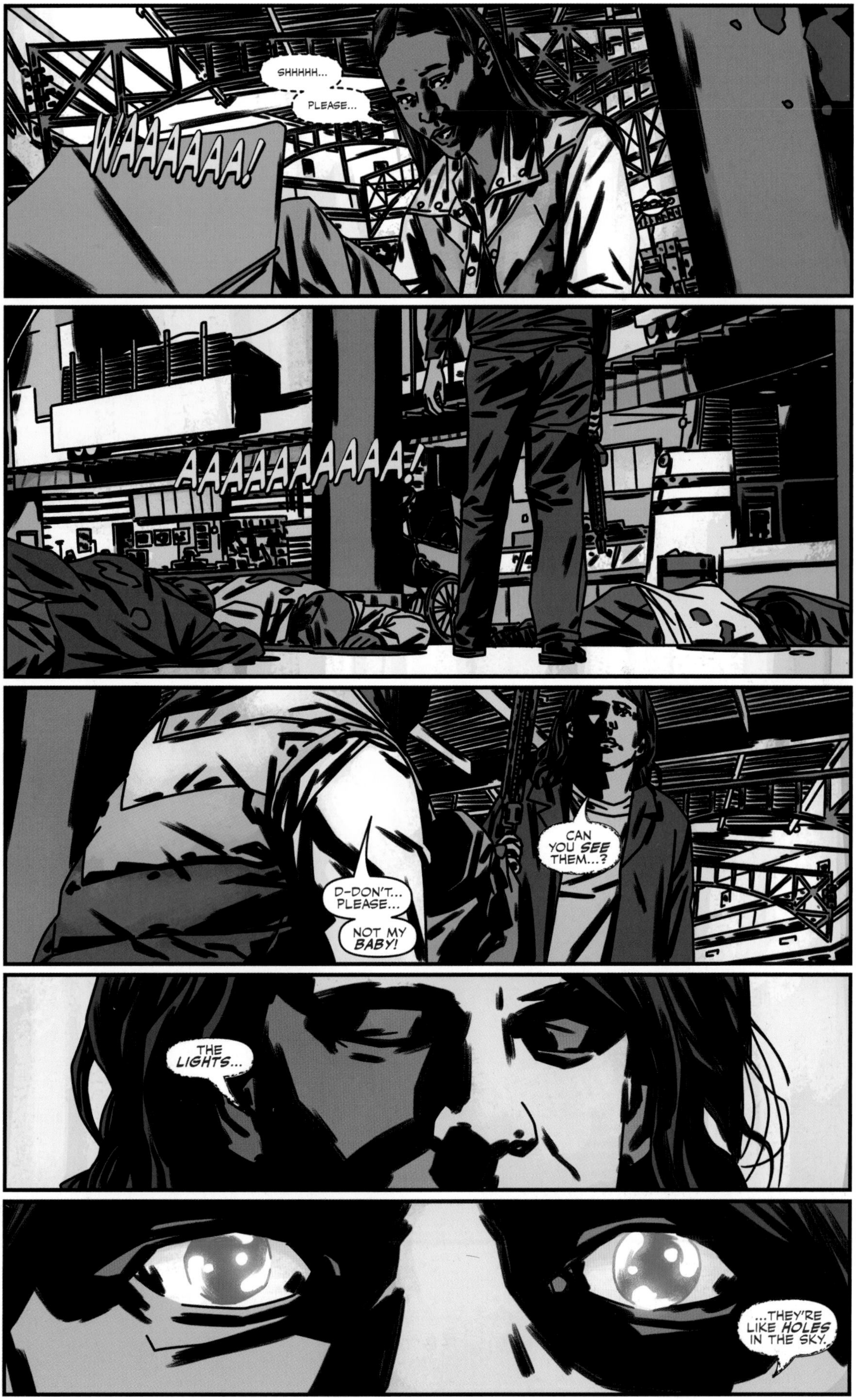
SHHHHH...
PLEASE...
WAAAAAA!
AAAAAAAAAA!
D-DON'T... PLEASE...
NOT MY BABY!
CAN YOU SEE THEM...?
THE LIGHTS...
...THEY'RE LIKE HOLES IN THE SKY.

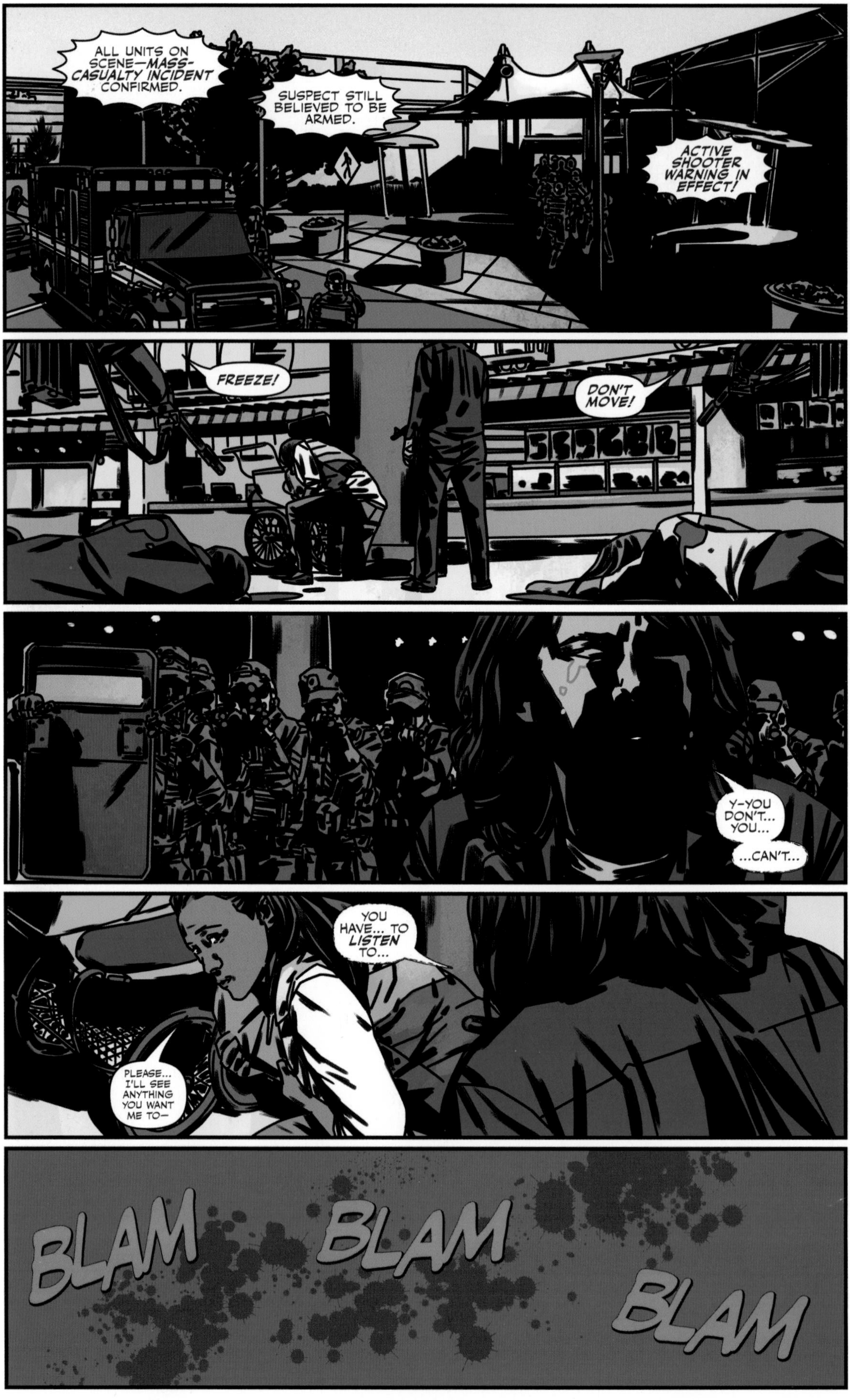
ALL UNITS ON SCENE—MASS-CASUALTY INCIDENT CONFIRMED.
SUSPECT STILL BELIEVED TO BE ARMED.
ACTIVE SHOOTER WARNING IN EFFECT!
FREEZE!
DON'T MOVE!
Y-YOU DON'T... YOU...
...CAN'T...
YOU HAVE... TO LISTEN TO...
PLEASE... I'LL SEE ANYTHING YOU WANT ME TO—
BLAM
BLAM
BLAM

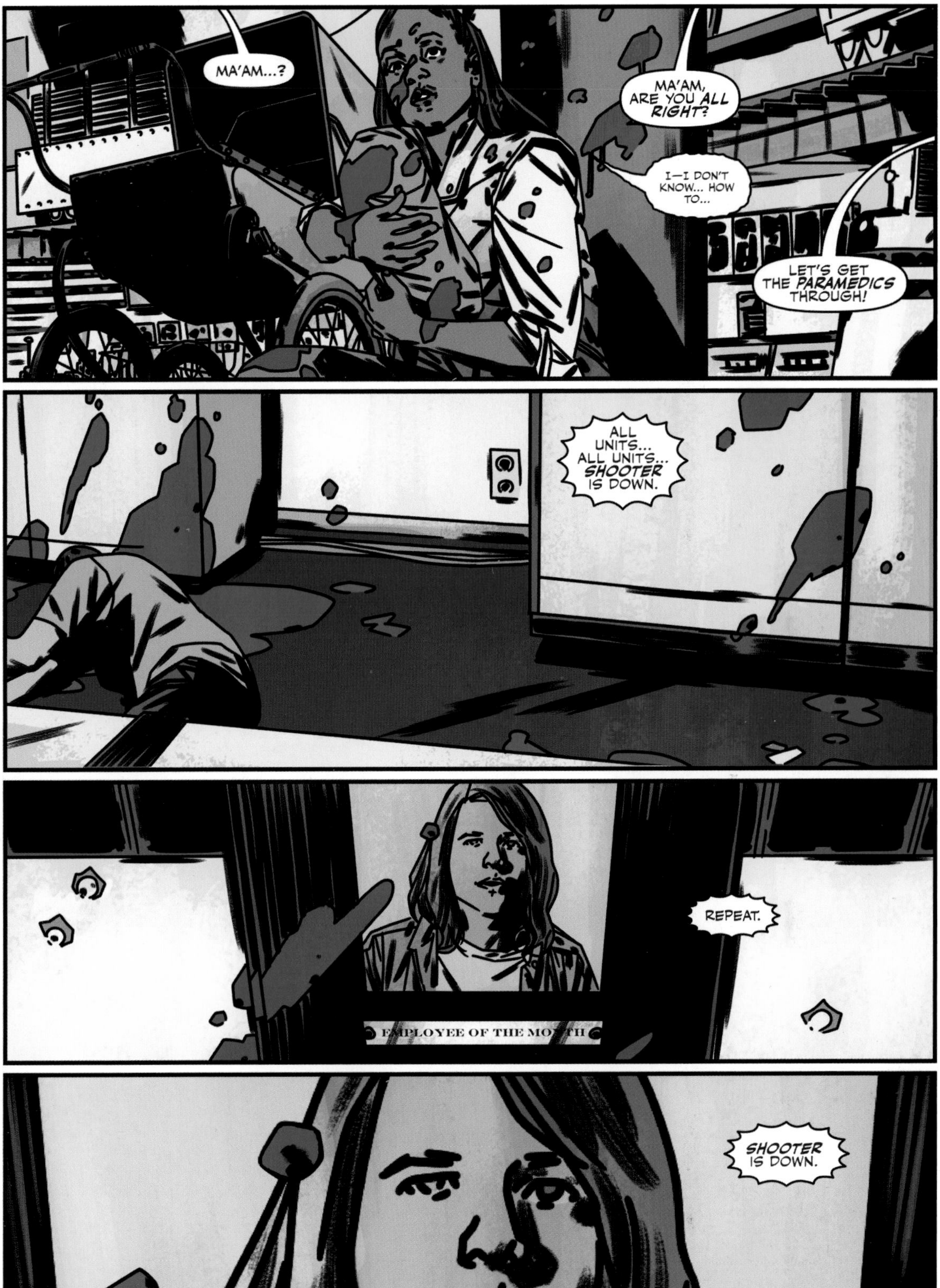
MA'AM...?
MA'AM, ARE YOU ALL RIGHT?
I—I DON'T KNOW... HOW TO...
LET'S GET THE PARAMEDICS THROUGH!
ALL UNITS... ALL UNITS... SHOOTER IS DOWN.
EMPLOYEE OF THE MONTH
REPEAT.
SHOOTER IS DOWN.

THE X FILES™

"ACTIVE SHOOTER"

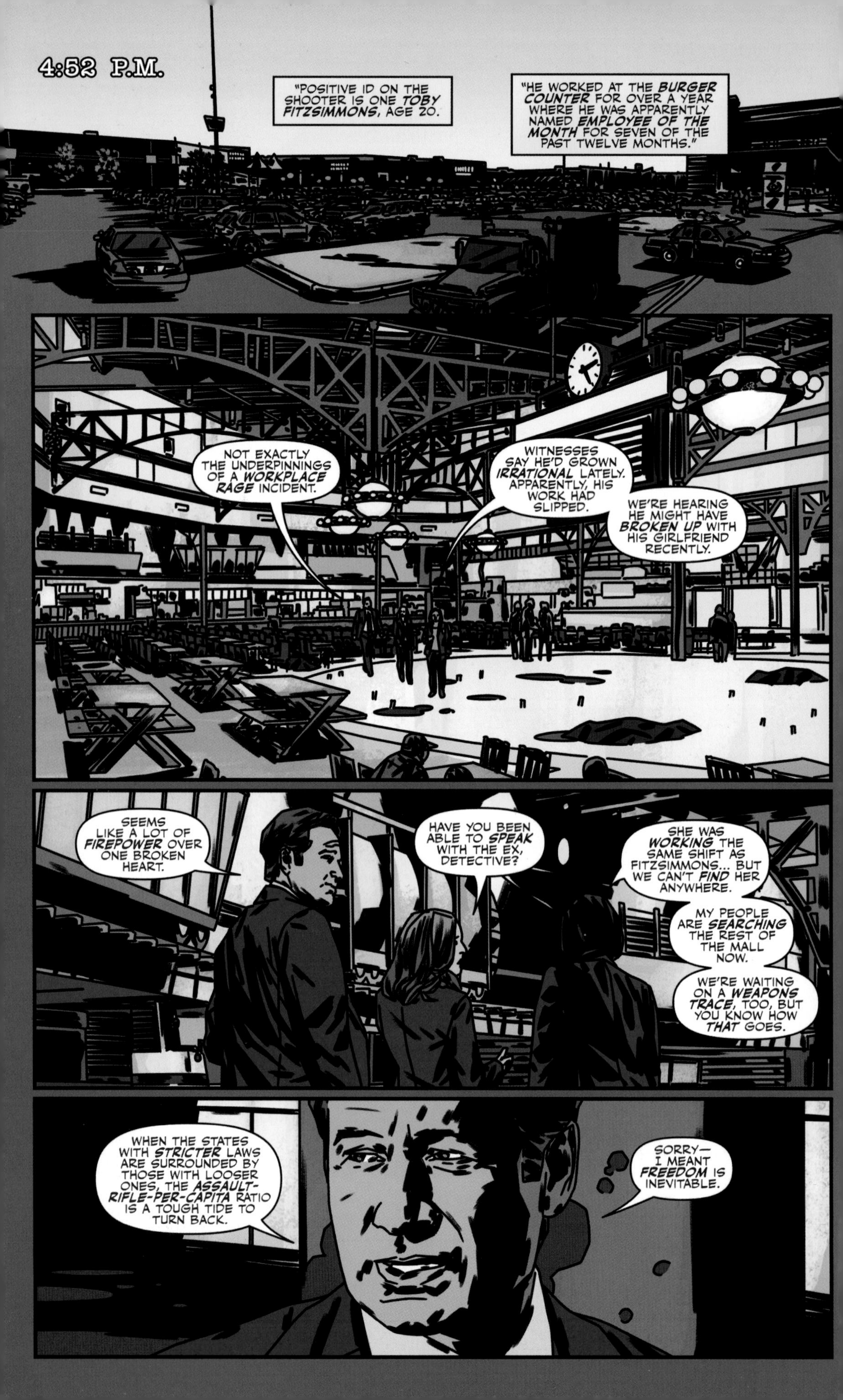
4:52 P.M.
"POSITIVE ID ON THE SHOOTER IS ONE TOBY FITZSIMMONS, AGE 20.
"HE WORKED AT THE BURGER COUNTER FOR OVER A YEAR WHERE HE WAS APPARENTLY NAMED EMPLOYEE OF THE MONTH FOR SEVEN OF THE PAST TWELVE MONTHS."
NOT EXACTLY THE UNDERPINNINGS OF A WORKPLACE RAGE INCIDENT.
WITNESSES SAY HE'D GROWN IRRATIONAL LATELY. APPARENTLY, HIS WORK HAD SLIPPED.
WE'RE HEARING HE MIGHT HAVE BROKEN UP WITH HIS GIRLFRIEND RECENTLY.
SEEMS LIKE A LOT OF FIREPOWER OVER ONE BROKEN HEART.
HAVE YOU BEEN ABLE TO SPEAK WITH THE EX, DETECTIVE?
SHE WAS WORKING THE SAME SHIFT AS FITZSIMMONS... BUT WE CAN'T FIND HER ANYWHERE.
MY PEOPLE ARE SEARCHING THE REST OF THE MALL NOW.
WE'RE WAITING ON A WEAPONS TRACE, TOO, BUT YOU KNOW HOW THAT GOES.
WHEN THE STATES WITH STRICTER LAWS ARE SURROUNDED BY THOSE WITH LOOSER ONES, THE ASSAULT-RIFLE-PER-CAPITA RATIO IS A TOUGH TIDE TO TURN BACK.
SORRY— I MEANT FREEDOM IS INEVITABLE.

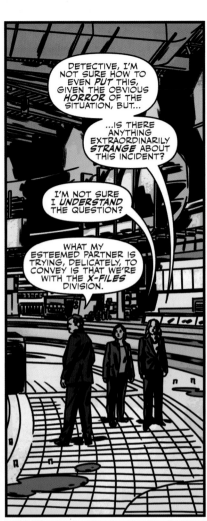

DETECTIVE, I'M NOT SURE HOW TO EVEN *PUT* THIS, GIVEN THE OBVIOUS *HORROR* OF THE SITUATION, BUT...

...IS THERE ANYTHING EXTRAORDINARILY *STRANGE* ABOUT THIS INCIDENT?

I'M NOT SURE I *UNDERSTAND* THE QUESTION?

WHAT MY ESTEEMED PARTNER IS TRYING, DELICATELY, TO CONVEY IS THAT WE'RE WITH THE *X-FILES* DIVISION.

IS HE FOR REAL?

QUITE OFTEN.

WE HANDLE THOSE CASES DEEMED HARD TO EXPLAIN FOR REASONS *BEYOND* THE NORMAL PROCESSES AND PRACTICES OF DISCOVERY AND INVESTIGATION.

THE *"SPOOKY ONES,"* IF YOU PREFER.

HONESTLY, IF YOU'RE RULING OUT *TERRORISM*...

...THE BULK OF WHAT I CAN REALLY DO HERE IS SUGGEST *AMERICA* NEEDS LESS FIREPOWER, MORE EMPATHY, AND THE OCCASIONAL *TIME OUT* IN THE CORNER EVERY NOW AND AGAIN.

CLIK

SA FOX MULDER

SA DANA SCULLY

PHA02 FIELD EXPERIMENT INITIATING

I'LL CALL MY *CAPTAIN* AND SEE IF HE KNOWS ANYTHING ABOUT WHY YOU'RE HERE.

THANK YOU, AGENT MULDER.

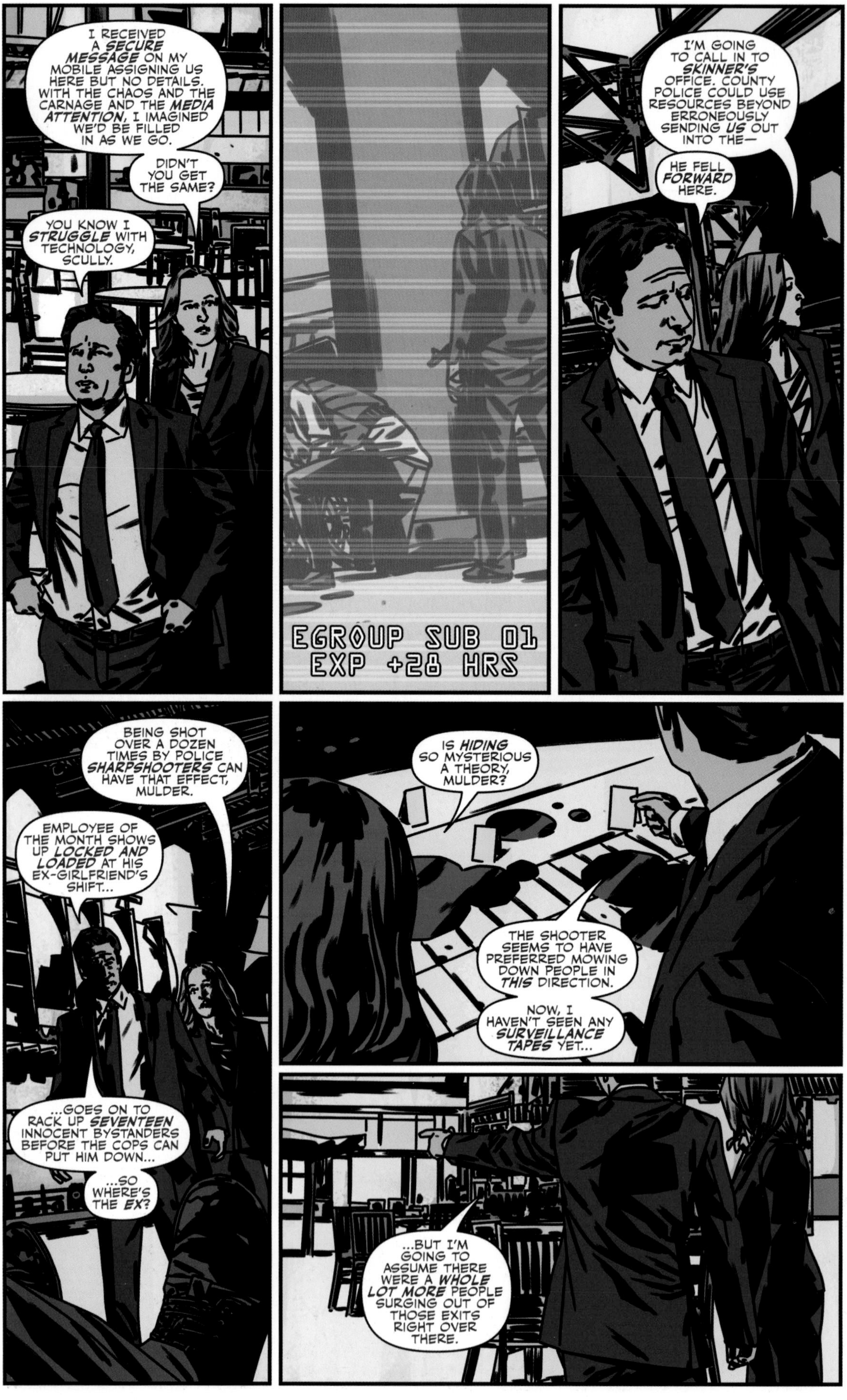
I RECEIVED A SECURE MESSAGE ON MY MOBILE ASSIGNING US HERE BUT NO DETAILS. WITH THE CHAOS AND THE CARNAGE AND THE MEDIA ATTENTION, I IMAGINED WE'D BE FILLED IN AS WE GO.
DIDN'T YOU GET THE SAME?
YOU KNOW I STRUGGLE WITH TECHNOLOGY, SCULLY.
EGROUP SUB 01
EXP +28 HRS
I'M GOING TO CALL IN TO SKINNER'S OFFICE. COUNTY POLICE COULD USE RESOURCES BEYOND ERRONEOUSLY SENDING US OUT INTO THE—
HE FELL FORWARD HERE.
BEING SHOT OVER A DOZEN TIMES BY POLICE SHARPSHOOTERS CAN HAVE THAT EFFECT, MULDER.
EMPLOYEE OF THE MONTH SHOWS UP LOCKED AND LOADED AT HIS EX-GIRLFRIEND'S SHIFT...
...GOES ON TO RACK UP SEVENTEEN INNOCENT BYSTANDERS BEFORE THE COPS CAN PUT HIM DOWN...
...SO WHERE'S THE EX?
IS HIDING SO MYSTERIOUS A THEORY, MULDER?
THE SHOOTER SEEMS TO HAVE PREFERRED MOWING DOWN PEOPLE IN THIS DIRECTION.
NOW, I HAVEN'T SEEN ANY SURVEILLANCE TAPES YET...
...BUT I'M GOING TO ASSUME THERE WERE A WHOLE LOT MORE PEOPLE SURGING OUT OF THOSE EXITS RIGHT OVER THERE.

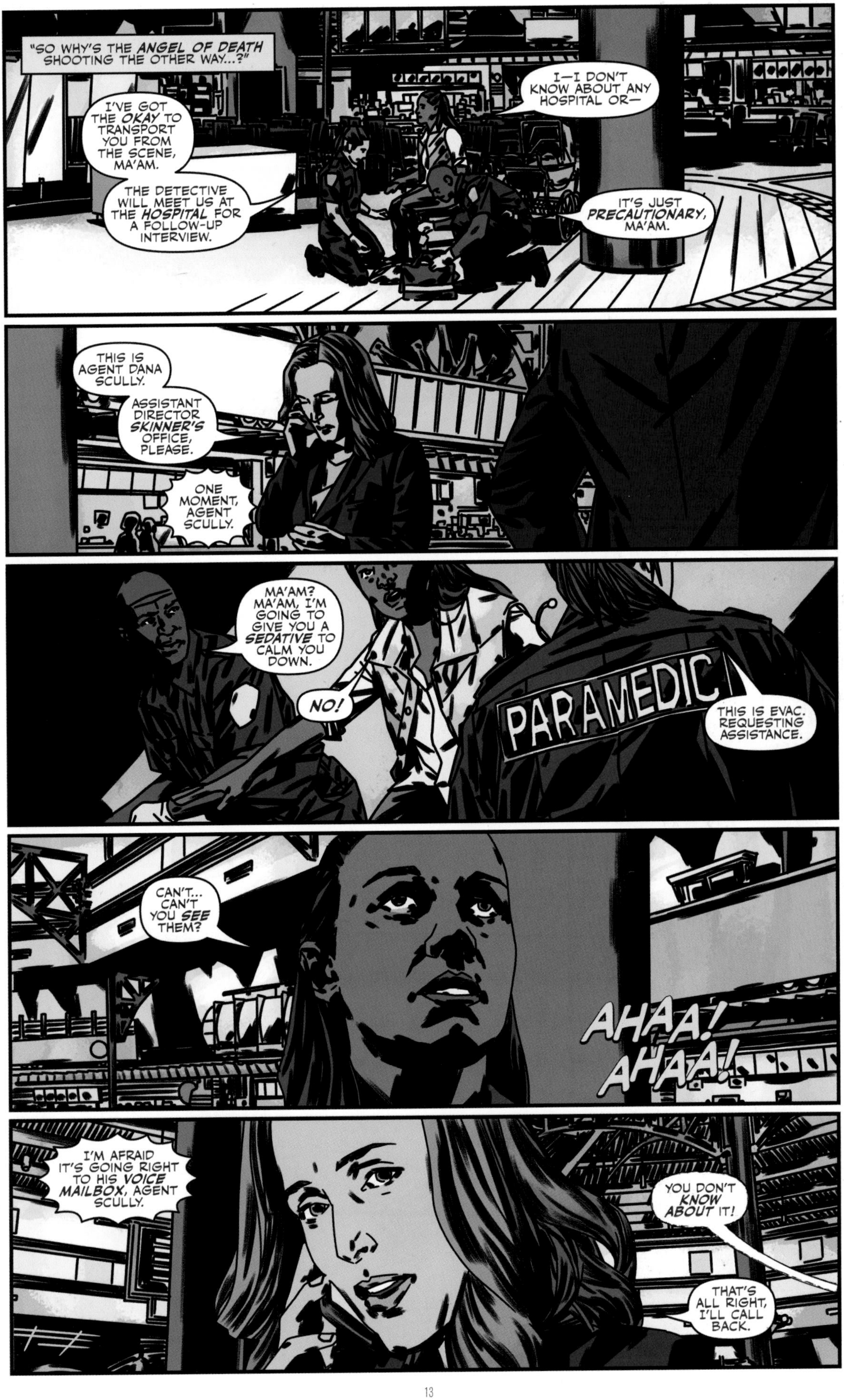

"SO WHY'S THE ANGEL OF DEATH SHOOTING THE OTHER WAY...?"
I'VE GOT THE OKAY TO TRANSPORT YOU FROM THE SCENE, MA'AM.
THE DETECTIVE WILL MEET US AT THE HOSPITAL FOR A FOLLOW-UP INTERVIEW.
I—I DON'T KNOW ABOUT ANY HOSPITAL OR—
IT'S JUST PRECAUTIONARY, MA'AM.
THIS IS AGENT DANA SCULLY.
ASSISTANT DIRECTOR SKINNER'S OFFICE, PLEASE.
ONE MOMENT, AGENT SCULLY.
MA'AM? MA'AM, I'M GOING TO GIVE YOU A SEDATIVE TO CALM YOU DOWN.
NO!
PARAMEDIC
THIS IS EVAC. REQUESTING ASSISTANCE.
CAN'T... CAN'T YOU SEE THEM?
AHAA! AHAA!
I'M AFRAID IT'S GOING RIGHT TO HIS VOICE MAILBOX, AGENT SCULLY.
YOU DON'T KNOW ABOUT IT!
THAT'S ALL RIGHT, I'LL CALL BACK.

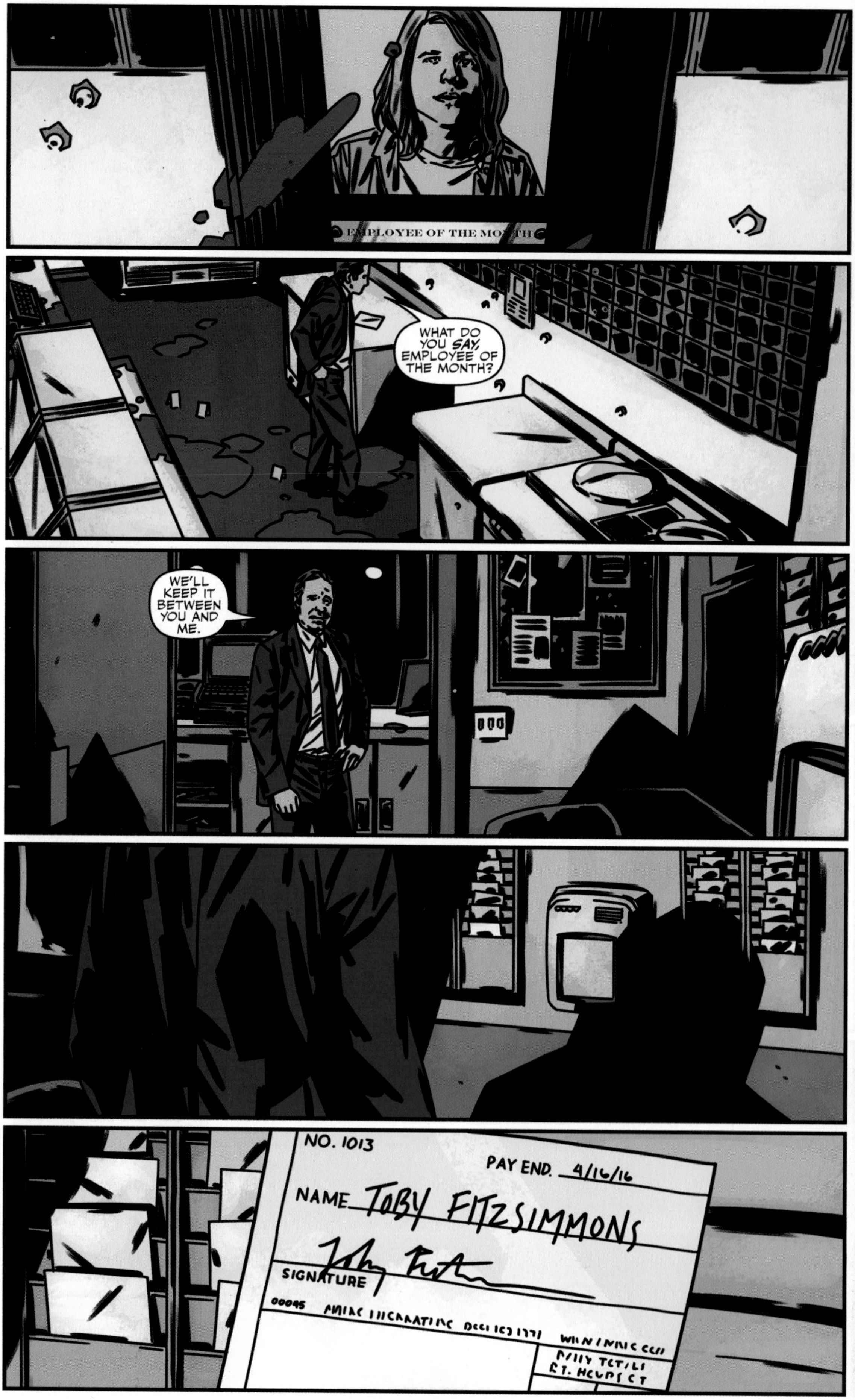
WHAT DO YOU *SAY*, EMPLOYEE OF THE MONTH?
WE'LL KEEP IT BETWEEN YOU AND ME.
NO. 1013
PAY END. 4/16/16
NAME TOBY FITZSIMMONS
SIGNATURE

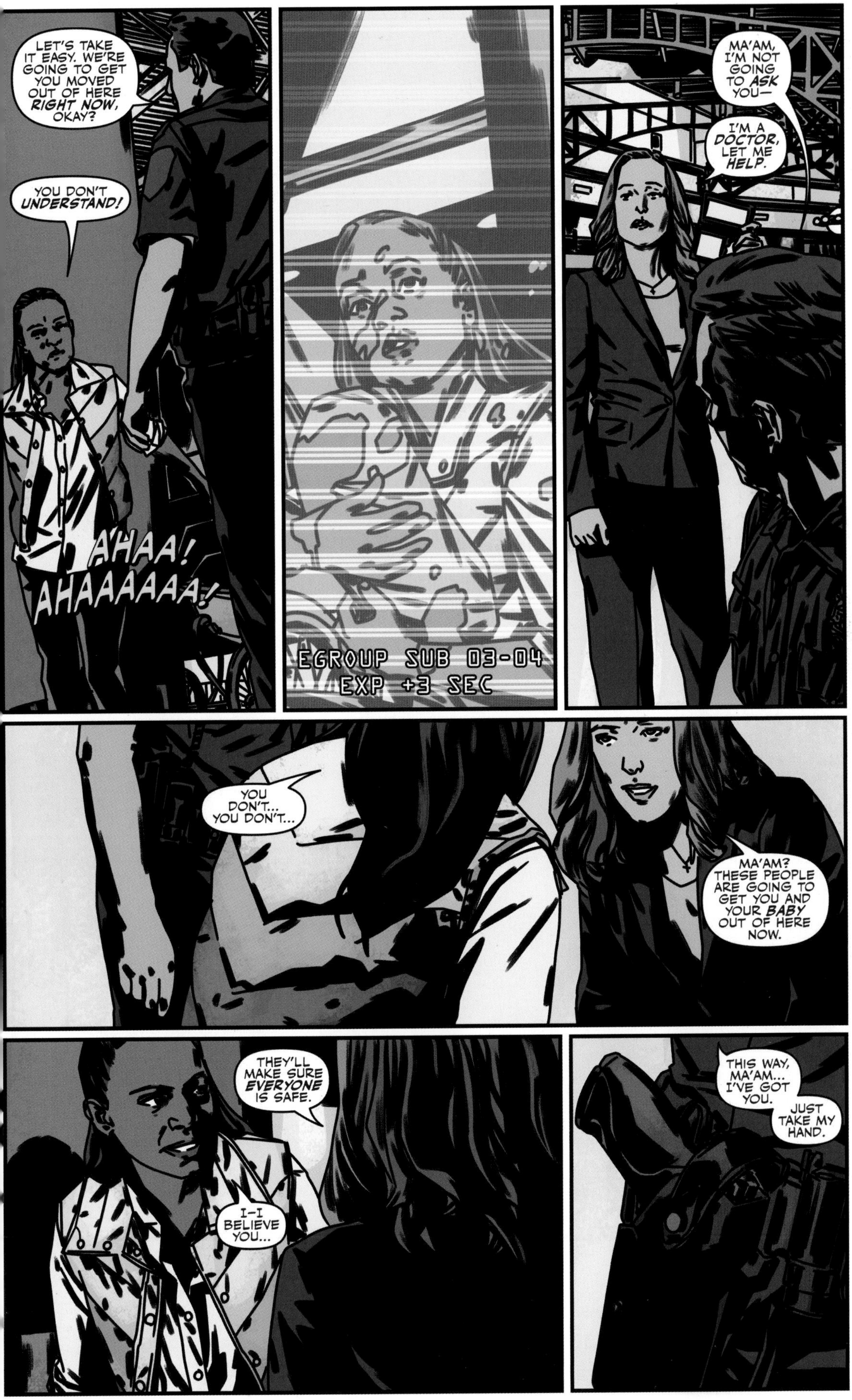
LET'S TAKE IT EASY. WE'RE GOING TO GET YOU MOVED OUT OF HERE RIGHT NOW, OKAY?
YOU DON'T UNDERSTAND!
AHAA! AHAAAAAA!
EGROUP SUB 03-04
EXP +3 SEC
MA'AM, I'M NOT GOING TO ASK YOU—
I'M A DOCTOR, LET ME HELP.
YOU DON'T... YOU DON'T...
MA'AM? THESE PEOPLE ARE GOING TO GET YOU AND YOUR BABY OUT OF HERE NOW.
THEY'LL MAKE SURE EVERYONE IS SAFE.
I-I BELIEVE YOU...
THIS WAY, MA'AM... I'VE GOT YOU.
JUST TAKE MY HAND.

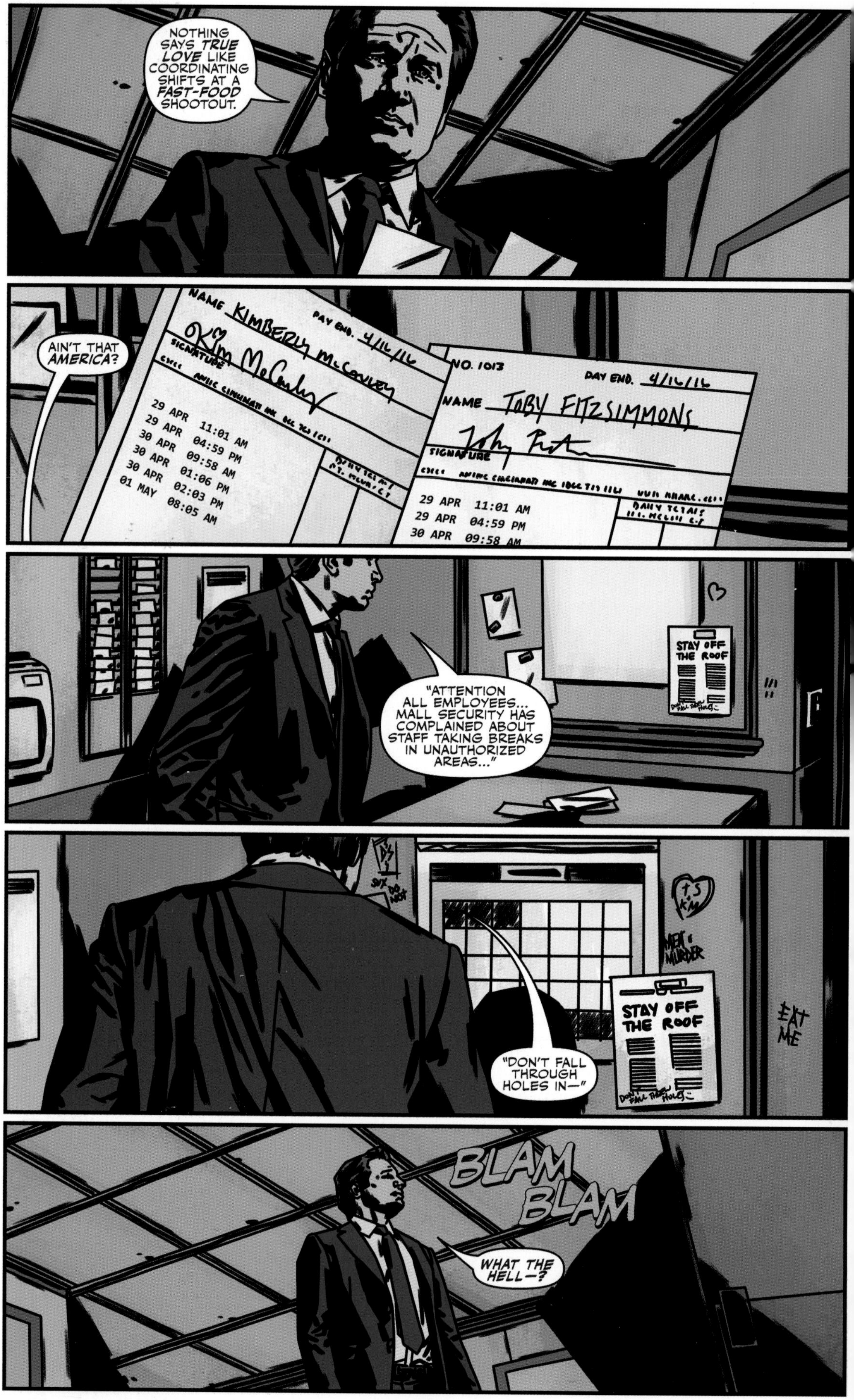

NOTHING SAYS TRUE LOVE LIKE COORDINATING SHIFTS AT A FAST-FOOD SHOOTOUT.
AIN'T THAT AMERICA?
NAME KIMBERLY McCAULEY
PAY END. 4/16/16
SIGNATURE
29 APR 11:01 AM
29 APR 04:59 PM
30 APR 09:58 AM
30 APR 01:06 PM
30 APR 02:03 PM
01 MAY 08:05 AM
NO. 1013
DAY END. 4/16/16
NAME TOBY FITZSIMMONS
SIGNATURE
29 APR 11:01 AM
29 APR 04:59 PM
30 APR 09:58 AM
STAY OFF THE ROOF
"ATTENTION ALL EMPLOYEES... MALL SECURITY HAS COMPLAINED ABOUT STAFF TAKING BREAKS IN UNAUTHORIZED AREAS..."
STAY OFF THE ROOF
EAT ME
"DON'T FALL THROUGH HOLES IN—"
BLAM BLAM
WHAT THE HELL—?

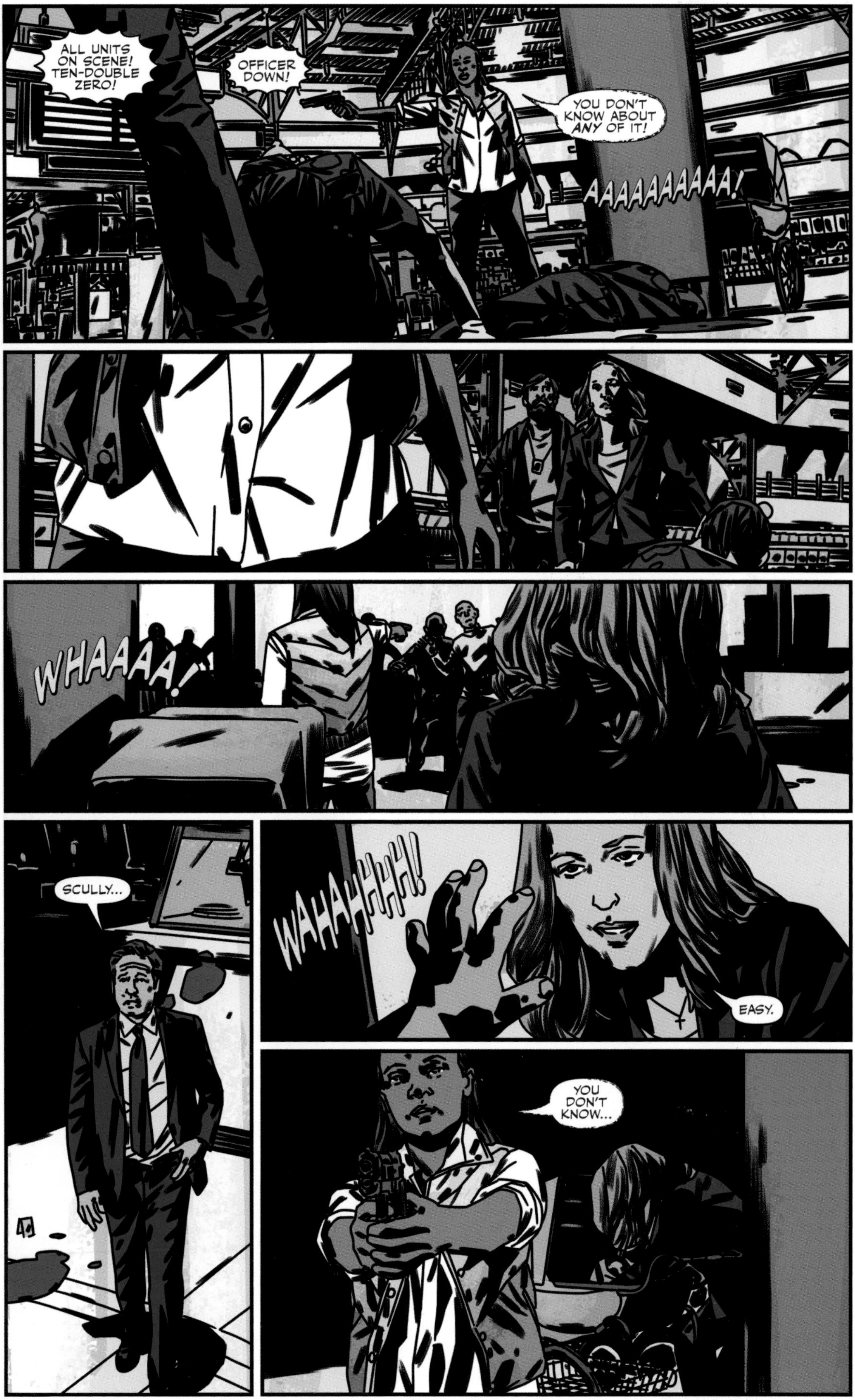
ALL UNITS ON SCENE! TEN-DOUBLE ZERO!
OFFICER DOWN!
YOU DON'T KNOW ABOUT ANY OF IT!
AAAAAAAAAA!
WHAAAA!
SCULLY...
WAHAHHHHH!
EASY.
YOU DON'T KNOW...

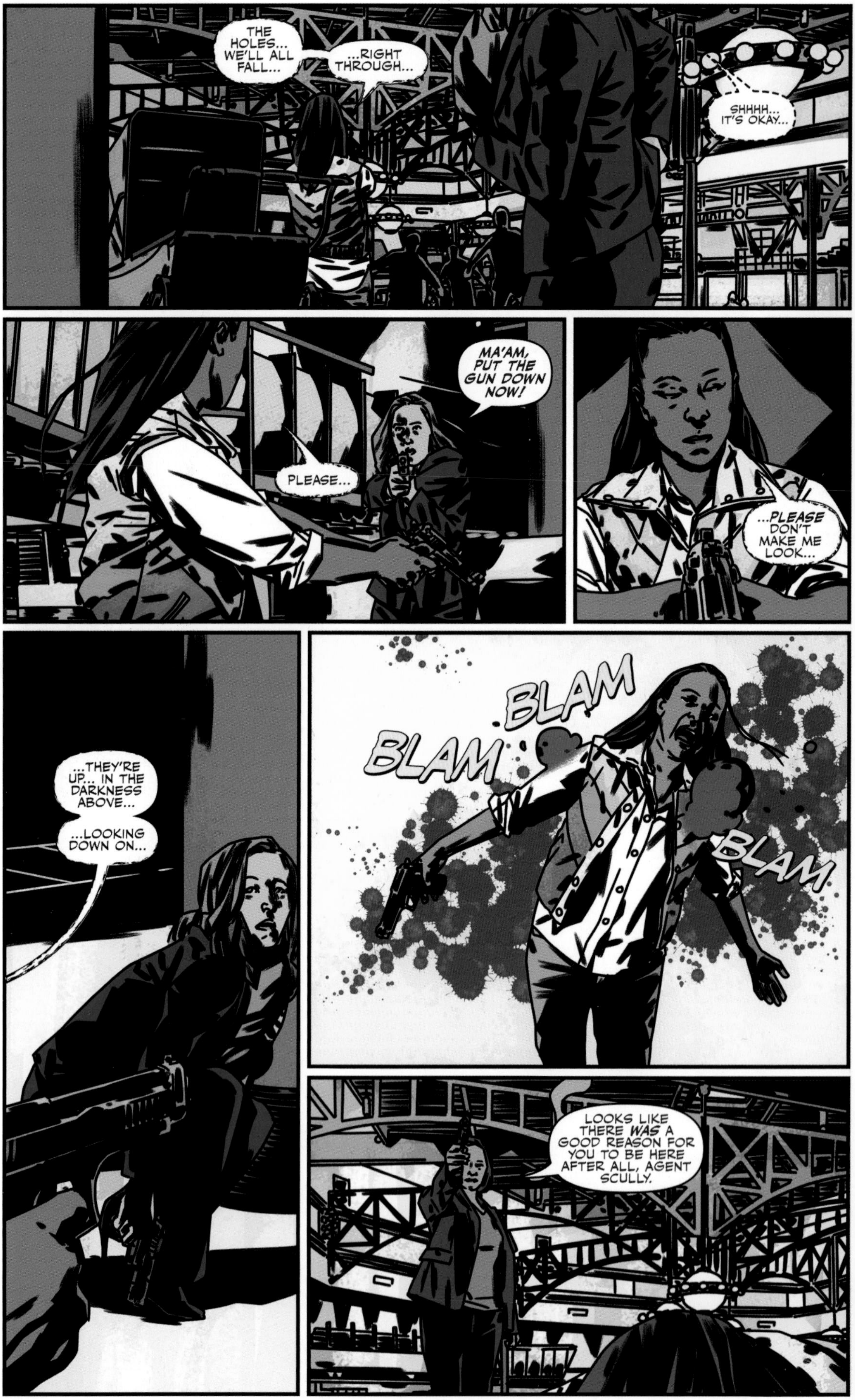
THE HOLES... WE'LL ALL FALL...
...RIGHT THROUGH...
SHHHH... IT'S OKAY...
MA'AM, PUT THE GUN DOWN NOW!
PLEASE...
...*PLEASE* DON'T MAKE ME LOOK...
...THEY'RE UP... IN THE DARKNESS ABOVE...
...LOOKING DOWN ON...
BLAM
BLAM
BLAM
LOOKS LIKE THERE *WAS* A GOOD REASON FOR YOU TO BE HERE AFTER ALL, AGENT SCULLY.

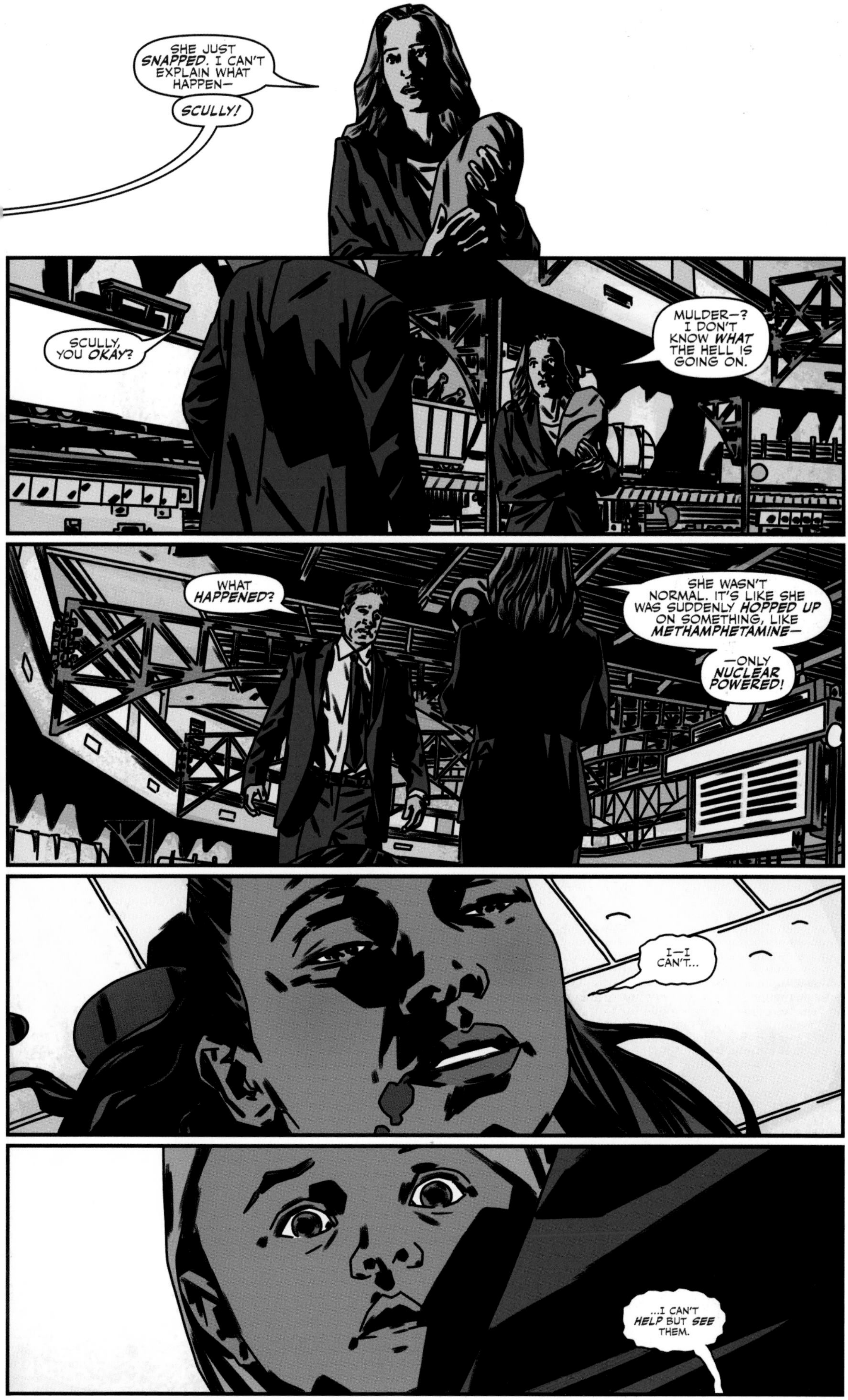
SHE JUST SNAPPED. I CAN'T EXPLAIN WHAT HAPPEN—
SCULLY!
SCULLY, YOU OKAY?
MULDER—? I DON'T KNOW WHAT THE HELL IS GOING ON.
WHAT HAPPENED?
SHE WASN'T NORMAL. IT'S LIKE SHE WAS SUDDENLY HOPPED UP ON SOMETHING, LIKE METHAMPHETAMINE—
—ONLY NUCLEAR POWERED!
I—I CAN'T...
...I CAN'T HELP BUT SEE THEM.

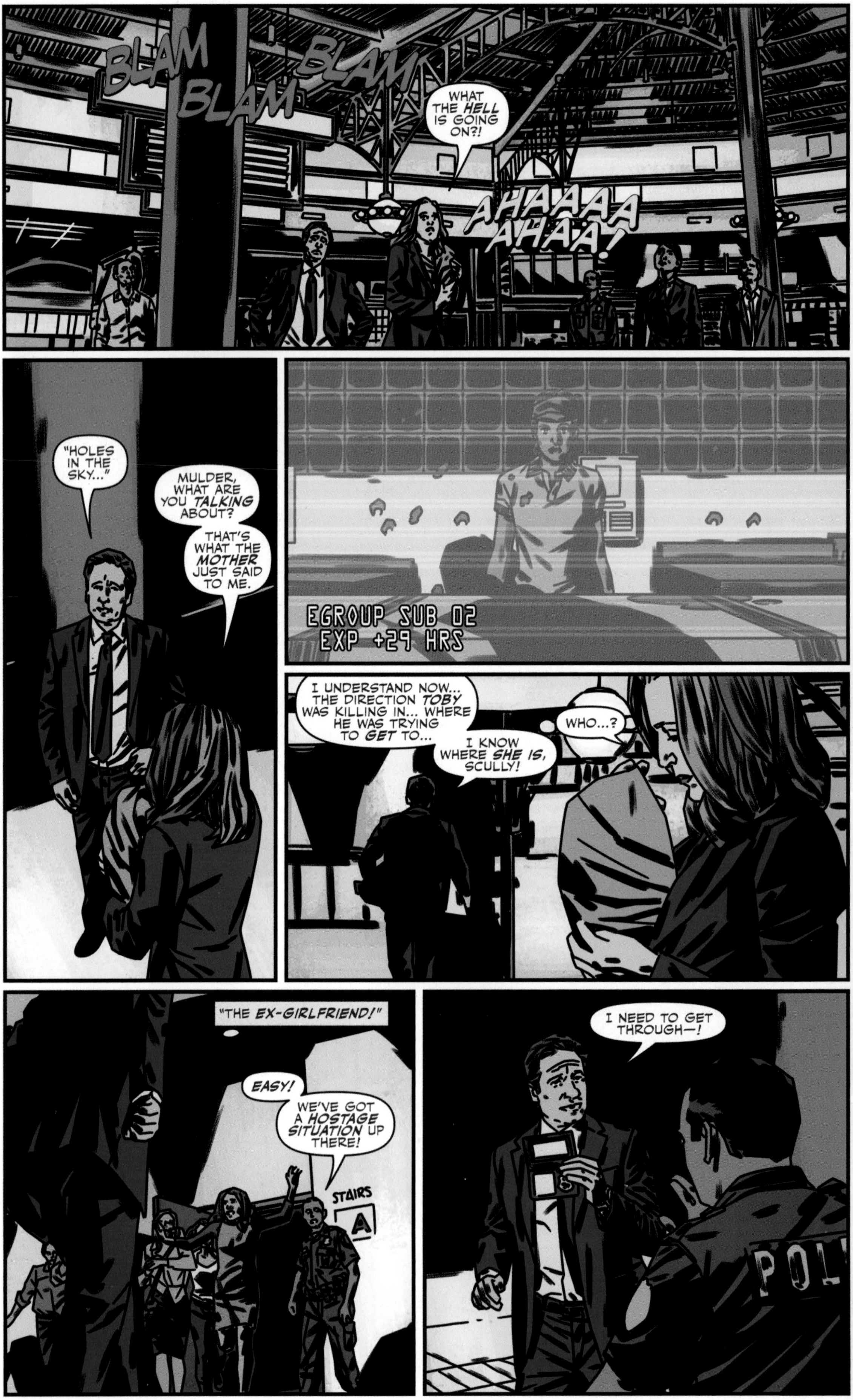
BLAM BLAM BLAM
WHAT THE HELL IS GOING ON?!
AHAAAAA AHAA!
"HOLES IN THE SKY..."
MULDER, WHAT ARE YOU TALKING ABOUT?
THAT'S WHAT THE MOTHER JUST SAID TO ME.
EGROUP SUB 02
EXP +29 HRS
I UNDERSTAND NOW... THE DIRECTION TOBY WAS KILLING IN... WHERE HE WAS TRYING TO GET TO...
WHO...?
I KNOW WHERE SHE IS, SCULLY!
"THE EX-GIRLFRIEND!"
EASY!
WE'VE GOT A HOSTAGE SITUATION UP THERE!
STAIRS
A
I NEED TO GET THROUGH—!
POL

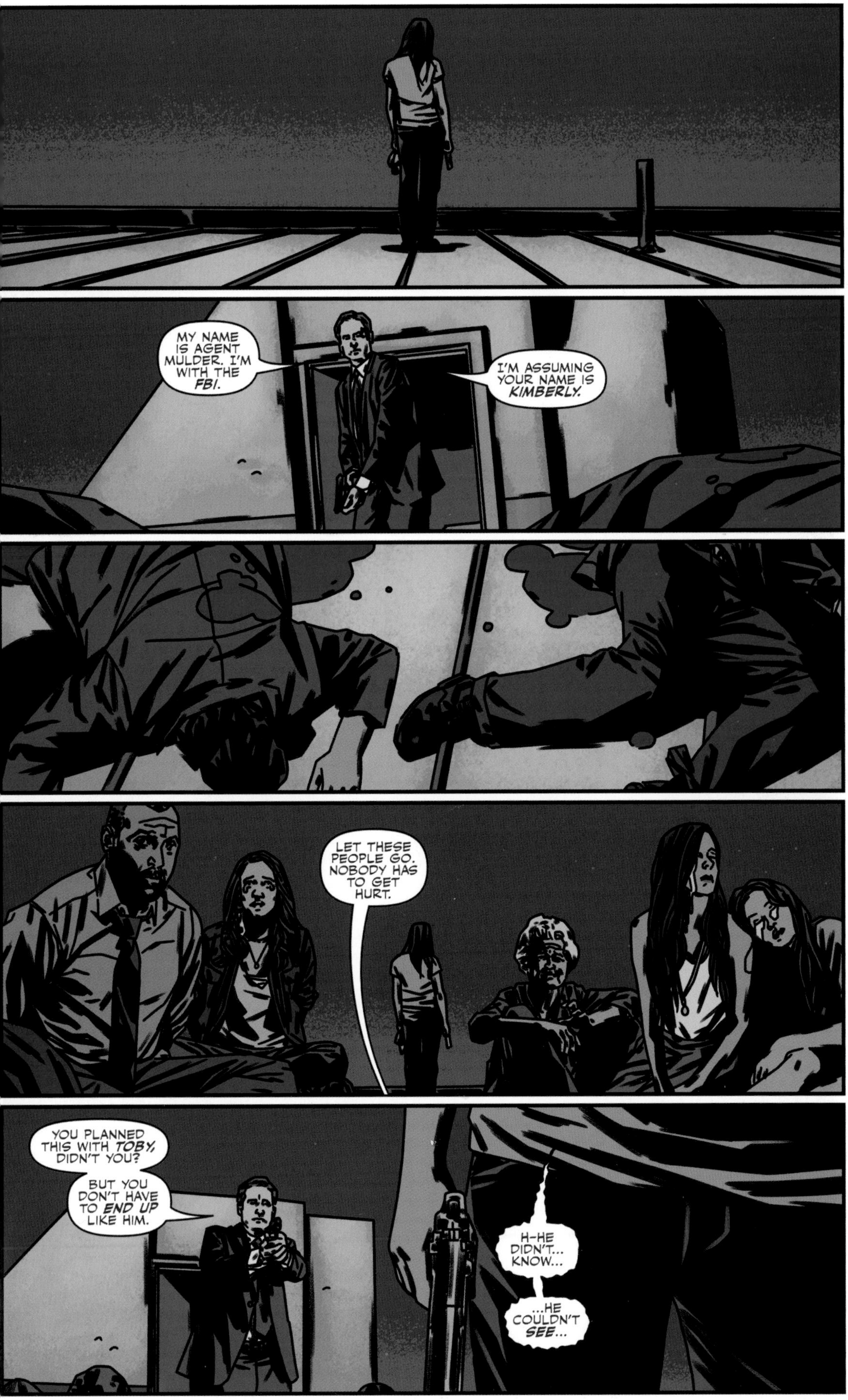
MY NAME IS AGENT MULDER. I'M WITH THE FBI.
I'M ASSUMING YOUR NAME IS KIMBERLY.
LET THESE PEOPLE GO. NOBODY HAS TO GET HURT.
YOU PLANNED THIS WITH TOBY, DIDN'T YOU?
BUT YOU DON'T HAVE TO END UP LIKE HIM.
H-HE DIDN'T... KNOW...
...HE COULDN'T SEE...

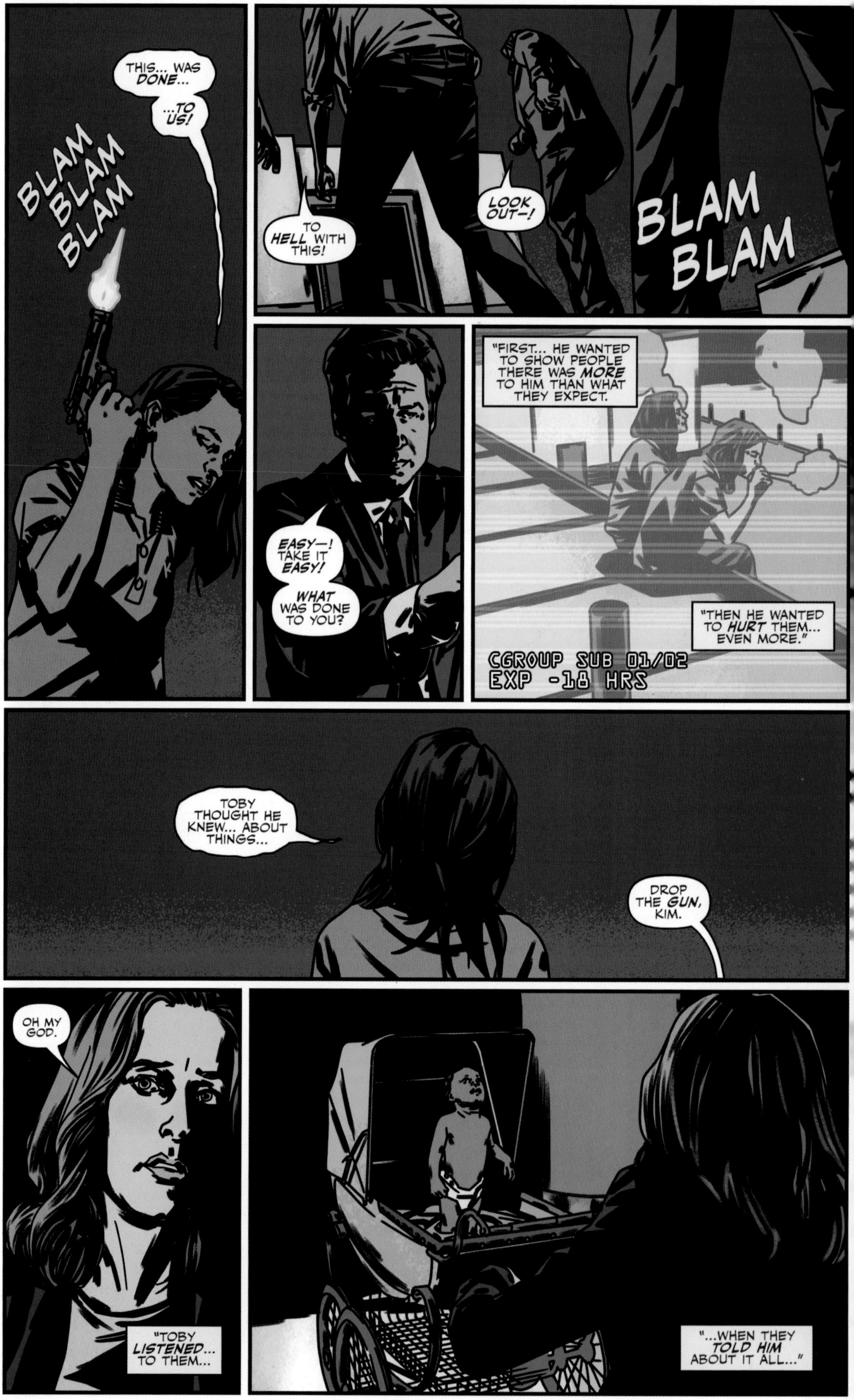

THIS... WAS DONE...
...TO US!
BLAM BLAM BLAM
TO HELL WITH THIS!
LOOK OUT—!
BLAM BLAM
EASY—! TAKE IT EASY!
WHAT WAS DONE TO YOU?
"FIRST... HE WANTED TO SHOW PEOPLE THERE WAS MORE TO HIM THAN WHAT THEY EXPECT.
"THEN HE WANTED TO HURT THEM... EVEN MORE."
CGROUP SUB 01/02
EXP -18 HRS
TOBY THOUGHT HE KNEW... ABOUT THINGS...
DROP THE GUN, KIM.
OH MY GOD.
"TOBY LISTENED... TO THEM...
"...WHEN THEY TOLD HIM ABOUT IT ALL..."

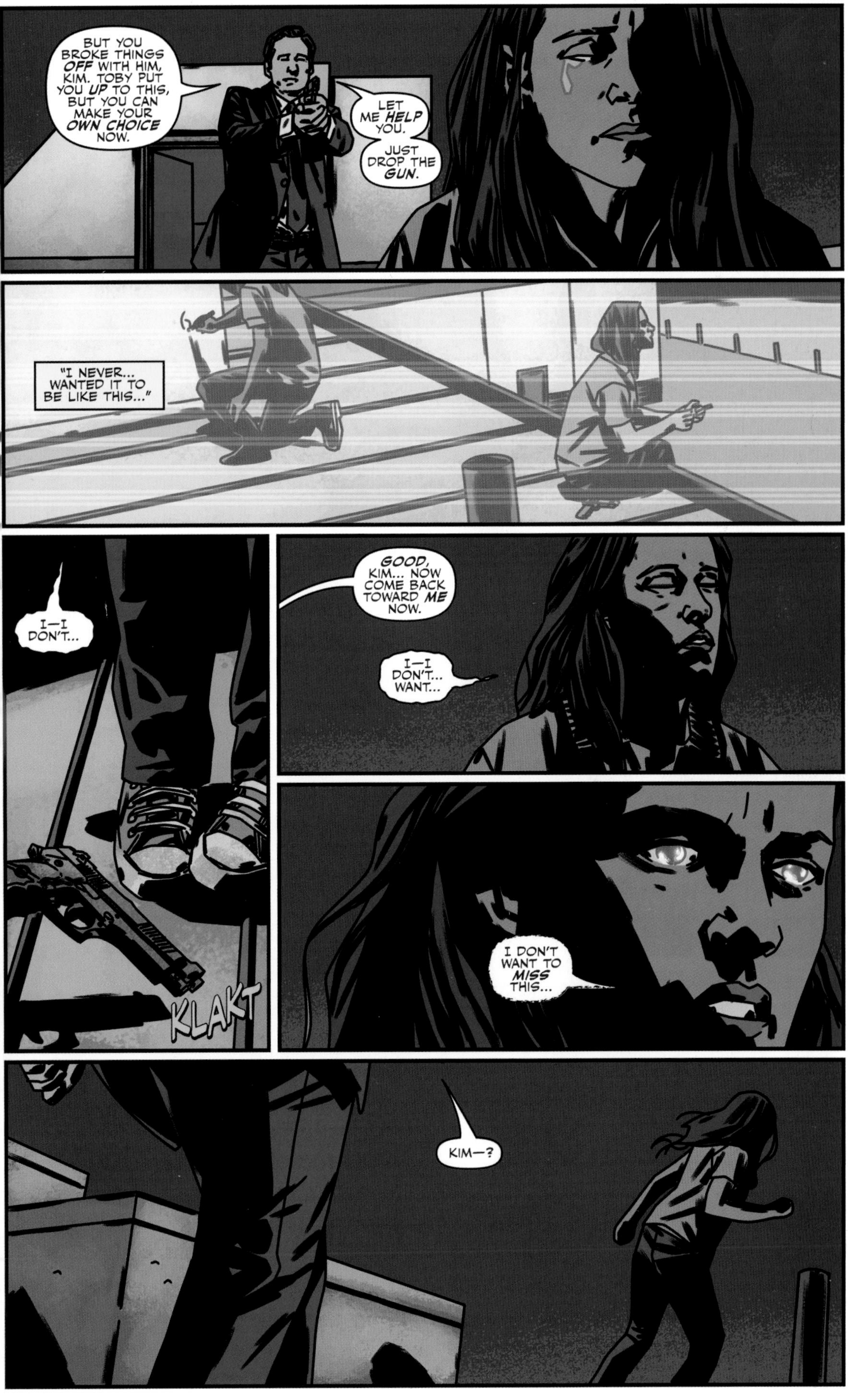
BUT YOU BROKE THINGS OFF WITH HIM, KIM. TOBY PUT YOU UP TO THIS, BUT YOU CAN MAKE YOUR OWN CHOICE NOW.
LET ME HELP YOU.
JUST DROP THE GUN.
"I NEVER... WANTED IT TO BE LIKE THIS..."
I—I DON'T...
KLAKT
GOOD, KIM... NOW COME BACK TOWARD ME NOW.
I—I DON'T... WANT...
I DON'T WANT TO MISS THIS...
KIM—?

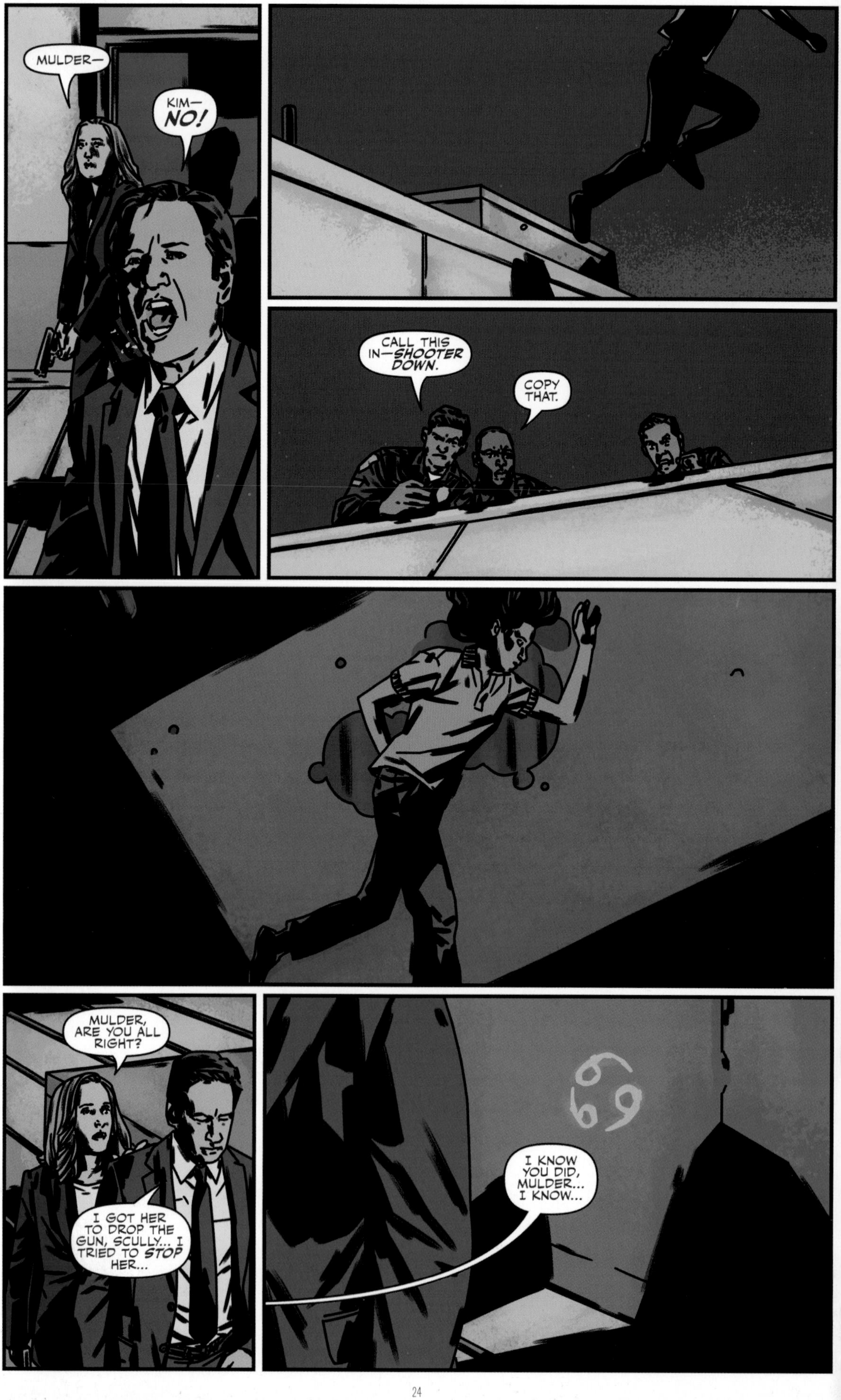
MULDER—
KIM— NO!
CALL THIS IN—SHOOTER DOWN.
COPY THAT.
MULDER, ARE YOU ALL RIGHT?
I GOT HER TO DROP THE GUN, SCULLY... I TRIED TO STOP HER...
I KNOW YOU DID, MULDER... I KNOW...

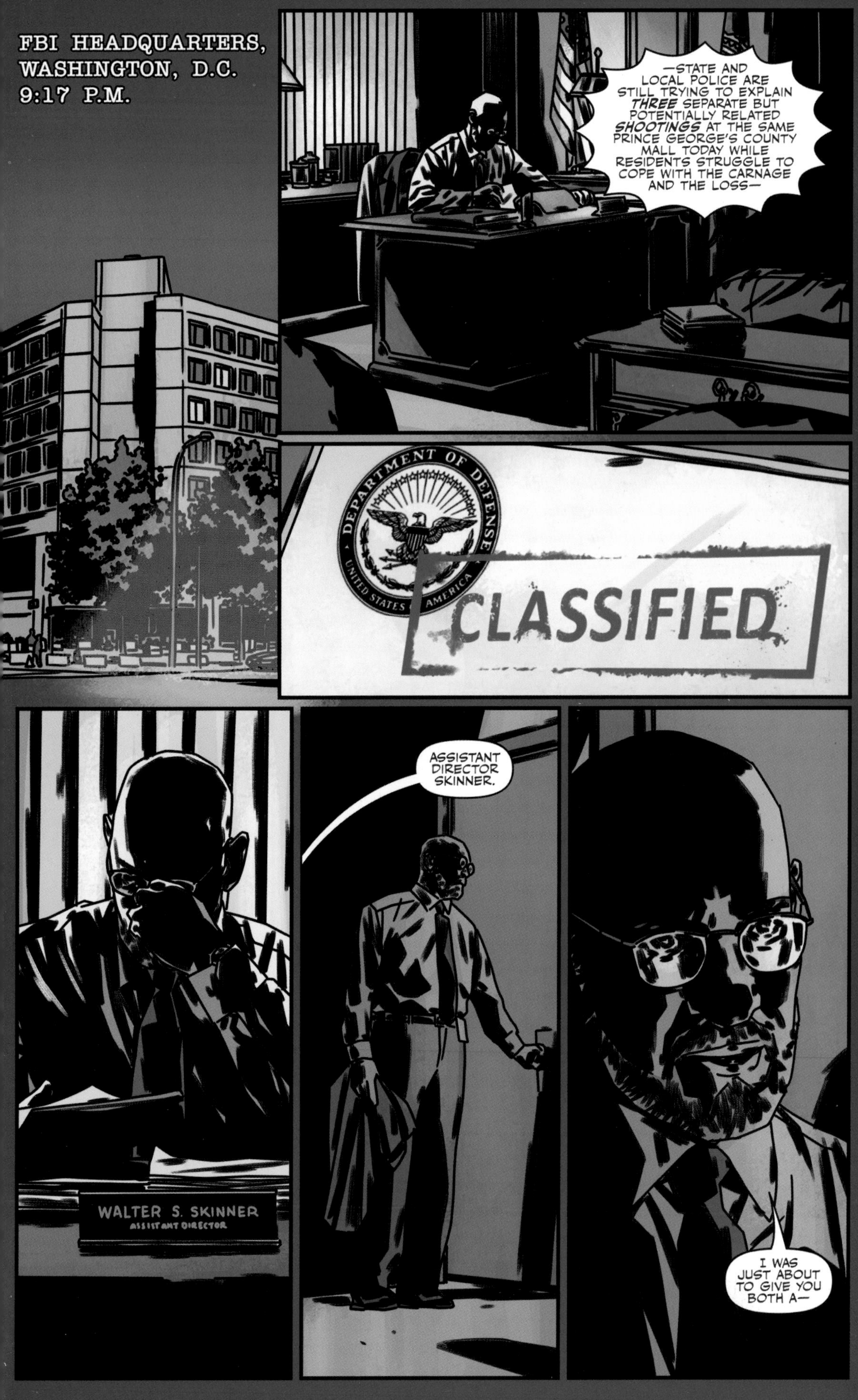
FBI HEADQUARTERS, WASHINGTON, D.C. 9:17 P.M.
—STATE AND LOCAL POLICE ARE STILL TRYING TO EXPLAIN THREE SEPARATE BUT POTENTIALLY RELATED SHOOTINGS AT THE SAME PRINCE GEORGE'S COUNTY MALL TODAY WHILE RESIDENTS STRUGGLE TO COPE WITH THE CARNAGE AND THE LOSS—
DEPARTMENT OF DEFENSE
UNITED STATES OF AMERICA
CLASSIFIED
WALTER S. SKINNER
ASSISTANT DIRECTOR
ASSISTANT DIRECTOR SKINNER.
I WAS JUST ABOUT TO GIVE YOU BOTH A—

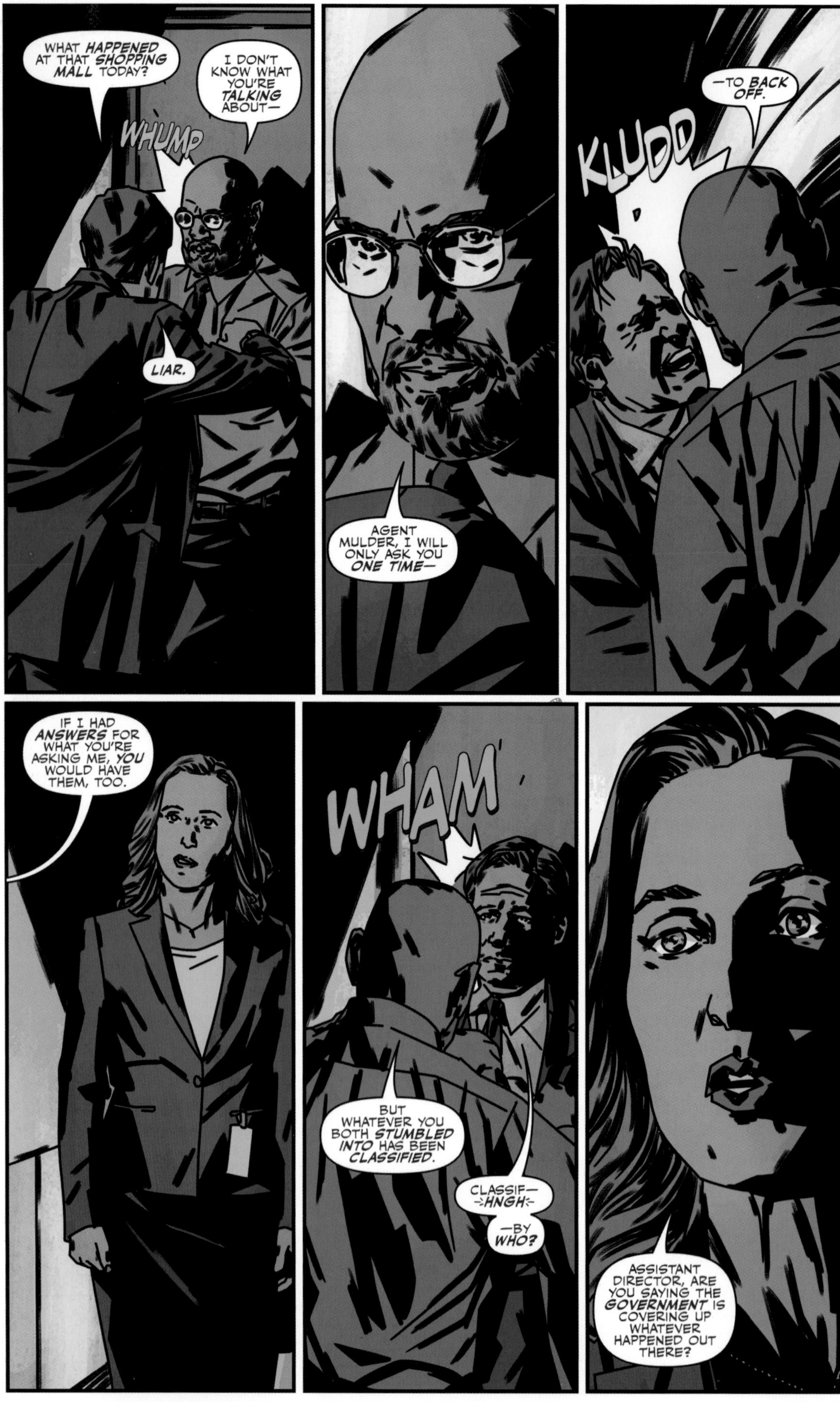
WHAT HAPPENED AT THAT SHOPPING MALL TODAY?
I DON'T KNOW WHAT YOU'RE TALKING ABOUT—
WHUMP
LIAR.
AGENT MULDER, I WILL ONLY ASK YOU ONE TIME—
—TO BACK OFF.
KLUDD
IF I HAD ANSWERS FOR WHAT YOU'RE ASKING ME, YOU WOULD HAVE THEM, TOO.
WHAM
BUT WHATEVER YOU BOTH STUMBLED INTO HAS BEEN CLASSIFIED.
CLASSIF— HNGH
—BY WHO?
ASSISTANT DIRECTOR, ARE YOU SAYING THE GOVERNMENT IS COVERING UP WHATEVER HAPPENED OUT THERE?

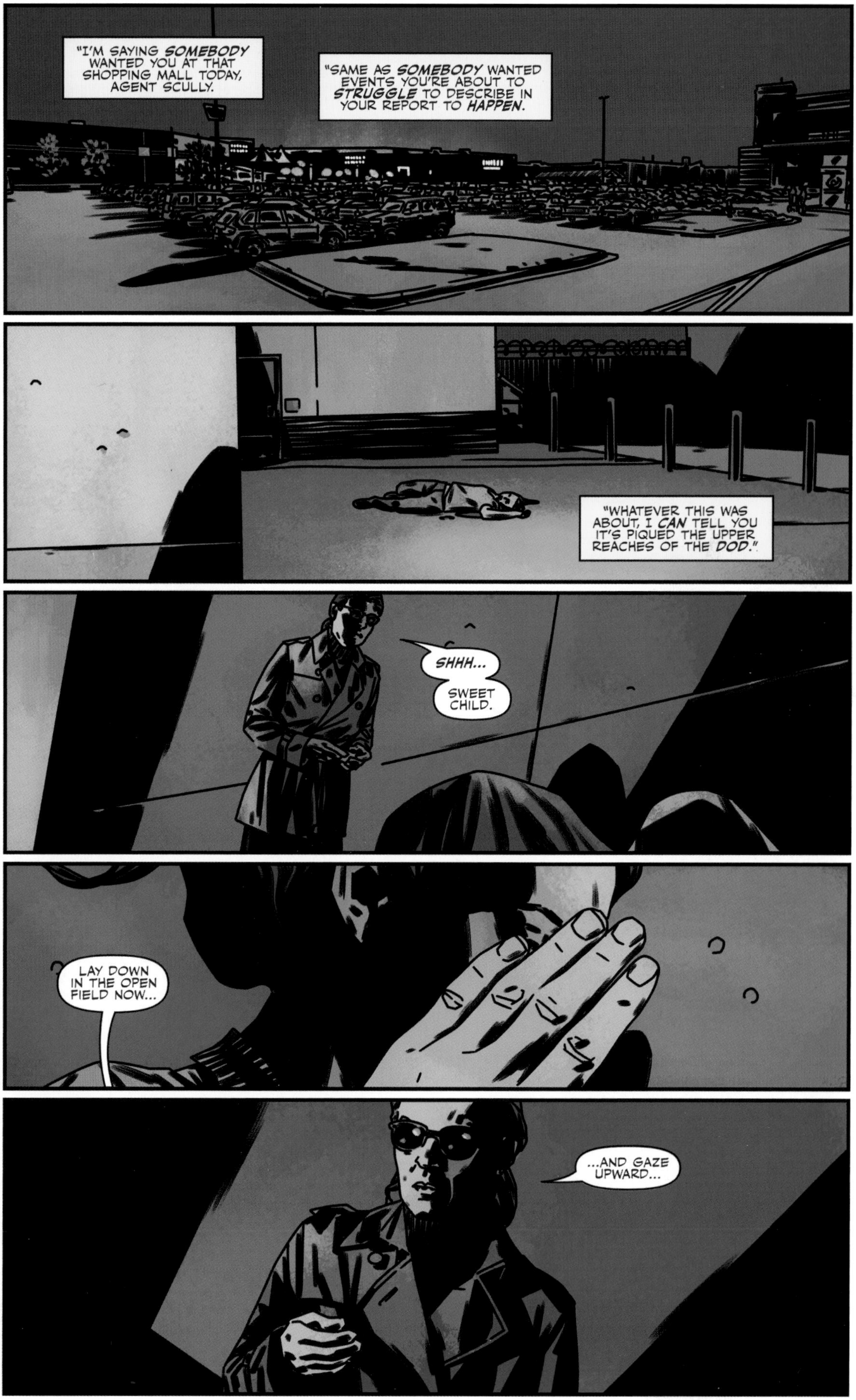

"I'M SAYING SOMEBODY WANTED YOU AT THAT SHOPPING MALL TODAY, AGENT SCULLY.
"SAME AS SOMEBODY WANTED EVENTS YOU'RE ABOUT TO STRUGGLE TO DESCRIBE IN YOUR REPORT TO HAPPEN.
"WHATEVER THIS WAS ABOUT, I CAN TELL YOU IT'S PIQUED THE UPPER REACHES OF THE DOD."
SHHH...
SWEET CHILD.
LAY DOWN IN THE OPEN FIELD NOW...
...AND GAZE UPWARD...

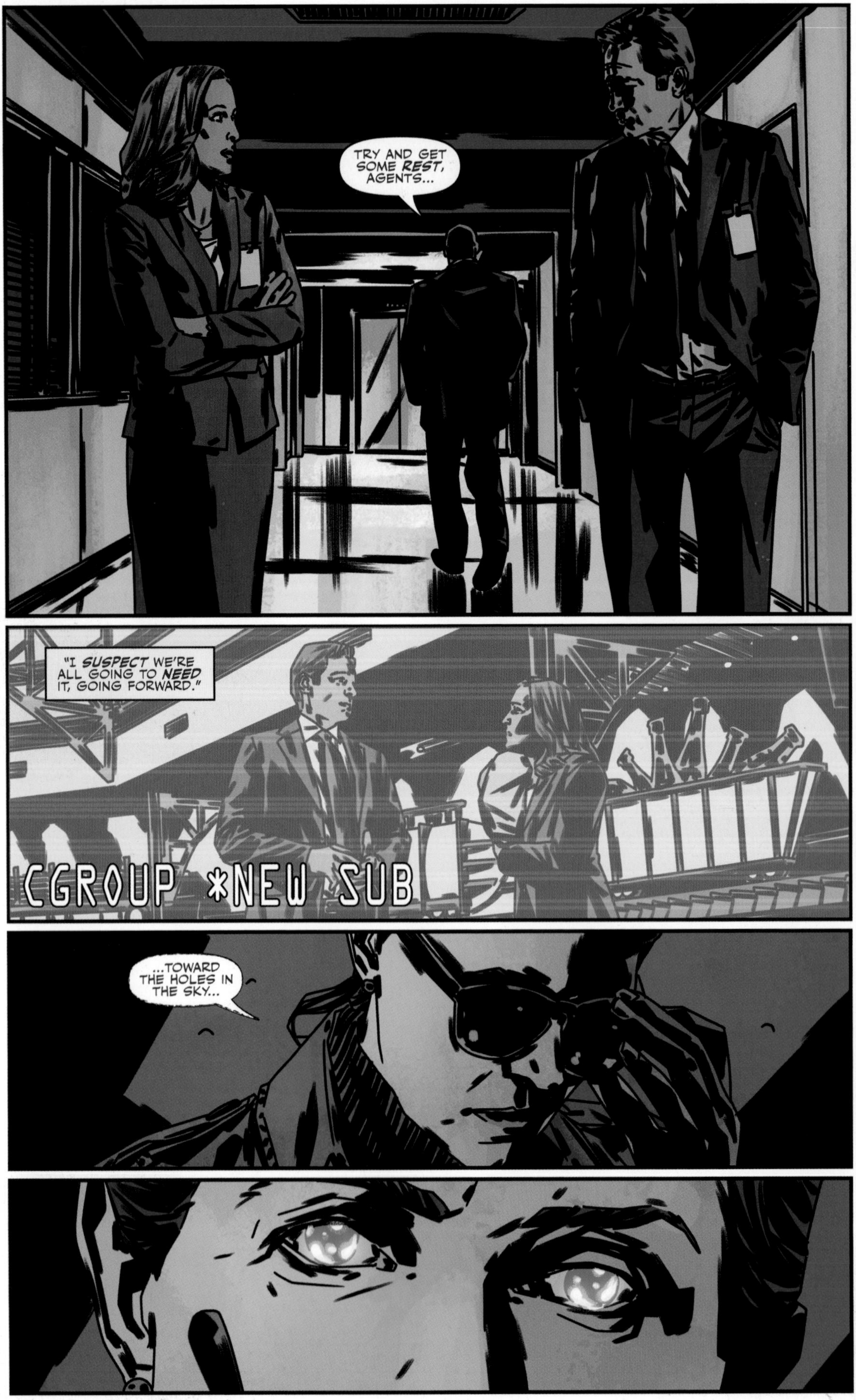
TRY AND GET SOME REST, AGENTS...
"I SUSPECT WE'RE ALL GOING TO NEED IT, GOING FORWARD."
CGROUP *NEW SUB
...TOWARD THE HOLES IN THE SKY...

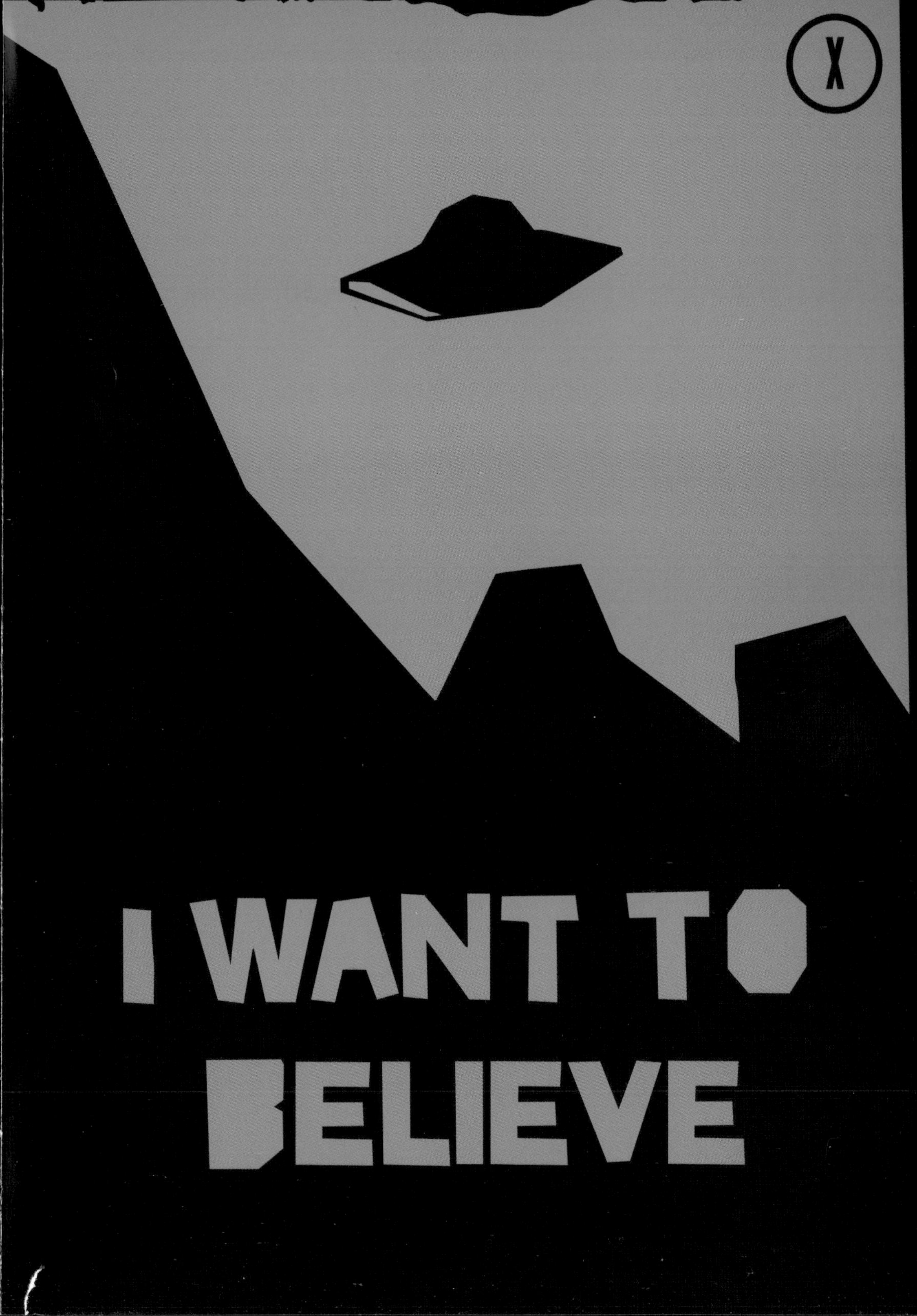
I WANT TO
BELIEVE

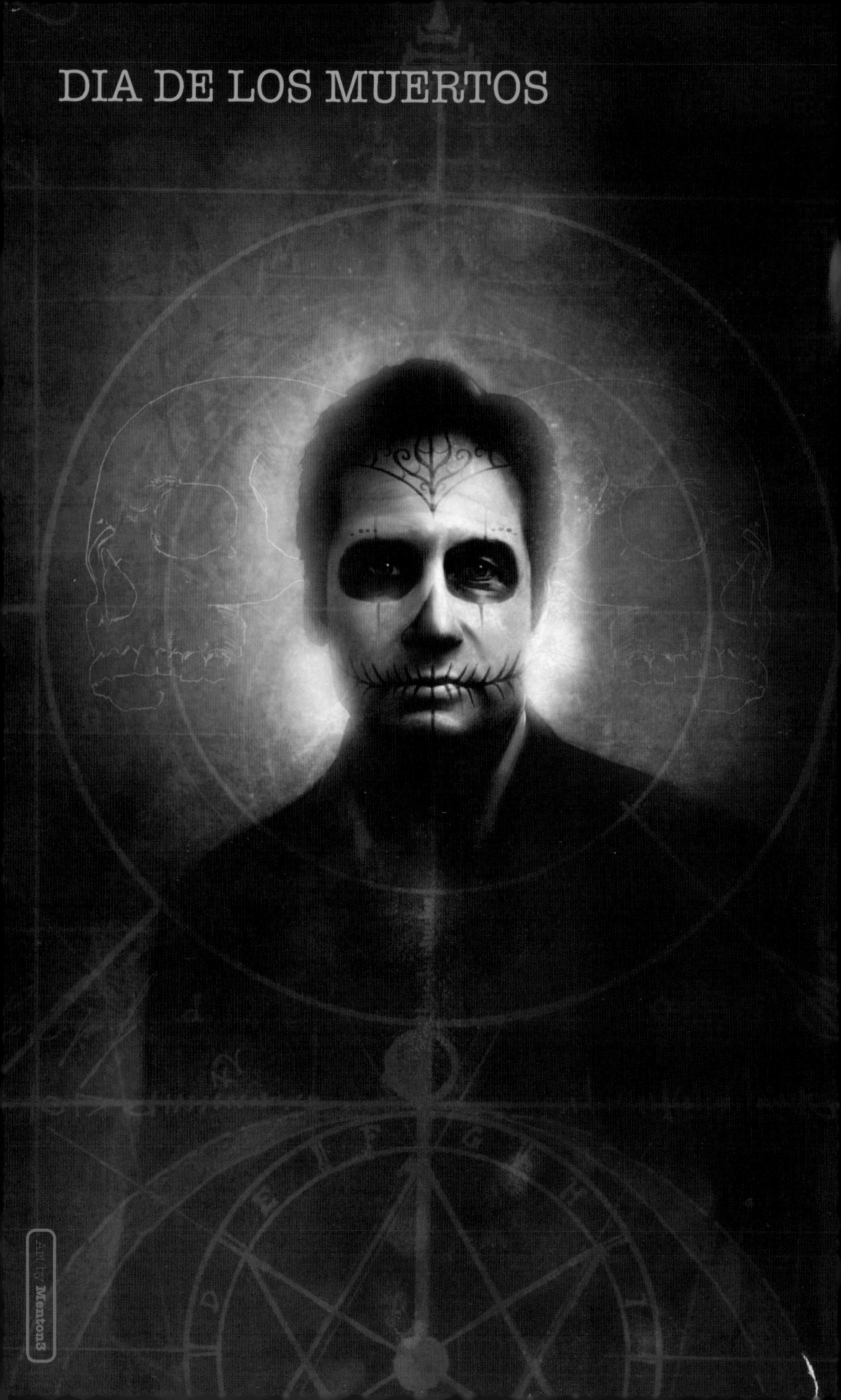
DIA DE LOS MUERTOS
Art by Menton3

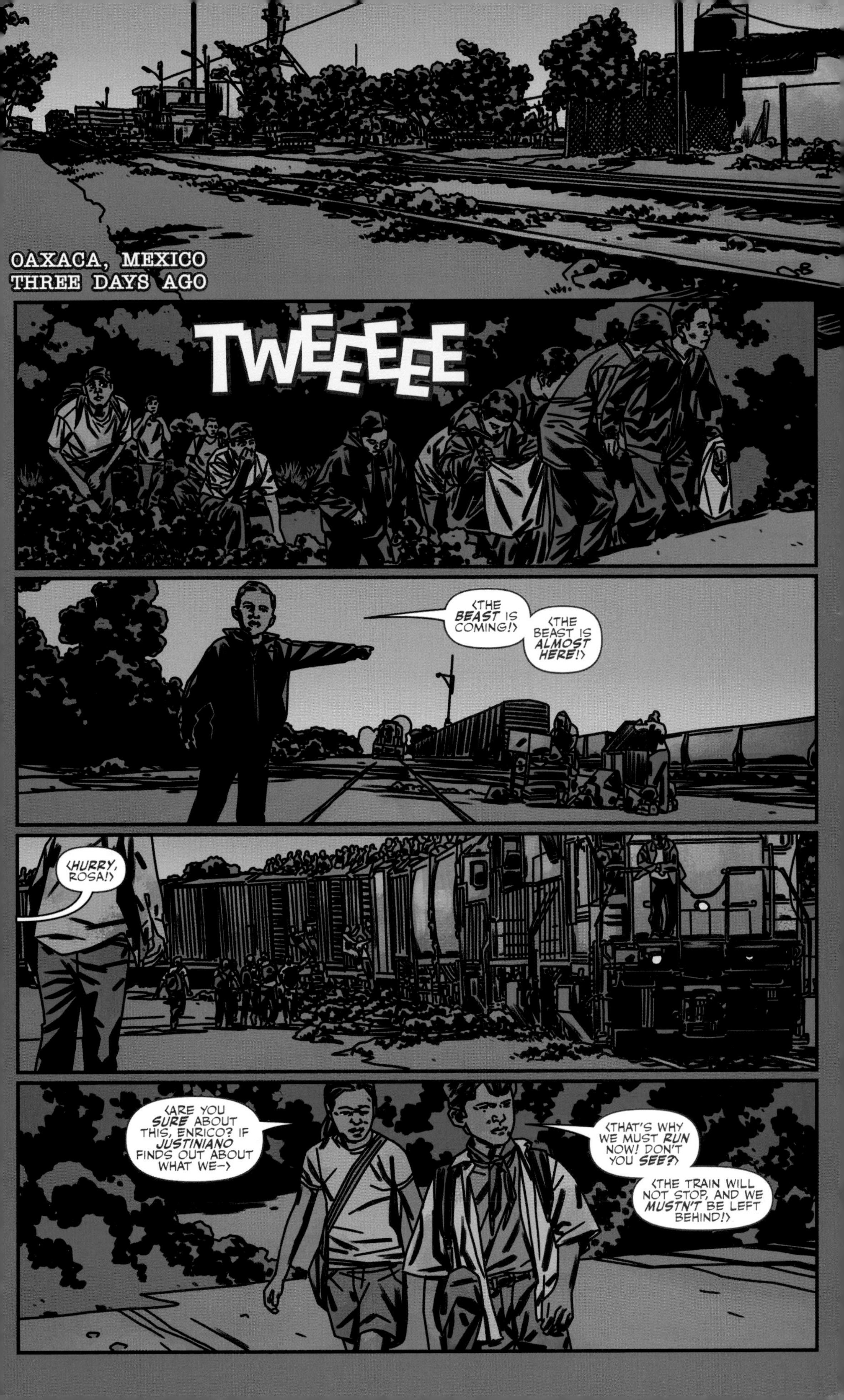
OAXACA, MEXICO
THREE DAYS AGO
TWEEEEE
‹THE BEAST IS COMING!›
‹THE BEAST IS ALMOST HERE!›
‹HURRY, ROSA!›
‹ARE YOU SURE ABOUT THIS, ENRICO? IF JUSTINIANO FINDS OUT ABOUT WHAT WE–›
‹THAT'S WHY WE MUST RUN NOW! DON'T YOU SEE?›
‹THE TRAIN WILL NOT STOP, AND WE MUSTN'T BE LEFT BEHIND!›

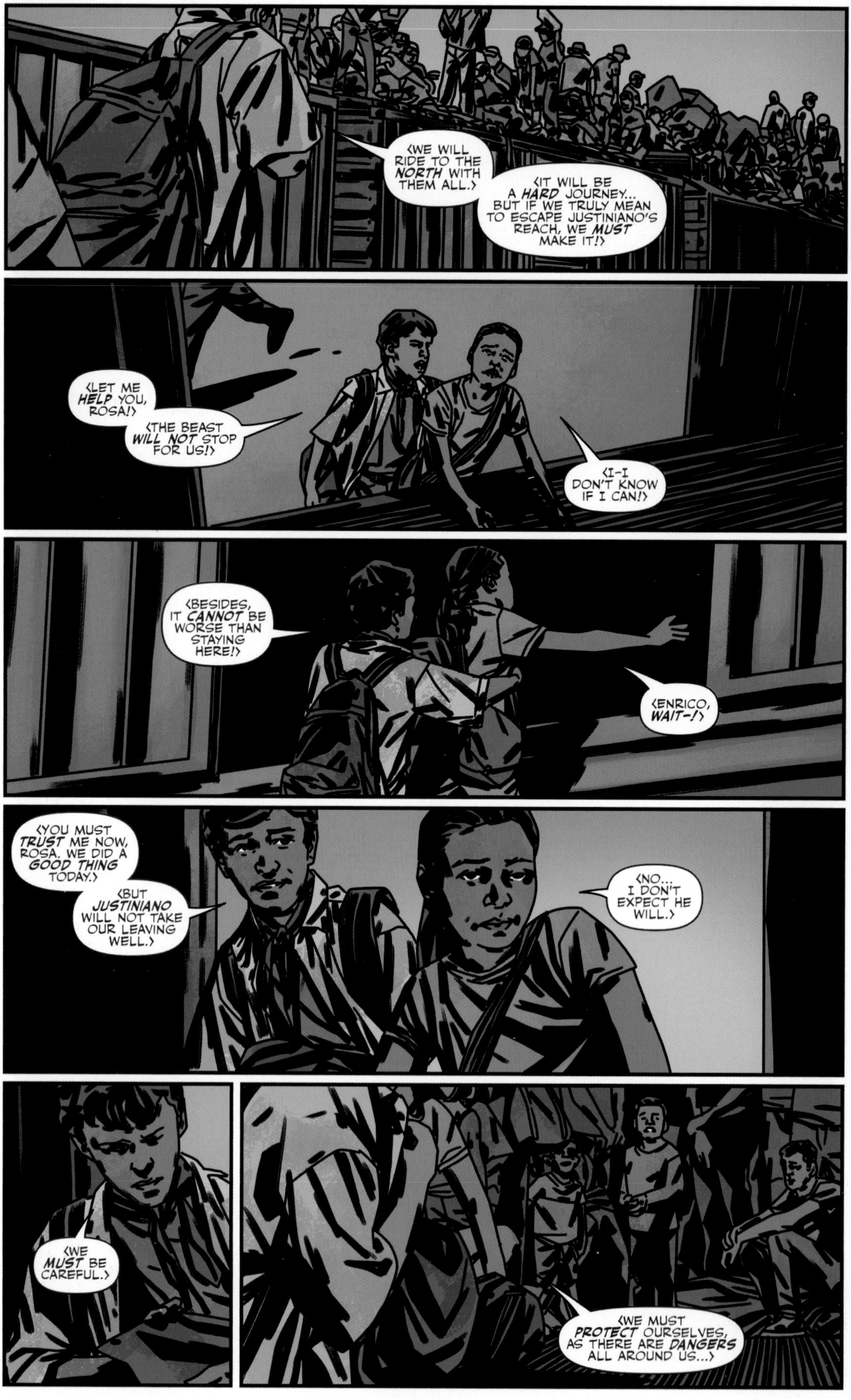
⟨WE WILL RIDE TO THE NORTH WITH THEM ALL.⟩
⟨IT WILL BE A HARD JOURNEY... BUT IF WE TRULY MEAN TO ESCAPE JUSTINIANO'S REACH, WE MUST MAKE IT!⟩
⟨LET ME HELP YOU, ROSA!⟩
⟨THE BEAST WILL NOT STOP FOR US!⟩
⟨I-I DON'T KNOW IF I CAN!⟩
⟨BESIDES, IT CANNOT BE WORSE THAN STAYING HERE!⟩
⟨ENRICO, WAIT-!⟩
⟨YOU MUST TRUST ME NOW, ROSA. WE DID A GOOD THING TODAY.⟩
⟨BUT JUSTINIANO WILL NOT TAKE OUR LEAVING WELL.⟩
⟨NO... I DON'T EXPECT HE WILL.⟩
⟨WE MUST BE CAREFUL.⟩
⟨WE MUST PROTECT OURSELVES, AS THERE ARE DANGERS ALL AROUND US...⟩

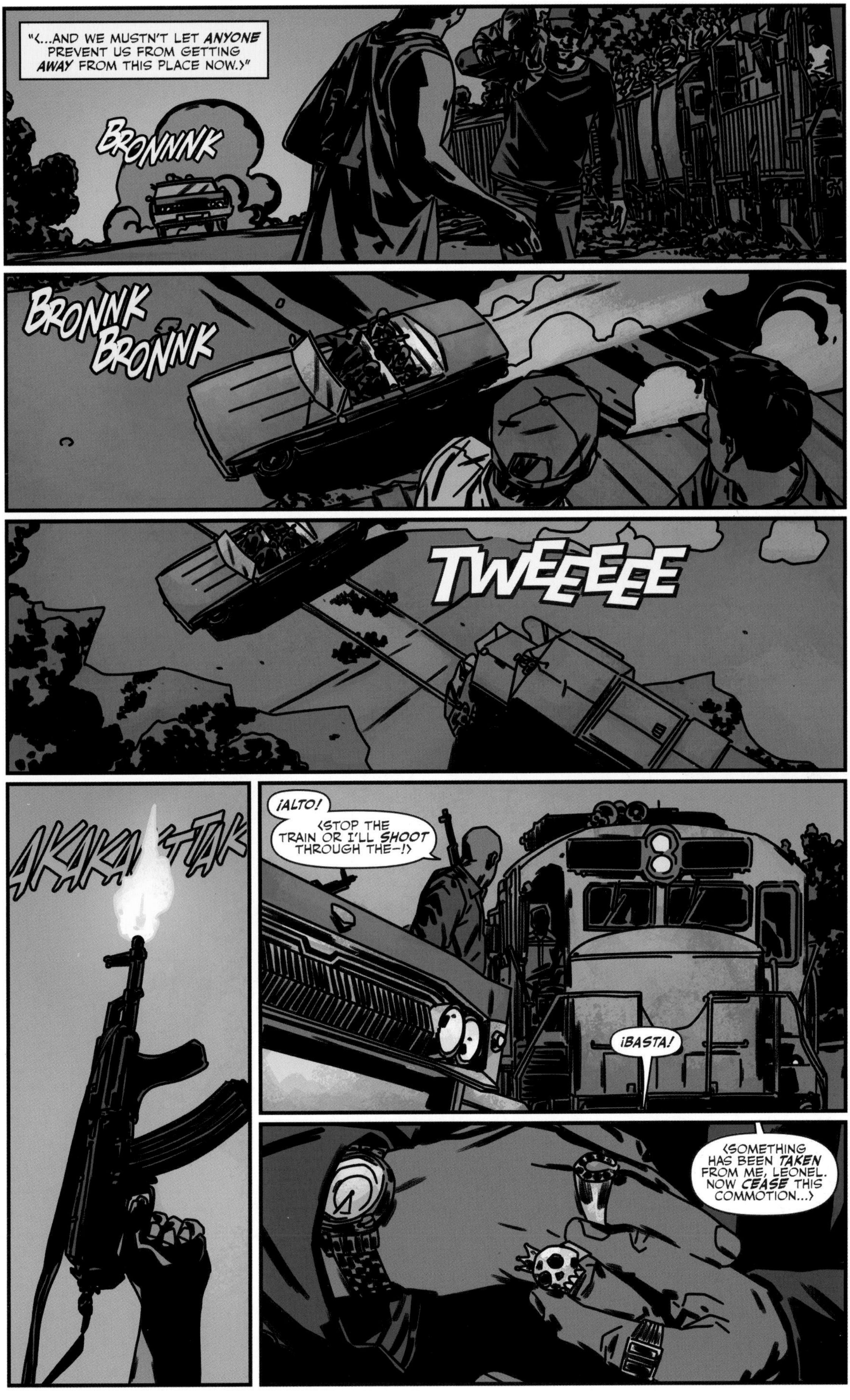
"‹...AND WE MUSTN'T LET ANYONE PREVENT US FROM GETTING AWAY FROM THIS PLACE NOW.›"
BRONNNK
BRONNK BRONNK
TWEEEEEE
¡ALTO!
‹STOP THE TRAIN OR I'LL SHOOT THROUGH THE–!›
¡BASTA!
‹SOMETHING HAS BEEN TAKEN FROM ME, LEONEL. NOW CEASE THIS COMMOTION...›

"<...AND GO AND TAKE IT *BACK* ALREADY.>

HOLA, MI AMIGOS!

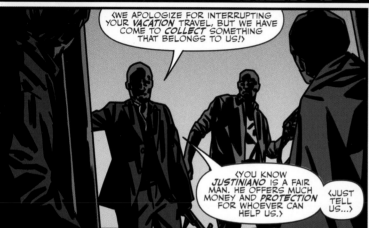

<WE APOLOGIZE FOR INTERRUPTING YOUR *VACATION* TRAVEL, BUT WE HAVE COME TO *COLLECT* SOMETHING THAT BELONGS TO US!>

<YOU KNOW *JUSTINIANO* IS A FAIR MAN. HE OFFERS MUCH MONEY AND *PROTECTION* FOR WHOEVER CAN HELP US.>

<JUST TELL US...>

<...*WHERE* IS THIS BOY AND HIS SISTER?>

<YOU KNOW WHAT WE CAN *DO* TO MAKE YOU TALK, AND WHAT WE CAN DO TO YOUR *FAMILIES*.>

<THESE THIEVES ARE NOT *WORTH* YOUR SILENCE...>

<DON'T BE *AFRAID*, ROSA. IT'S LIKE I WAS TOLD...>

<...OUR *OFFERING* WAS FAIR.>

<...*OR* YOUR *TONGUES!*>

<YOU MUST *TRY* TO NOT BE AFRAID, ROSA.>

<THINGS ARE IN THE HANDS OF THE *SAINTS* NOW.>

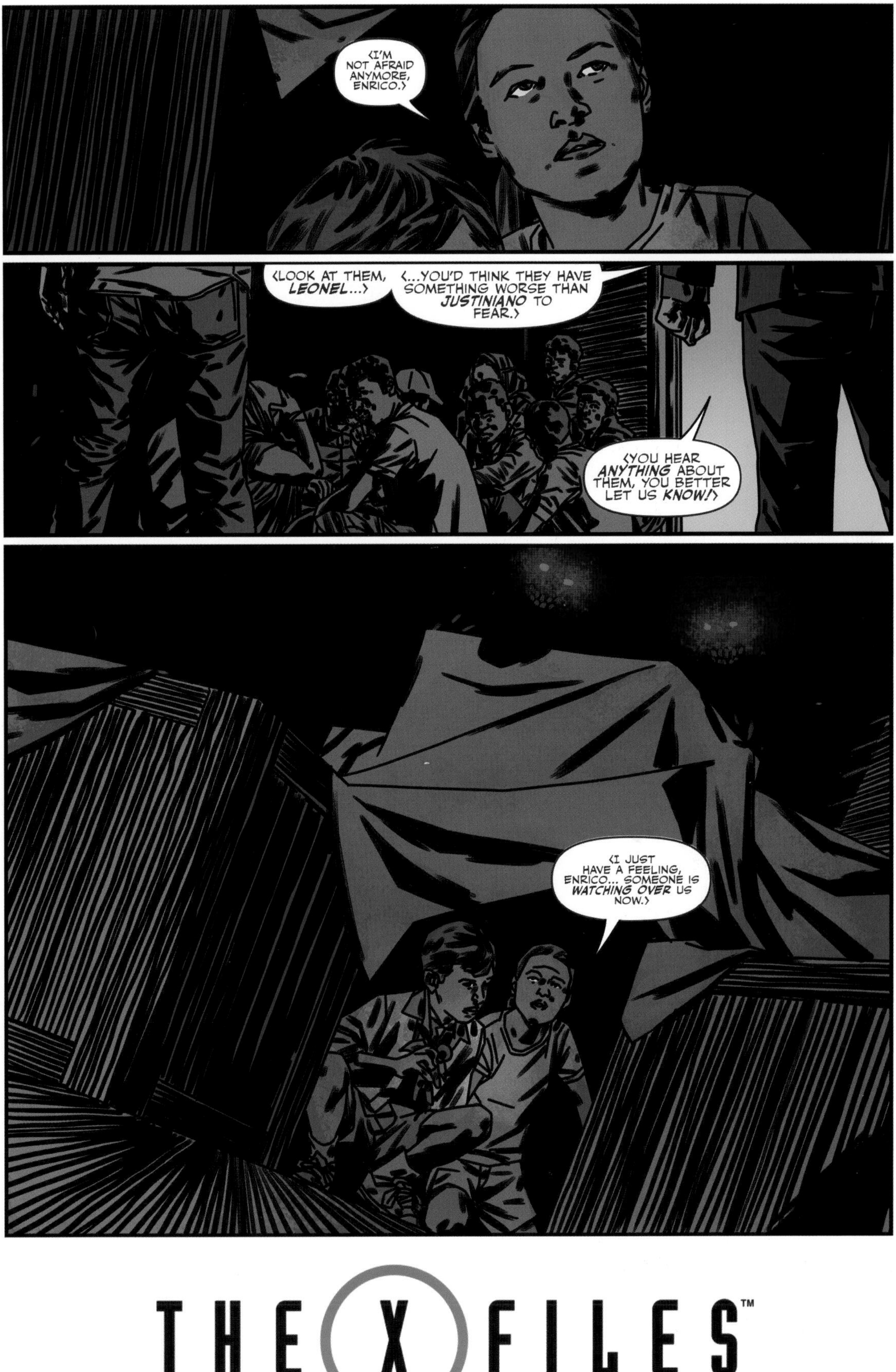
‹I'M NOT AFRAID ANYMORE, ENRICO.›
‹LOOK AT THEM, LEONEL...›
‹...YOU'D THINK THEY HAVE SOMETHING WORSE THAN JUSTINIANO TO FEAR.›
‹YOU HEAR ANYTHING ABOUT THEM, YOU BETTER LET US KNOW!›
‹I JUST HAVE A FEELING, ENRICO... SOMEONE IS WATCHING OVER US NOW.›

THE X FILES™

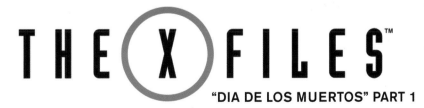

"DIA DE LOS MUERTOS" PART 1

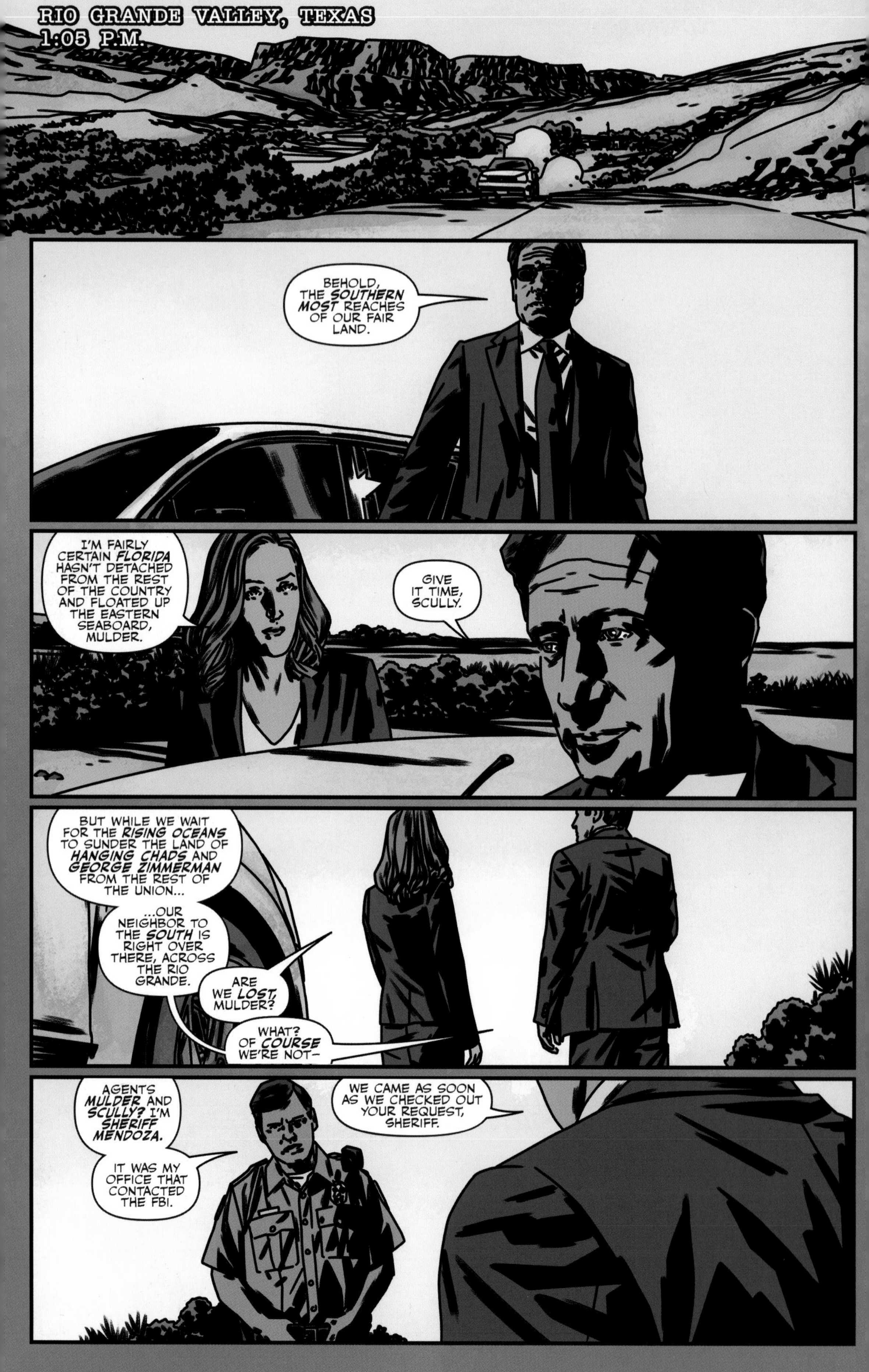
RIO GRANDE VALLEY, TEXAS
1:05 P.M.
BEHOLD, THE SOUTHERN MOST REACHES OF OUR FAIR LAND.
I'M FAIRLY CERTAIN FLORIDA HASN'T DETACHED FROM THE REST OF THE COUNTRY AND FLOATED UP THE EASTERN SEABOARD, MULDER.
GIVE IT TIME, SCULLY.
BUT WHILE WE WAIT FOR THE RISING OCEANS TO SUNDER THE LAND OF HANGING CHADS AND GEORGE ZIMMERMAN FROM THE REST OF THE UNION...
...OUR NEIGHBOR TO THE SOUTH IS RIGHT OVER THERE, ACROSS THE RIO GRANDE.
ARE WE LOST, MULDER?
WHAT? OF COURSE WE'RE NOT--
AGENTS MULDER AND SCULLY? I'M SHERIFF MENDOZA.
IT WAS MY OFFICE THAT CONTACTED THE FBI.
WE CAME AS SOON AS WE CHECKED OUT YOUR REQUEST, SHERIFF.

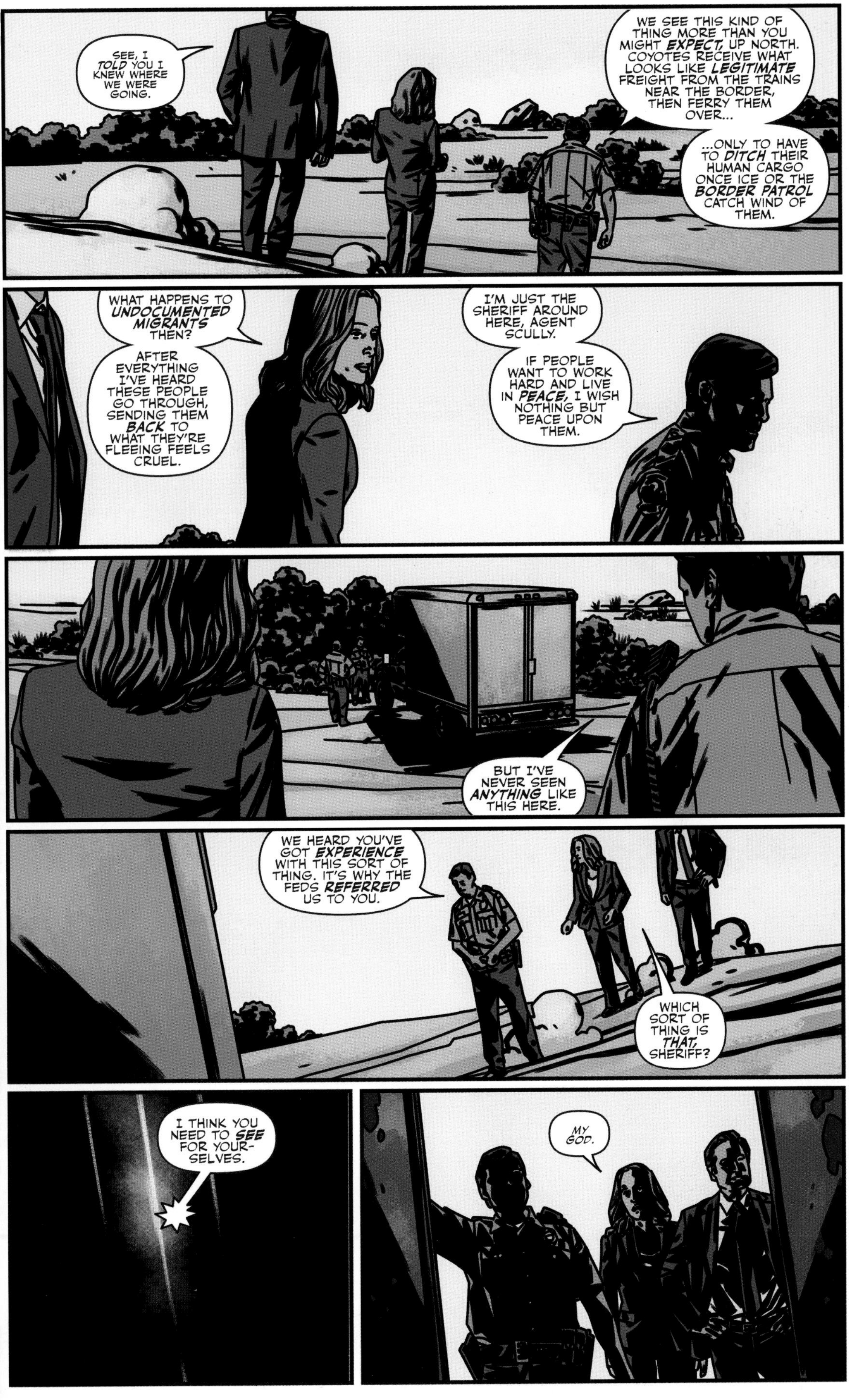
SEE, I TOLD YOU I KNEW WHERE WE WERE GOING.
WE SEE THIS KIND OF THING MORE THAN YOU MIGHT EXPECT, UP NORTH. COYOTES RECEIVE WHAT LOOKS LIKE LEGITIMATE FREIGHT FROM THE TRAINS NEAR THE BORDER, THEN FERRY THEM OVER...
...ONLY TO HAVE TO DITCH THEIR HUMAN CARGO ONCE ICE OR THE BORDER PATROL CATCH WIND OF THEM.
WHAT HAPPENS TO UNDOCUMENTED MIGRANTS THEN?
AFTER EVERYTHING I'VE HEARD THESE PEOPLE GO THROUGH, SENDING THEM BACK TO WHAT THEY'RE FLEEING FEELS CRUEL.
I'M JUST THE SHERIFF AROUND HERE, AGENT SCULLY.
IF PEOPLE WANT TO WORK HARD AND LIVE IN PEACE, I WISH NOTHING BUT PEACE UPON THEM.
BUT I'VE NEVER SEEN ANYTHING LIKE THIS HERE.
WE HEARD YOU'VE GOT EXPERIENCE WITH THIS SORT OF THING. IT'S WHY THE FEDS REFERRED US TO YOU.
WHICH SORT OF THING IS THAT, SHERIFF?
I THINK YOU NEED TO SEE FOR YOURSELVES.
MY GOD.

WE PULLED 37 *BODIES* OUT OF THERE, EARLIER THIS MORNING.

NONE OF THEM WITH *ANY* IDENTIFICATION, AND *ALL OF THEM* JUST RIPPED TO PIECES.

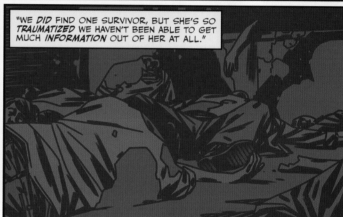

"WE *DID* FIND ONE SURVIVOR, BUT SHE'S SO *TRAUMATIZED* WE HAVEN'T BEEN ABLE TO GET MUCH *INFORMATION* OUT OF HER AT ALL."

JUDGING BY THE *WHOLE-SALE SLAUGHTER* SHE WOULD APPEAR TO HAVE WITNESSED, THAT DOESN'T SURPRISE ME.

THAT'S BY *DESIGN* SOMETIMES, TOO. *WIPE OUT* AN ENTIRE GROUP OF AND YOU SEND A *MESSAGE*.

BUT IF YOU'RE WILLING TO LEAVE A *WITNESS* TO IT ALL...

"...FOLKS JUST *KNOW* YOU'RE NOT PLAYING AROUND."

WHAT ABOUT THE *DRIVER* OF THE TRUCK?

LOOKS LIKE *HE* MET THE SAME FATE AS HIS HUMAN CARGO.

NOT MUCH *OF* HIM LEFT, IN ANY CASE.

THESE *GANGS*... THEY'RE ALL CONNECTED TO THE *CARTELS*, EITHER INDIRECTLY OR EVEN UNDER THEIR *DIRECT COMMAND*, THESE DAYS.

YOU THINK THE *CARTELS* DID THIS?

WHAT WOULD THEY *GAIN* FROM THE MASS MURDER OF *DESPERATE IMMIGRANTS* ON AMERICAN SOIL?

WE DON'T KNOW WHO THESE MIGRANTS *WERE*, AGENT SCULLY.

BUT IF I HAD A *NICKEL* FOR EVERY TIME I COULDN'T WRAP MY HEAD AROUND HOW THESE *MONSTERS* DO THEIR BUSINESS, IT'D PUSH ME TOWARD THAT *RETIREMENT* MY WIFE KEEPS ASKING ABOUT.

SCULLY, COME TAKE A *LOOK* AT THIS.

THERE'S NO *SHORTAGE* OF THINGS TO LOOK AT, UNFORTUNATELY.

THANK YOU, MULDER... THEY'RE *LOVELY?*

THEY'RE *MARIGOLDS*. SYMBOLS OF LIFE'S FRAGILE, FLEETING BEAUTY.

THEY FIGURE PROMINENTLY IN MEXICAN *DAY OF THE DEAD* RITUALS, GUIDING THE SPIRITS TO *ALTARS* LEFT FOR THEM BY THE LIVING.

SO WERE THEY LEFT BY THE *KILLERS* OR THE *VICTIMS?*

THEREIN LIES ONE OF A NUMBER OF *MYSTERIES*, MY DEAR *GUMSHOE*...

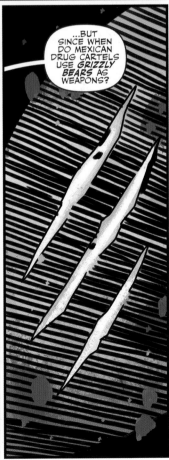

...BUT SINCE WHEN DO MEXICAN DRUG CARTELS USE *GRIZZLY BEARS* AS WEAPONS?

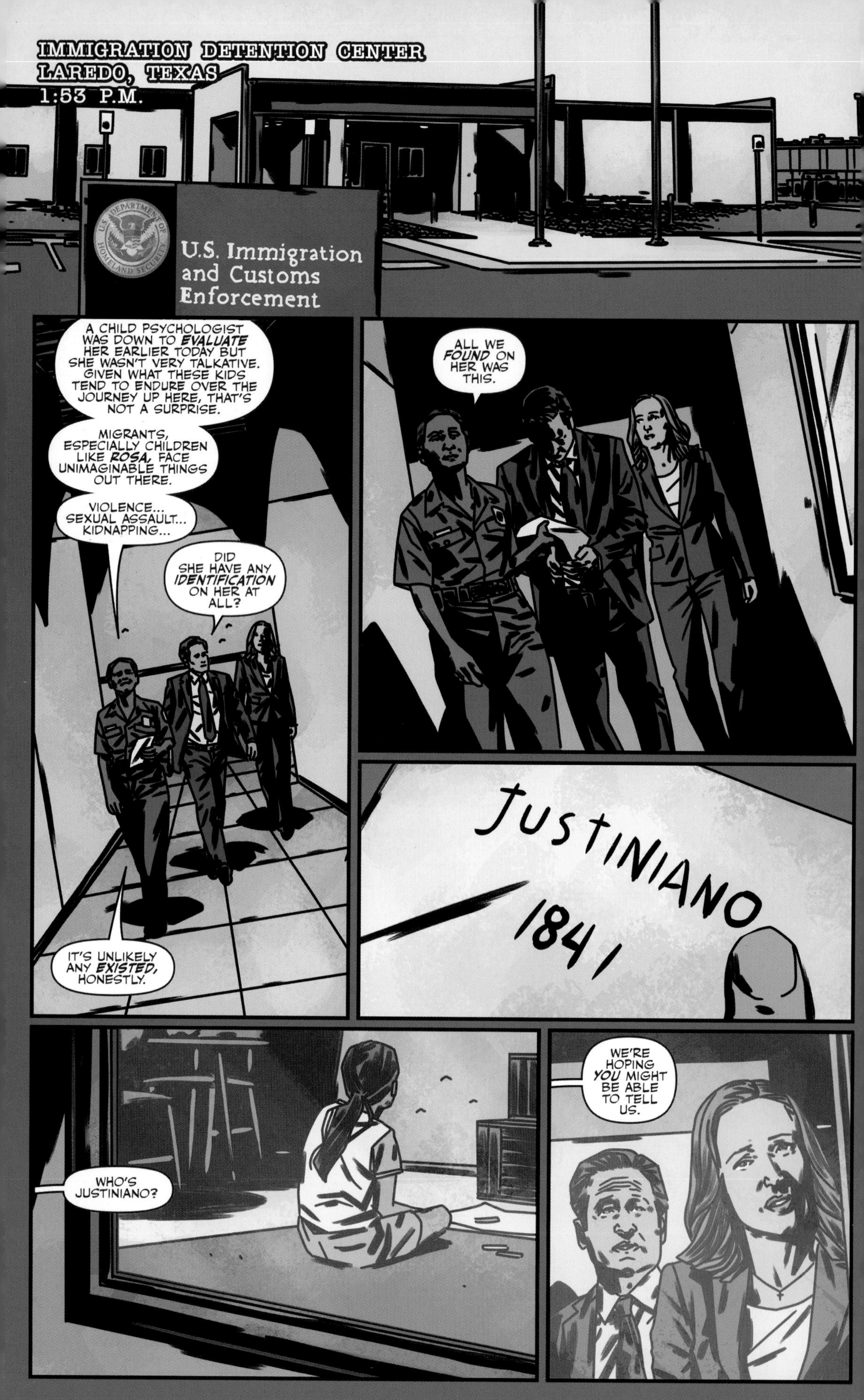
IMMIGRATION DETENTION CENTER
LAREDO, TEXAS
1:53 P.M.
U.S. Immigration and Customs Enforcement
U.S. DEPARTMENT OF HOMELAND SECURITY
A CHILD PSYCHOLOGIST WAS DOWN TO EVALUATE HER EARLIER TODAY BUT SHE WASN'T VERY TALKATIVE. GIVEN WHAT THESE KIDS TEND TO ENDURE OVER THE JOURNEY UP HERE, THAT'S NOT A SURPRISE.
MIGRANTS, ESPECIALLY CHILDREN LIKE ROSA, FACE UNIMAGINABLE THINGS OUT THERE.
VIOLENCE... SEXUAL ASSAULT... KIDNAPPING...
DID SHE HAVE ANY IDENTIFICATION ON HER AT ALL?
IT'S UNLIKELY ANY EXISTED, HONESTLY.
ALL WE FOUND ON HER WAS THIS.
JUSTINIANO
1841
WHO'S JUSTINIANO?
WE'RE HOPING YOU MIGHT BE ABLE TO TELL US.

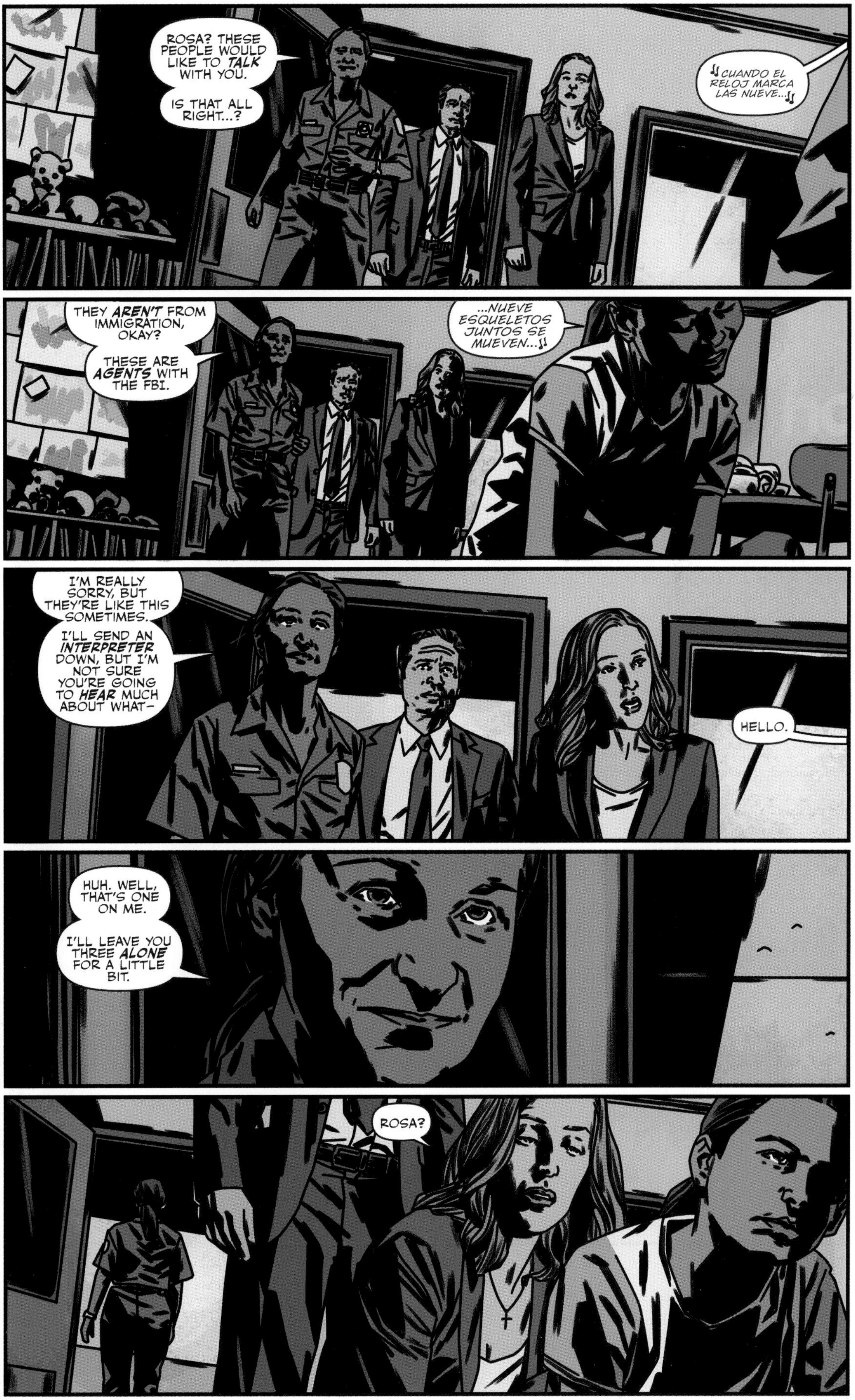

ROSA? THESE PEOPLE WOULD LIKE TO TALK WITH YOU.
IS THAT ALL RIGHT...?
♪ CUANDO EL RELOJ MARCA LAS NUEVE... ♪
THEY AREN'T FROM IMMIGRATION, OKAY?
THESE ARE AGENTS WITH THE FBI.
...NUEVE ESQUELETOS JUNTOS SE MUEVEN... ♪
I'M REALLY SORRY, BUT THEY'RE LIKE THIS SOMETIMES.
I'LL SEND AN INTERPRETER DOWN, BUT I'M NOT SURE YOU'RE GOING TO HEAR MUCH ABOUT WHAT-
HELLO.
HUH. WELL, THAT'S ONE ON ME.
I'LL LEAVE YOU THREE ALONE FOR A LITTLE BIT.
ROSA?

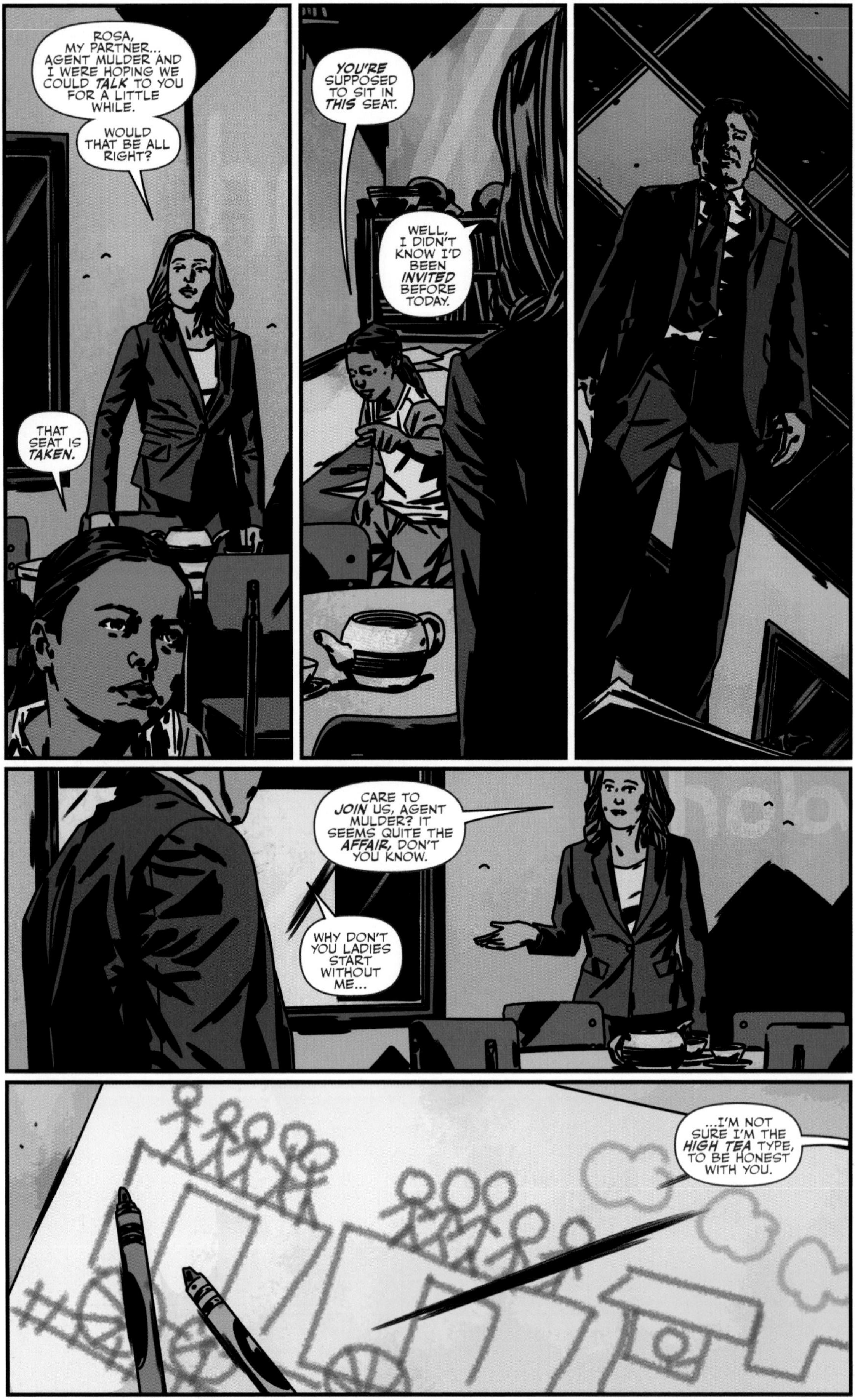

ROSA, MY PARTNER... AGENT MULDER AND I WERE HOPING WE COULD TALK TO YOU FOR A LITTLE WHILE.
WOULD THAT BE ALL RIGHT?
THAT SEAT IS TAKEN.
YOU'RE SUPPOSED TO SIT IN THIS SEAT.
WELL, I DIDN'T KNOW I'D BEEN INVITED BEFORE TODAY.
CARE TO JOIN US, AGENT MULDER? IT SEEMS QUITE THE AFFAIR, DON'T YOU KNOW.
WHY DON'T YOU LADIES START WITHOUT ME...
...I'M NOT SURE I'M THE HIGH TEA TYPE, TO BE HONEST WITH YOU.

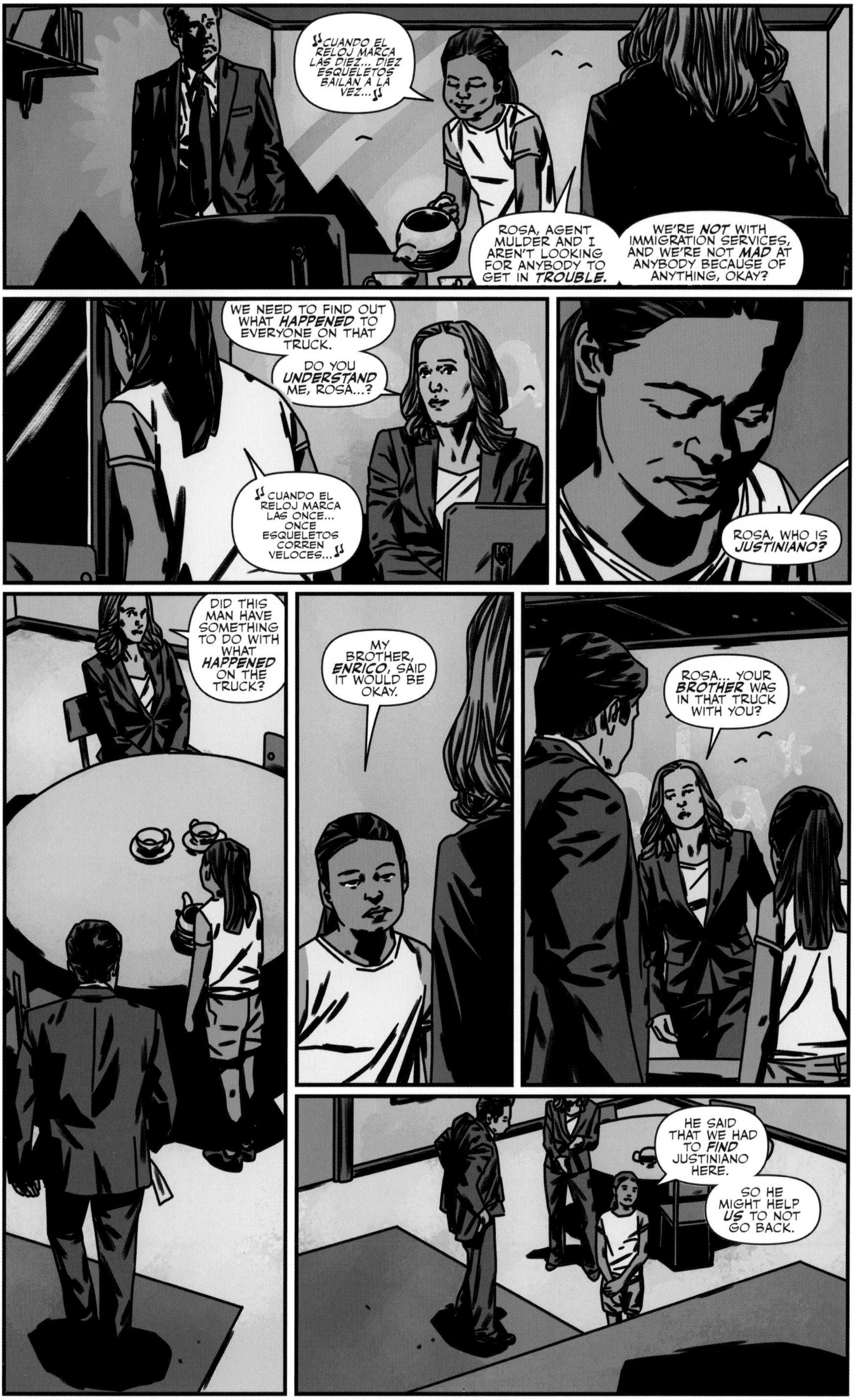
♫CUANDO EL RELOJ MARCA LAS DIEZ... DIEZ ESQUELETOS BAILAN A LA VEZ...♫
ROSA, AGENT MULDER AND I AREN'T LOOKING FOR ANYBODY TO GET IN TROUBLE.
WE'RE NOT WITH IMMIGRATION SERVICES, AND WE'RE NOT MAD AT ANYBODY BECAUSE OF ANYTHING, OKAY?
WE NEED TO FIND OUT WHAT HAPPENED TO EVERYONE ON THAT TRUCK.
DO YOU UNDERSTAND ME, ROSA...?
♫CUANDO EL RELOJ MARCA LAS ONCE... ONCE ESQUELETOS CORREN VELOCES...♫
ROSA, WHO IS JUSTINIANO?
DID THIS MAN HAVE SOMETHING TO DO WITH WHAT HAPPENED ON THE TRUCK?
MY BROTHER, ENRICO, SAID IT WOULD BE OKAY.
ROSA... YOUR BROTHER WAS IN THAT TRUCK WITH YOU?
HE SAID THAT WE HAD TO FIND JUSTINIANO HERE.
SO HE MIGHT HELP US TO NOT GO BACK.

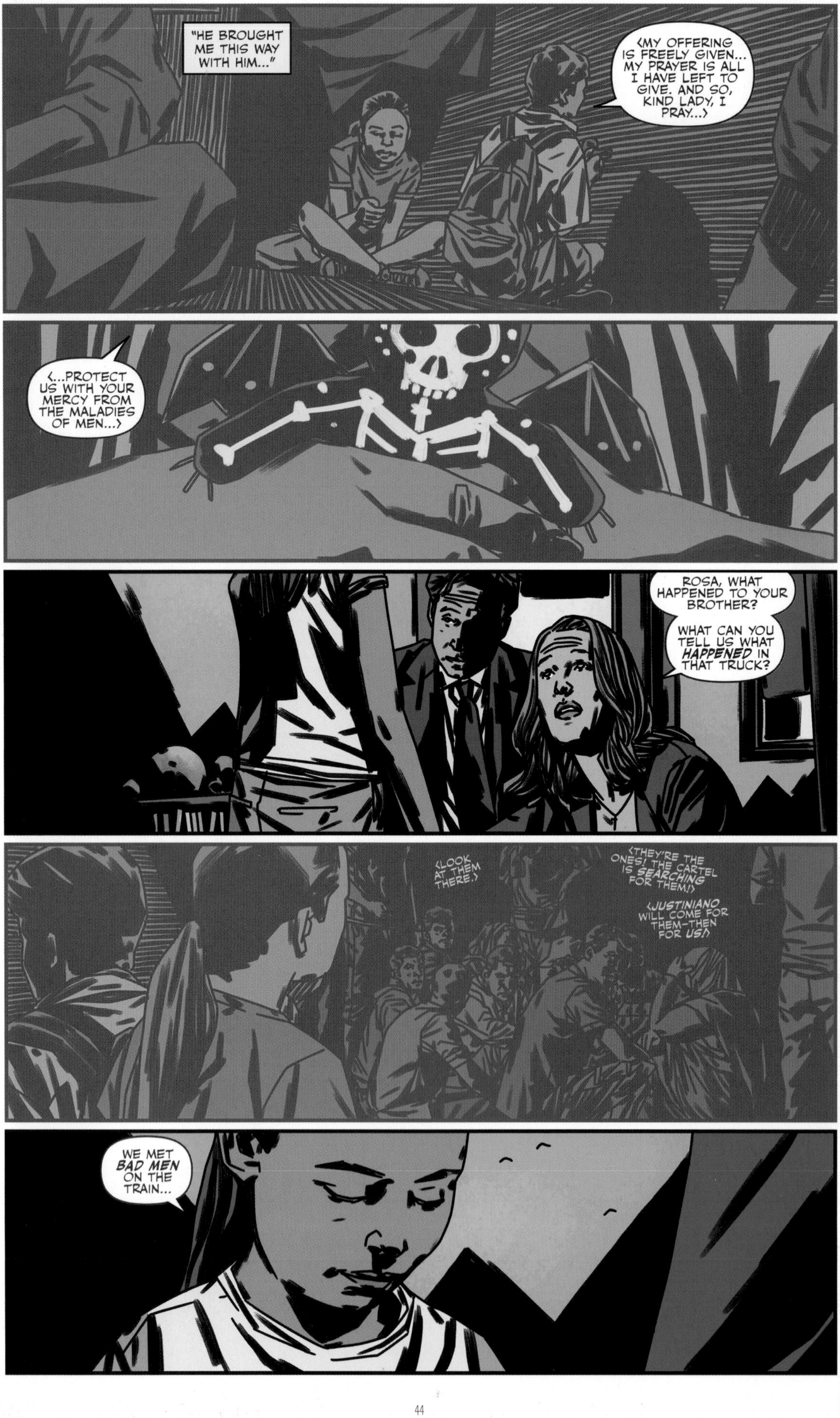
"HE BROUGHT ME THIS WAY WITH HIM..."
‹MY OFFERING IS FREELY GIVEN... MY PRAYER IS ALL I HAVE LEFT TO GIVE. AND SO, KIND LADY, I PRAY...›
‹...PROTECT US WITH YOUR MERCY FROM THE MALADIES OF MEN...›
ROSA, WHAT HAPPENED TO YOUR BROTHER?
WHAT CAN YOU TELL US WHAT HAPPENED IN THAT TRUCK?
‹LOOK AT THEM THERE.›
‹THEY'RE THE ONES! THE CARTEL IS SEARCHING FOR THEM!›
‹JUSTINIANO WILL COME FOR THEM—THEN FOR US!›
WE MET BAD MEN ON THE TRAIN...

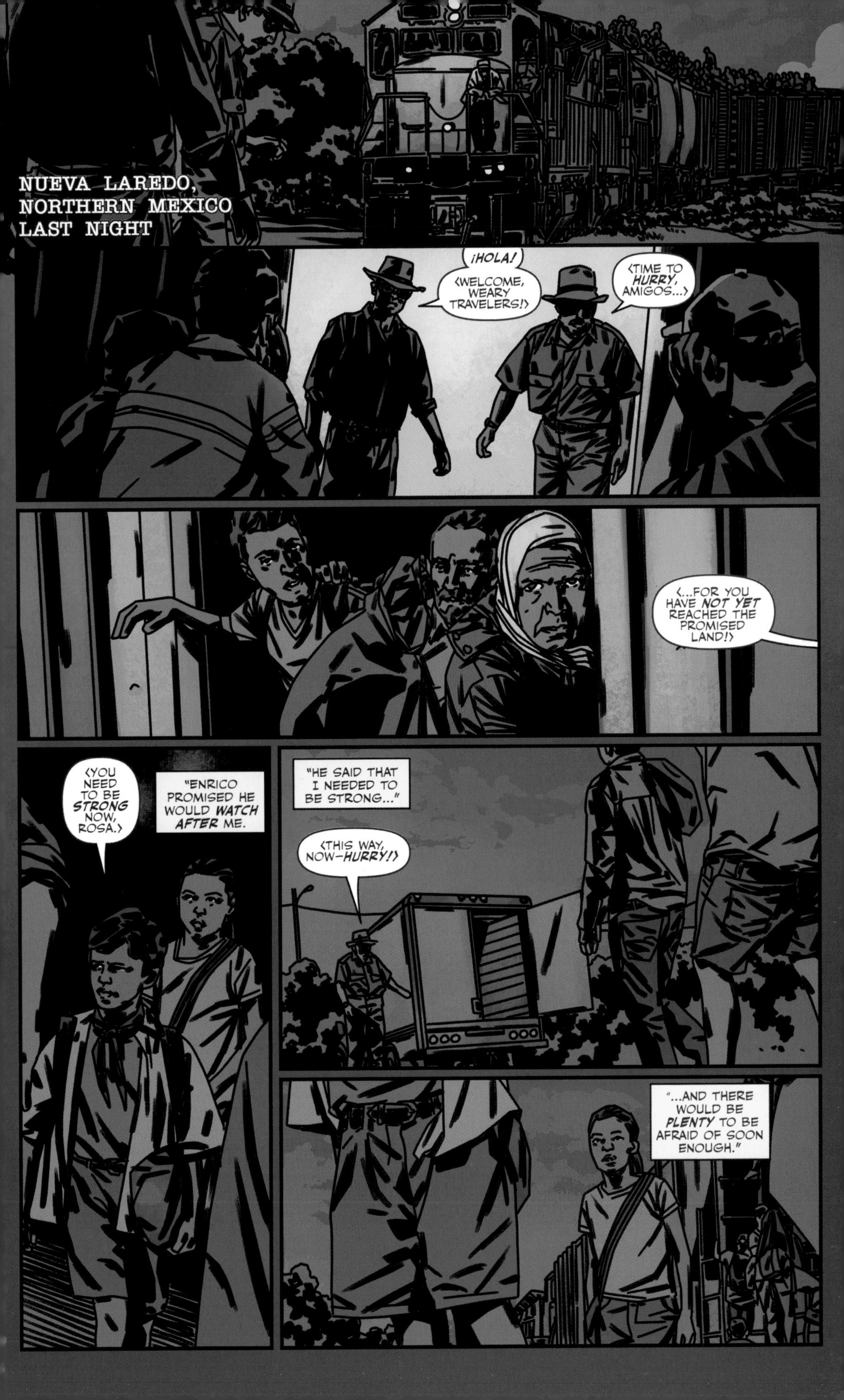
NUEVA LAREDO,
NORTHERN MEXICO
LAST NIGHT
¡HOLA!
‹WELCOME, WEARY TRAVELERS!›
‹TIME TO HURRY, AMIGOS...›
‹...FOR YOU HAVE NOT YET REACHED THE PROMISED LAND!›
‹YOU NEED TO BE STRONG NOW, ROSA.›
"ENRICO PROMISED HE WOULD WATCH AFTER ME.
"HE SAID THAT I NEEDED TO BE STRONG..."
‹THIS WAY, NOW–HURRY!›
"...AND THERE WOULD BE PLENTY TO BE AFRAID OF SOON ENOUGH."

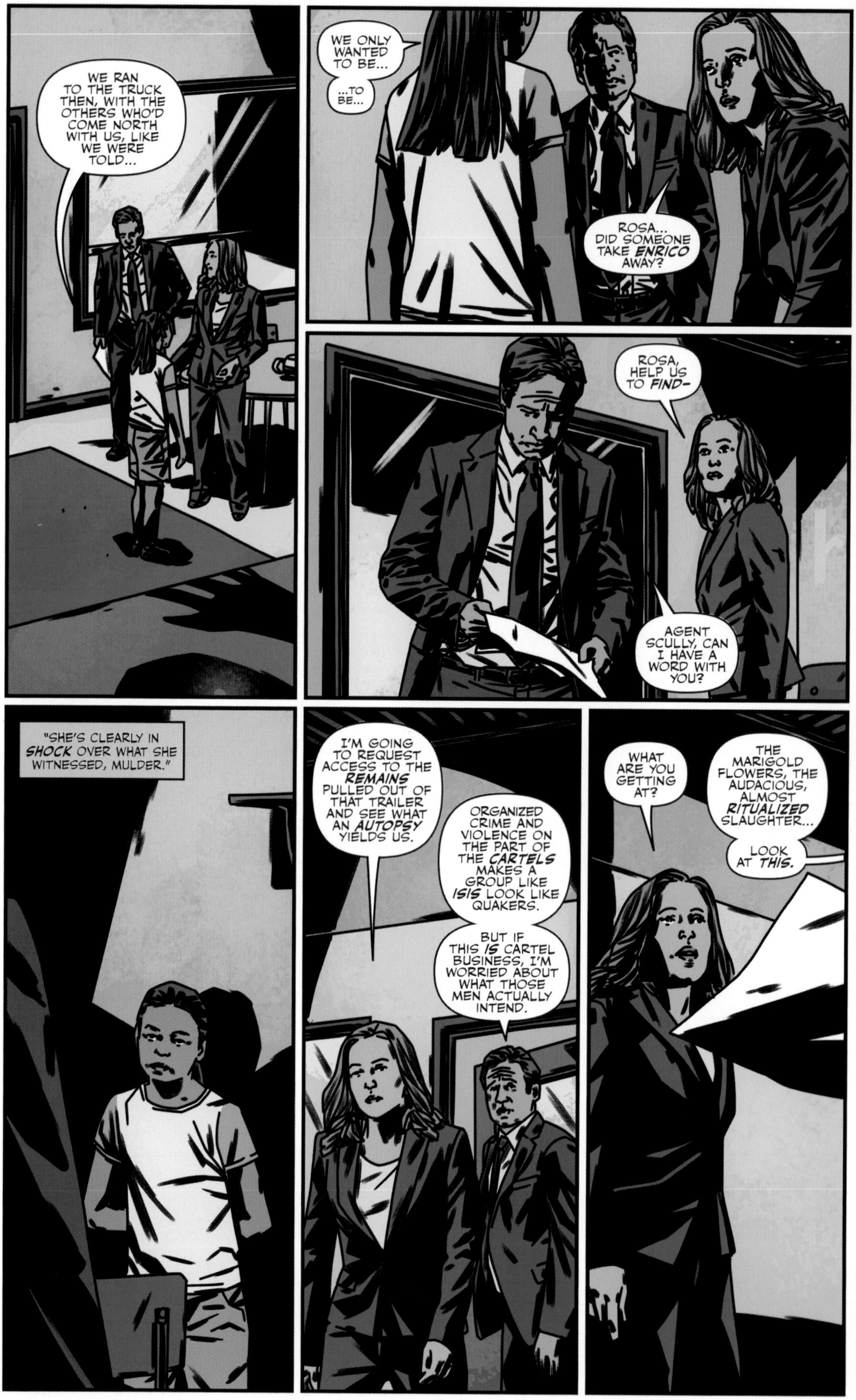
WE RAN TO THE TRUCK THEN, WITH THE OTHERS WHO'D COME NORTH WITH US, LIKE WE WERE TOLD...
WE ONLY WANTED TO BE...
...TO BE...
ROSA... DID SOMEONE TAKE ENRICO AWAY?
ROSA, HELP US TO FIND-
AGENT SCULLY, CAN I HAVE A WORD WITH YOU?
"SHE'S CLEARLY IN SHOCK OVER WHAT SHE WITNESSED, MULDER."
I'M GOING TO REQUEST ACCESS TO THE REMAINS PULLED OUT OF THAT TRAILER AND SEE WHAT AN AUTOPSY YIELDS US.
ORGANIZED CRIME AND VIOLENCE ON THE PART OF THE CARTELS MAKES A GROUP LIKE ISIS LOOK LIKE QUAKERS.
BUT IF THIS IS CARTEL BUSINESS, I'M WORRIED ABOUT WHAT THOSE MEN ACTUALLY INTEND.
WHAT ARE YOU GETTING AT?
THE MARIGOLD FLOWERS, THE AUDACIOUS, ALMOST RITUALIZED SLAUGHTER...
LOOK AT THIS.

IT'S NOT YOUR TYPICAL "HOUSE WITHOUT WINDOWS" DRAWING THAT MAKES IT TO THE SCHOOL PSYCHOLOGIST...

...BUT SEE THE *SKULLS* AND OTHER DAY OF THE DEAD TOUCHES SHE'S DRAWING?

THE CARTELS FETISHIZE *SANTA MUERTE*, THE *DEATH ANGEL*.

THEY OFFER HER TRIBUTE AND PRAYER, AND THEY REVEL IN THE *BLOOD* SPILLED IN HER NAME.

SEE *THAT...?*

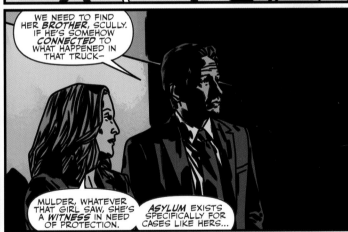

WE NEED TO FIND HER *BROTHER*, SCULLY. IF HE'S SOMEHOW *CONNECTED* TO WHAT HAPPENED IN THAT TRUCK—

MULDER, WHATEVER THAT GIRL SAW, SHE'S A *WITNESS* IN NEED OF PROTECTION.

ASYLUM EXISTS SPECIFICALLY FOR CASES LIKE HERS...

"...BUT WHAT YOU'RE SUGGESTING MAY *EXPOSE* HER TO DEPORTATION."

YOU HEAD OVER TO THE *MORGUE*, THEN *CHECK* THE CRIMINAL DATABASE AND ONGOING INVESTIGATIONS WITH NARCOTICS AND SEE WHAT *"JUSTINIANO"* TURNS UP.

WHAT ARE *YOU* GOING TO DO?

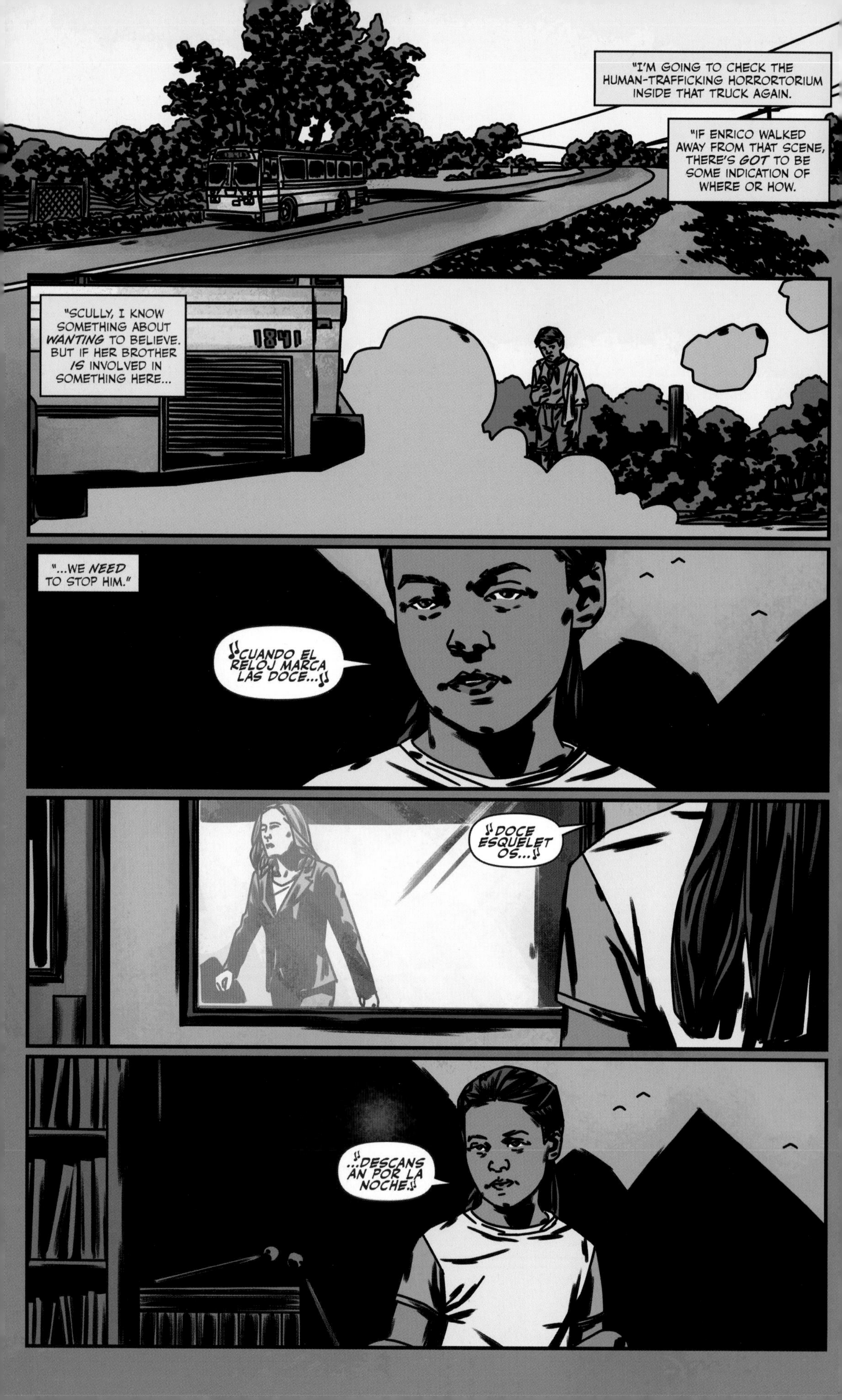
"I'M GOING TO CHECK THE HUMAN-TRAFFICKING HORRORTORIUM INSIDE THAT TRUCK AGAIN.
"IF ENRICO WALKED AWAY FROM THAT SCENE, THERE'S GOT TO BE SOME INDICATION OF WHERE OR HOW.
1841
"SCULLY, I KNOW SOMETHING ABOUT WANTING TO BELIEVE. BUT IF HER BROTHER IS INVOLVED IN SOMETHING HERE...
"...WE NEED TO STOP HIM."
♪CUANDO EL RELOJ MARCA LAS DOCE...♪
♪DOCE ESQUELET OS...♪
♪...DESCANS AN POR LA NOCHE.♪

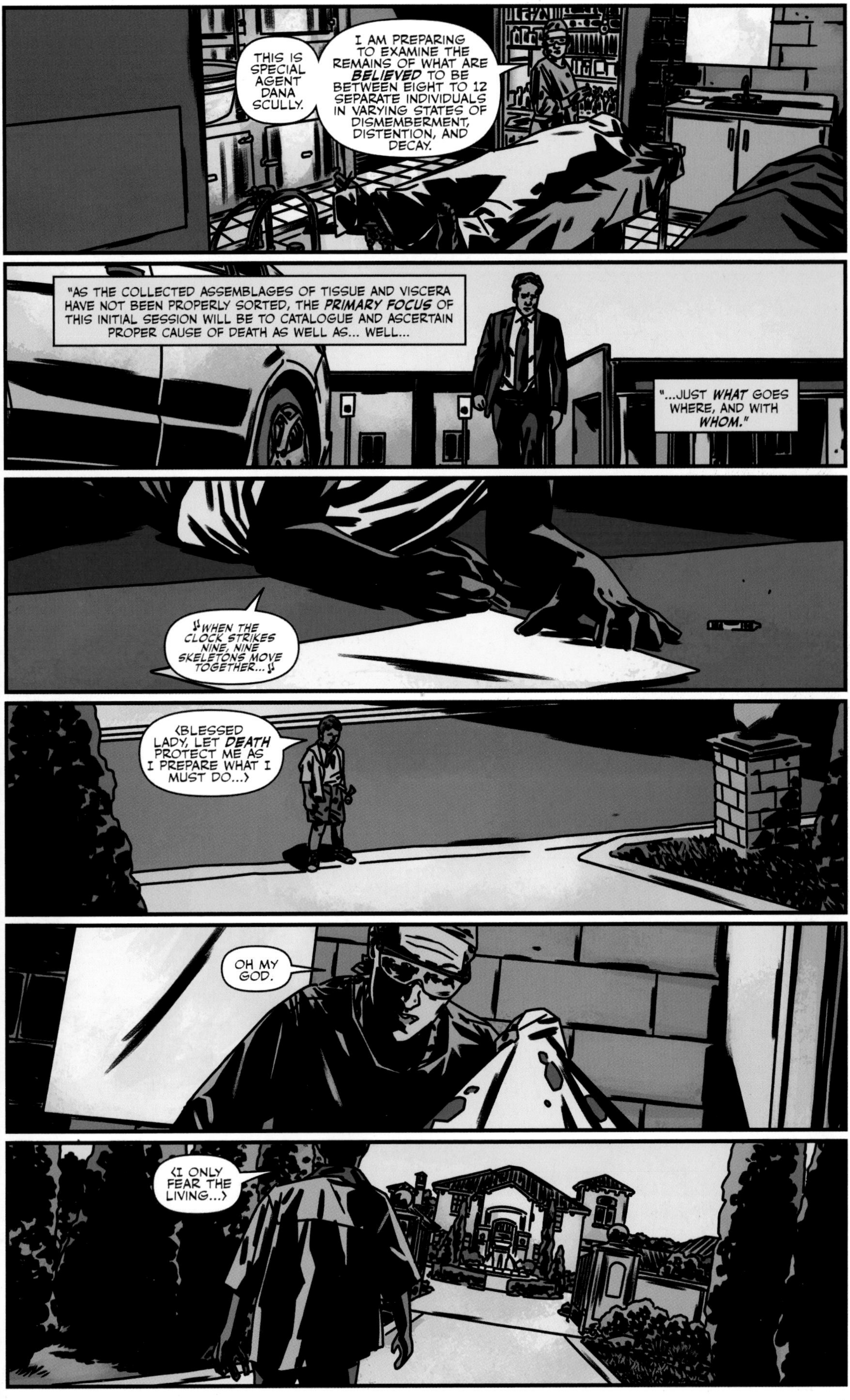
THIS IS SPECIAL AGENT DANA SCULLY.
I AM PREPARING TO EXAMINE THE REMAINS OF WHAT ARE BELIEVED TO BE BETWEEN EIGHT TO 12 SEPARATE INDIVIDUALS IN VARYING STATES OF DISMEMBERMENT, DISTENTION, AND DECAY.
"AS THE COLLECTED ASSEMBLAGES OF TISSUE AND VISCERA HAVE NOT BEEN PROPERLY SORTED, THE PRIMARY FOCUS OF THIS INITIAL SESSION WILL BE TO CATALOGUE AND ASCERTAIN PROPER CAUSE OF DEATH AS WELL AS... WELL...
"...JUST WHAT GOES WHERE, AND WITH WHOM."
♫ WHEN THE CLOCK STRIKES NINE, NINE SKELETONS MOVE TOGETHER... ♫
‹BLESSED LADY, LET DEATH PROTECT ME AS I PREPARE WHAT I MUST DO...›
OH MY GOD.
‹I ONLY FEAR THE LIVING...›

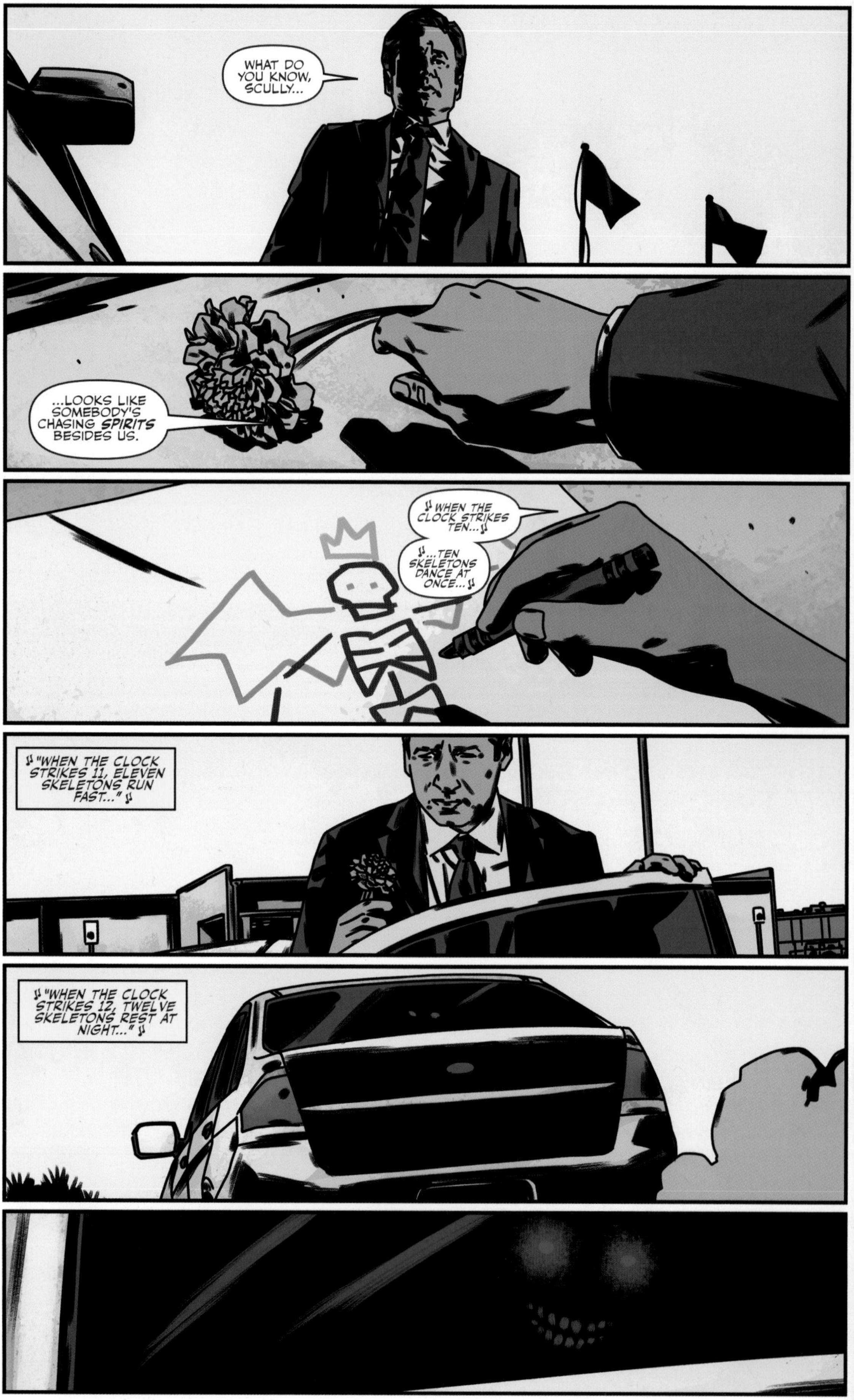
WHAT DO YOU KNOW, SCULLY...
...LOOKS LIKE SOMEBODY'S CHASING ***SPIRITS*** BESIDES US.
♫ WHEN THE CLOCK STRIKES TEN... ♫
♫ ...TEN SKELETONS DANCE AT ONCE... ♫
♫ "WHEN THE CLOCK STRIKES 11, ELEVEN SKELETONS RUN FAST..." ♫
♫ "WHEN THE CLOCK STRIKES 12, TWELVE SKELETONS REST AT NIGHT..." ♫

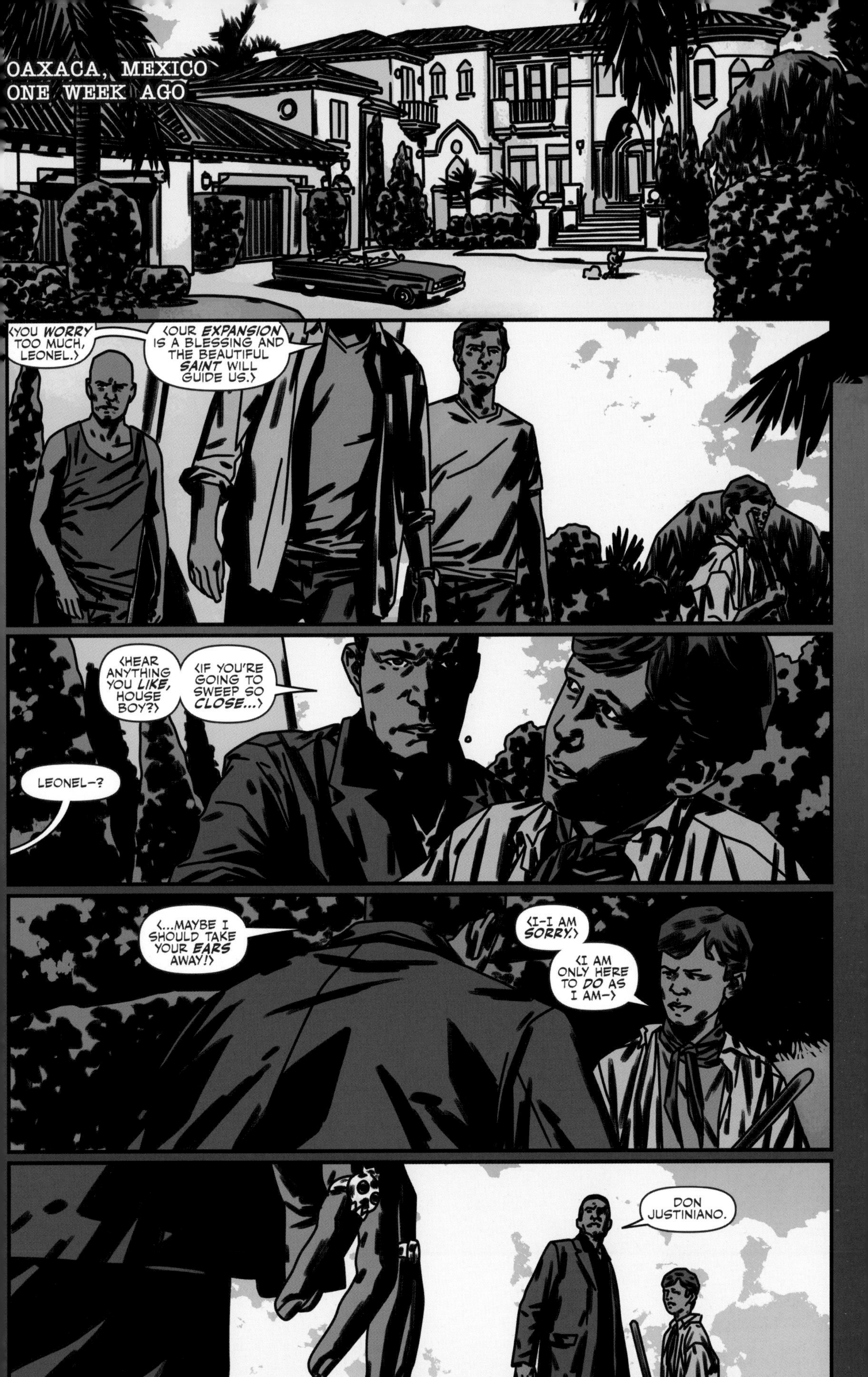
OAXACA, MEXICO
ONE WEEK AGO
‹YOU WORRY TOO MUCH, LEONEL.›
‹OUR EXPANSION IS A BLESSING AND THE BEAUTIFUL SAINT WILL GUIDE US.›
‹HEAR ANYTHING YOU LIKE, HOUSE BOY?›
‹IF YOU'RE GOING TO SWEEP SO CLOSE...›
LEONEL–?
‹...MAYBE I SHOULD TAKE YOUR EARS AWAY!›
‹I–I AM SORRY.›
‹I AM ONLY HERE TO DO AS I AM–›
DON JUSTINIANO.

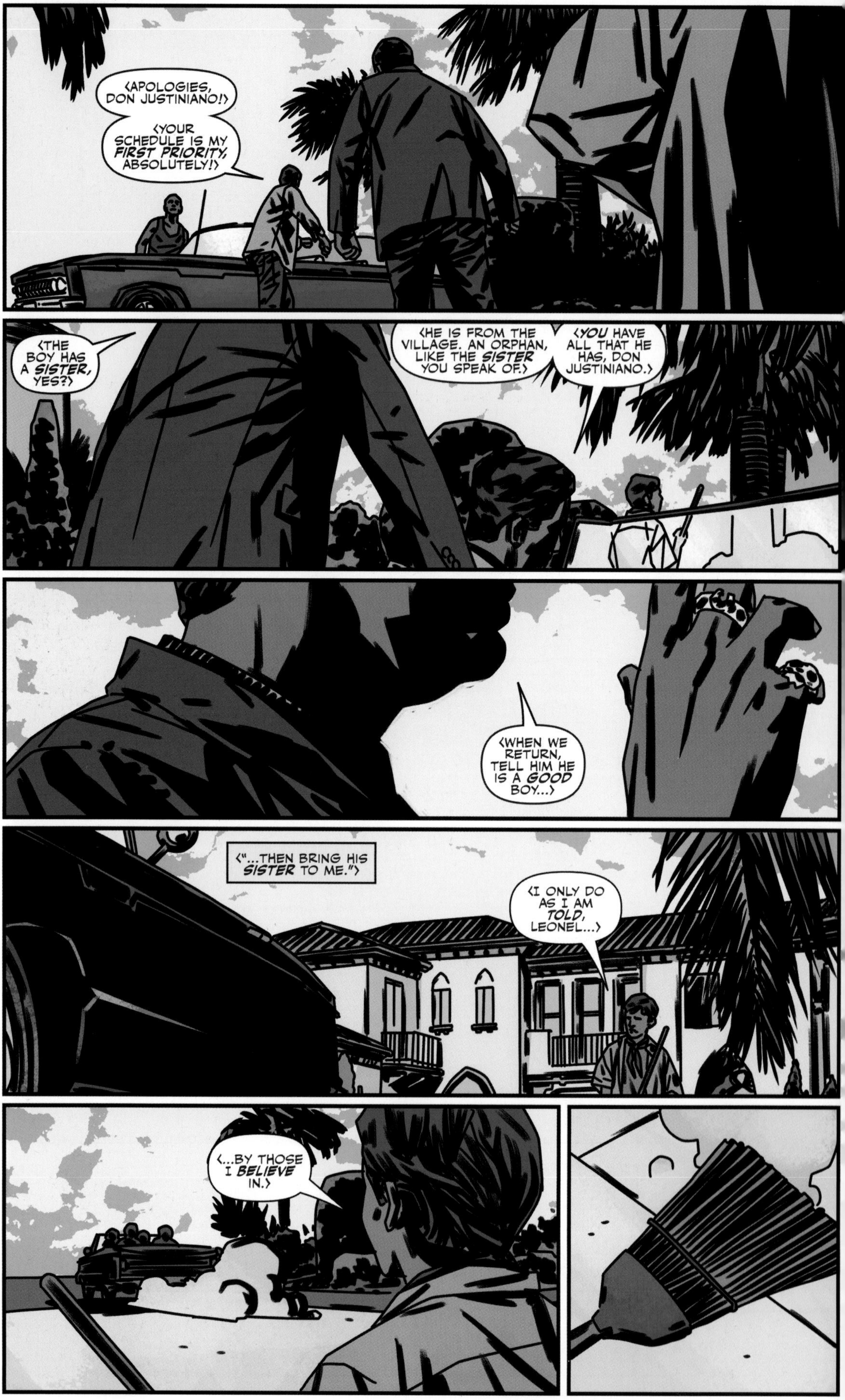
‹APOLOGIES, DON JUSTINIANO!›
‹YOUR SCHEDULE IS MY *FIRST PRIORITY*, ABSOLUTELY!›
‹THE BOY HAS A *SISTER*, YES?›
‹HE IS FROM THE VILLAGE. AN ORPHAN, LIKE THE *SISTER* YOU SPEAK OF.›
‹*YOU* HAVE ALL THAT HE HAS, DON JUSTINIANO.›
‹WHEN WE RETURN, TELL HIM HE IS A *GOOD* BOY...›
‹"...THEN BRING HIS *SISTER* TO ME."›
‹I ONLY DO AS I AM *TOLD*, LEONEL...›
‹...BY THOSE I *BELIEVE* IN.›

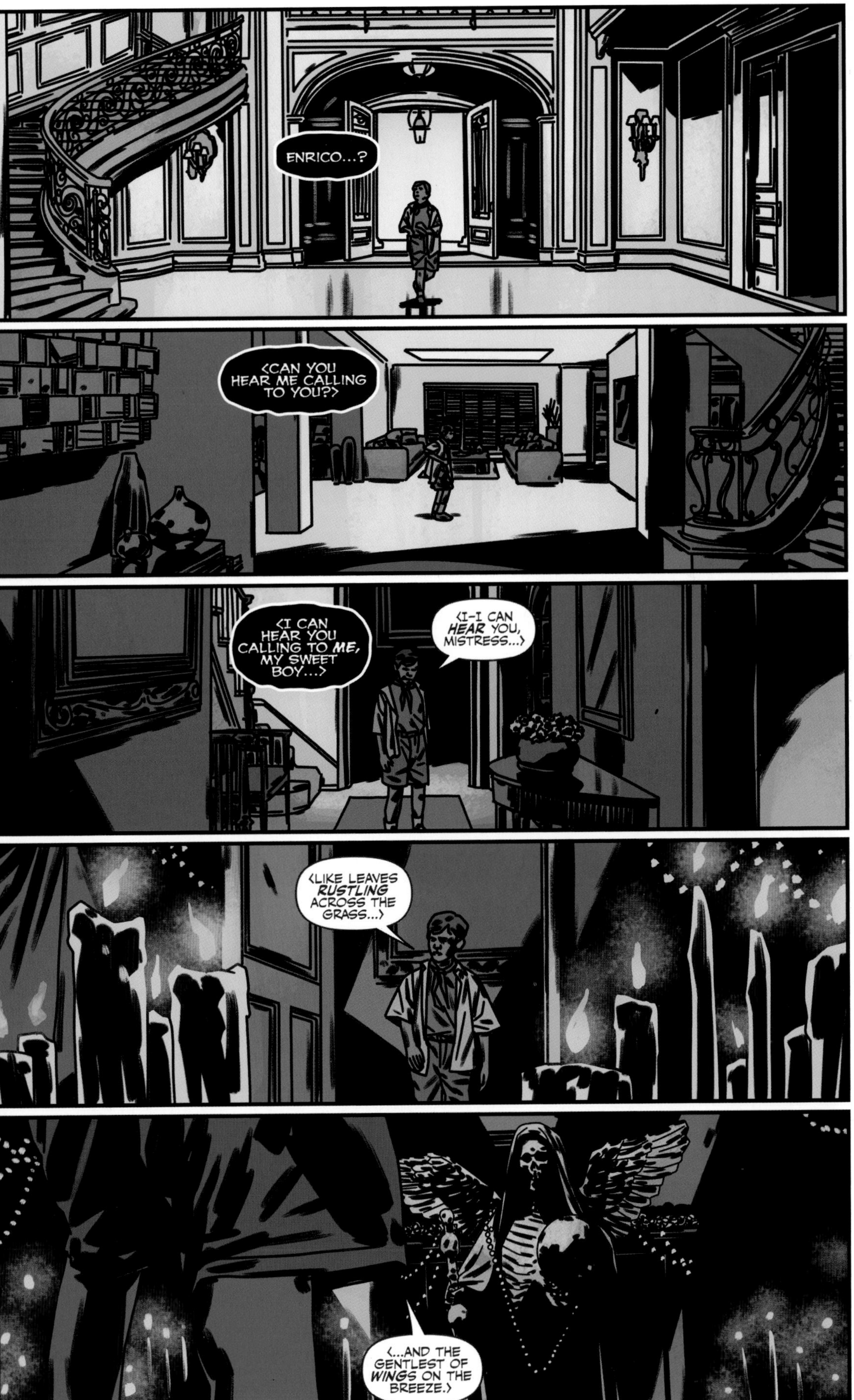
ENRICO...?
<CAN YOU HEAR ME CALLING TO YOU?>
<I CAN HEAR YOU CALLING TO *ME*, MY SWEET BOY...>
<I-I CAN *HEAR* YOU, MISTRESS...>
<LIKE LEAVES *RUSTLING* ACROSS THE GRASS...>
<...AND THE GENTLEST OF *WINGS* ON THE BREEZE.>

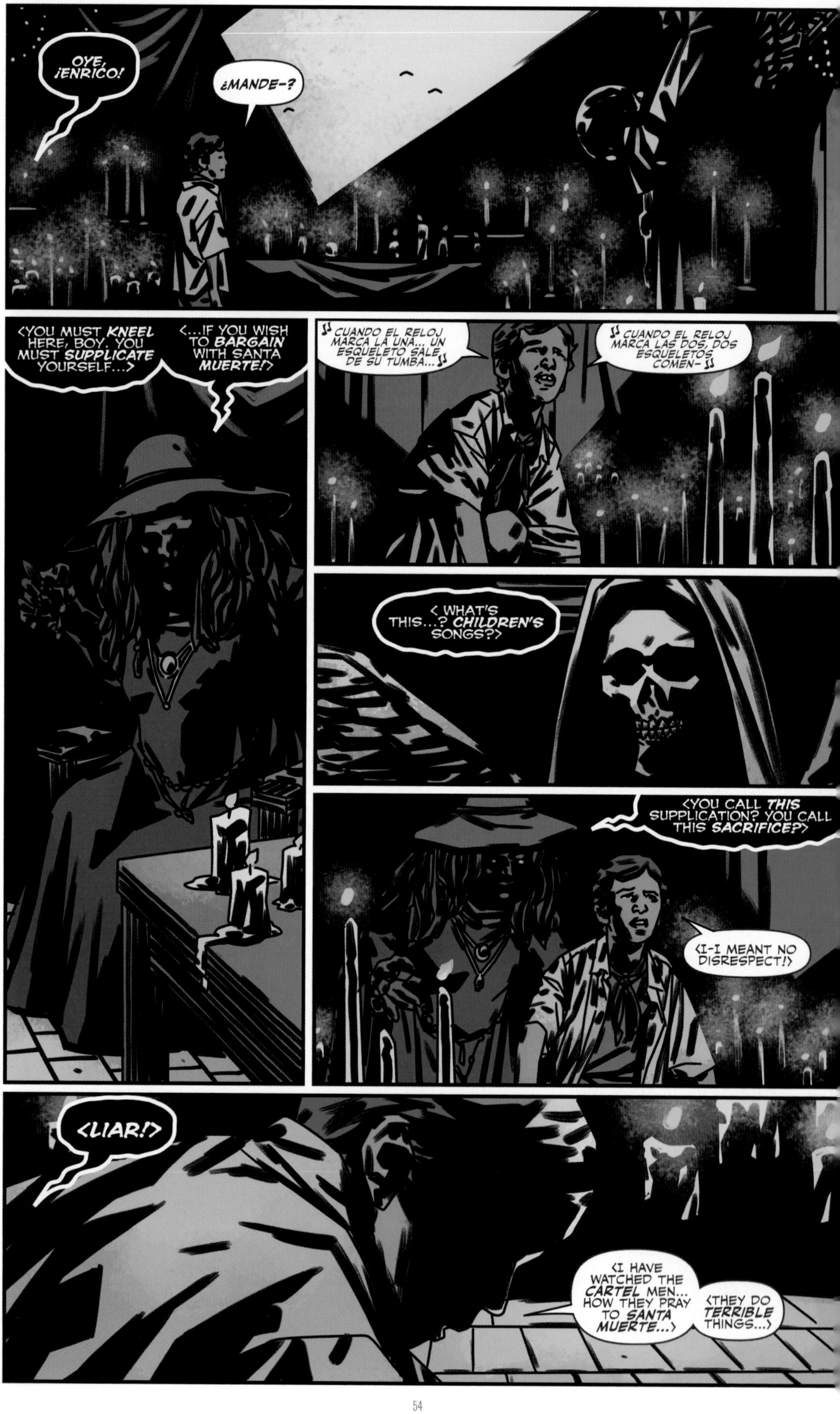
OYE, ¡ENRICO!
¿MANDE-?
<YOU MUST KNEEL HERE, BOY. YOU MUST SUPPLICATE YOURSELF...>
<...IF YOU WISH TO BARGAIN WITH SANTA MUERTE!>
♫ CUANDO EL RELOJ MARCA LA UNA... UN ESQUELETO SALE DE SU TUMBA... ♫
♫ CUANDO EL RELOJ MARCA LAS DOS, DOS ESQUELETOS COMEN- ♫
< WHAT'S THIS...? CHILDREN'S SONGS?>
<YOU CALL THIS SUPPLICATION? YOU CALL THIS SACRIFICE?>
<I-I MEANT NO DISRESPECT!>
<LIAR!>
<I HAVE WATCHED THE CARTEL MEN... HOW THEY PRAY TO SANTA MUERTE...>
<THEY DO TERRIBLE THINGS...>

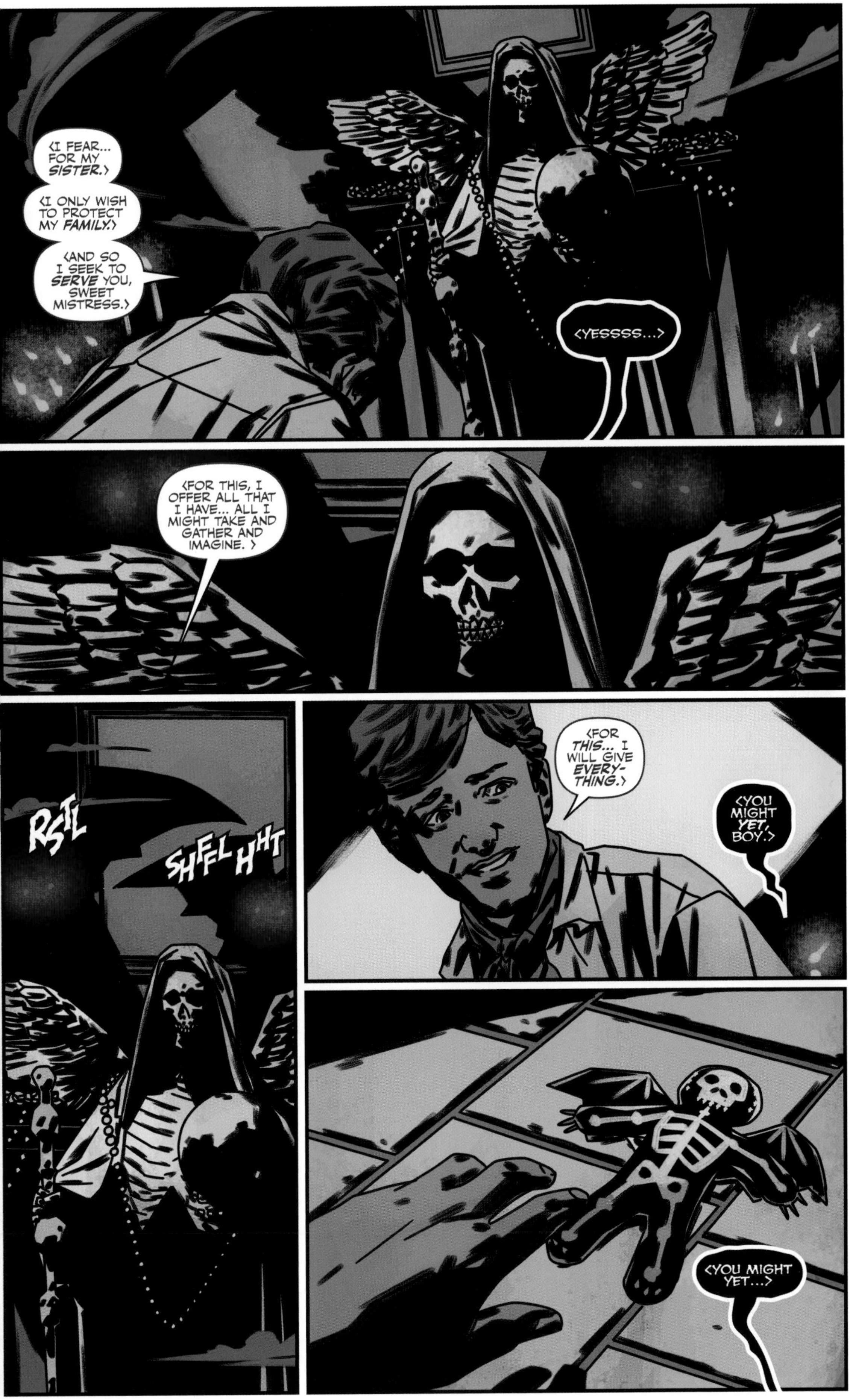
<I FEAR... FOR MY SISTER.>
<I ONLY WISH TO PROTECT MY FAMILY.>
<AND SO I SEEK TO SERVE YOU, SWEET MISTRESS.>
<YESSSS...>
<FOR THIS, I OFFER ALL THAT I HAVE... ALL I MIGHT TAKE AND GATHER AND IMAGINE.>
RSTL
SHFFL HHT
<FOR THIS... I WILL GIVE EVERY-THING.>
<YOU MIGHT YET, BOY.>
<YOU MIGHT YET...>

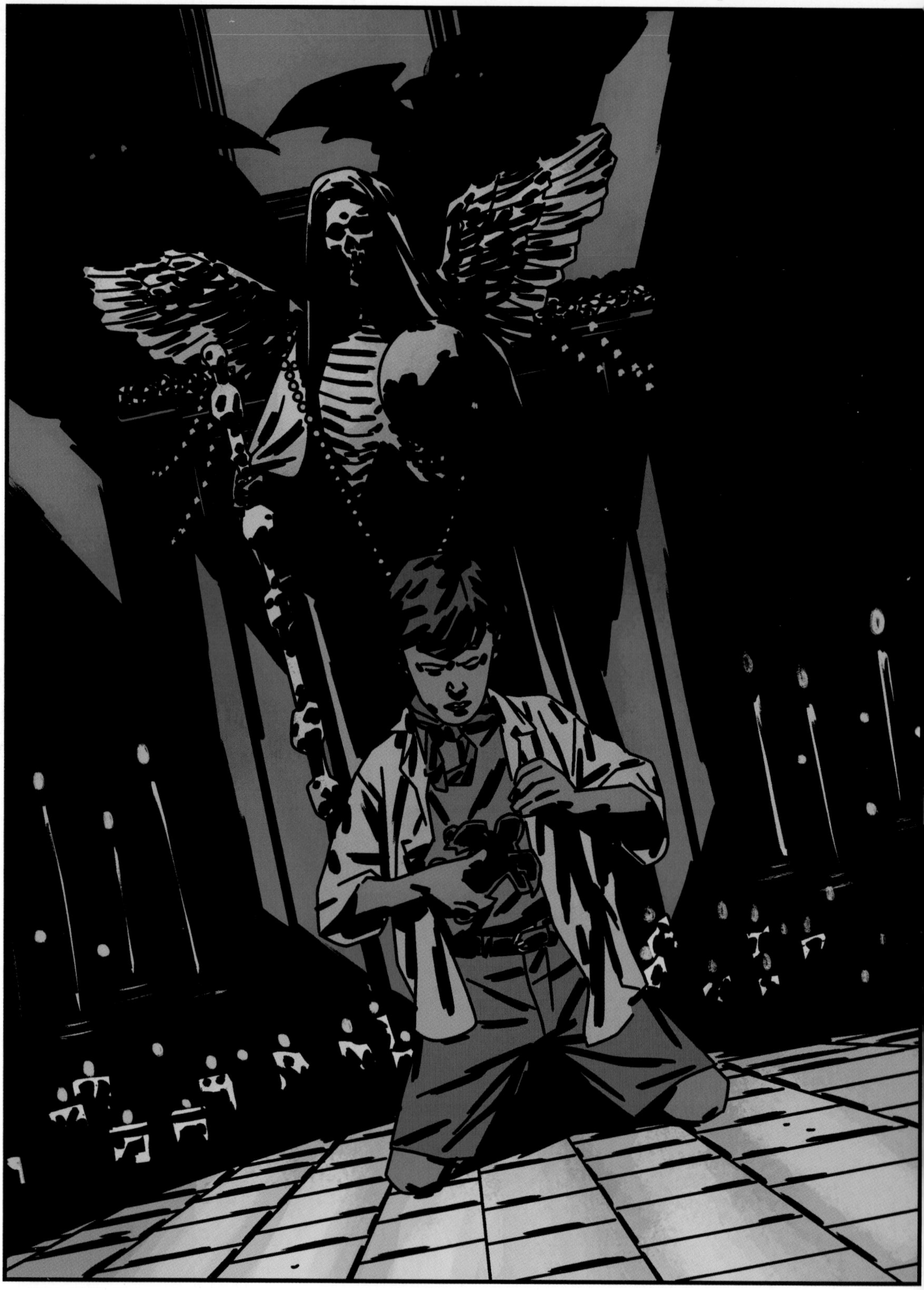

THE X FILES™

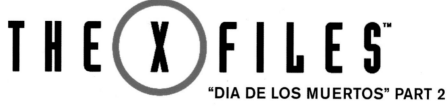

"DIA DE LOS MUERTOS" PART 2

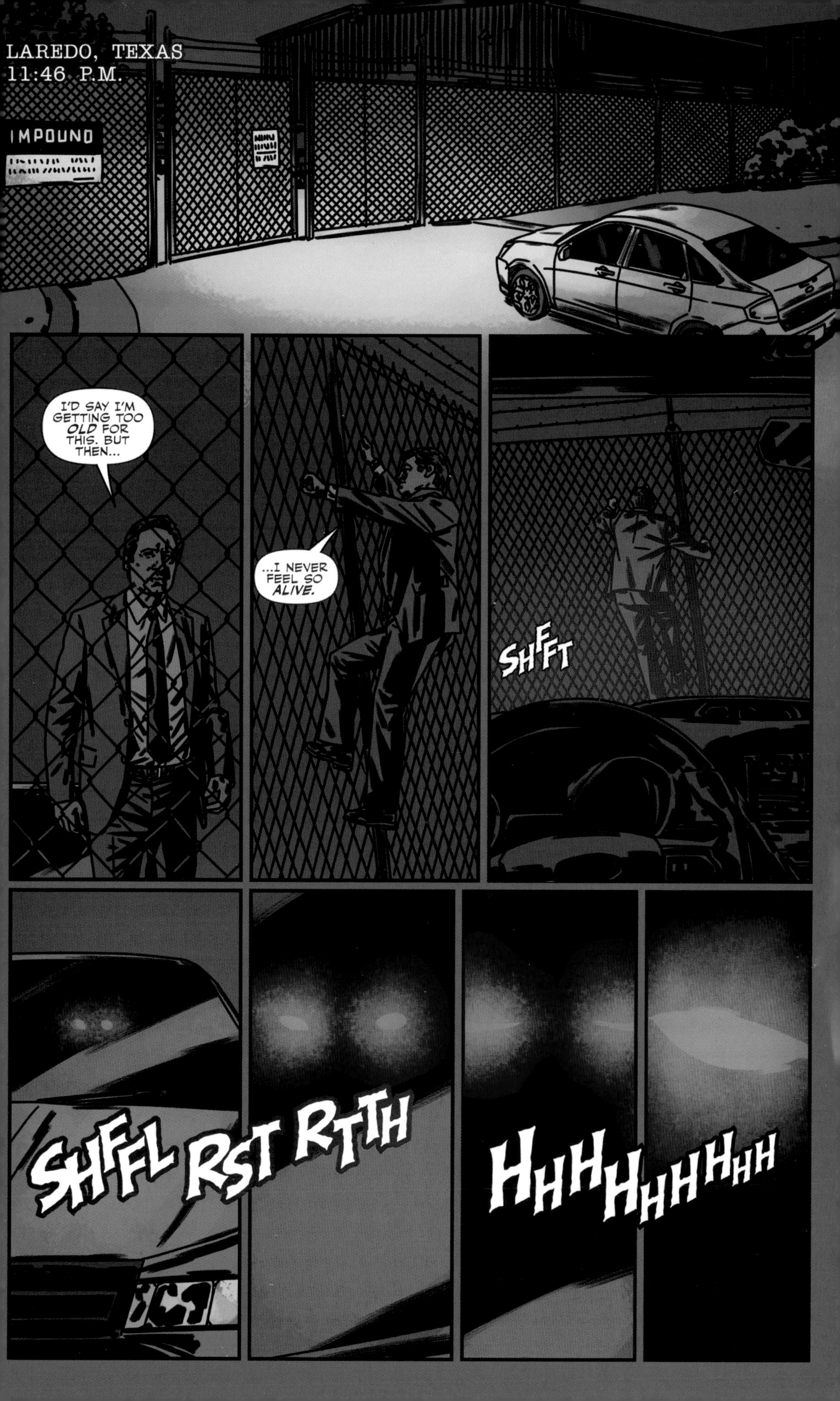
LAREDO, TEXAS
11:46 P.M.
IMPOUND
I'D SAY I'M GETTING TOO OLD FOR THIS. BUT THEN...
...I NEVER FEEL SO ALIVE.
SHFFT
SHFFL RST RTTH
HHHHHHHHH

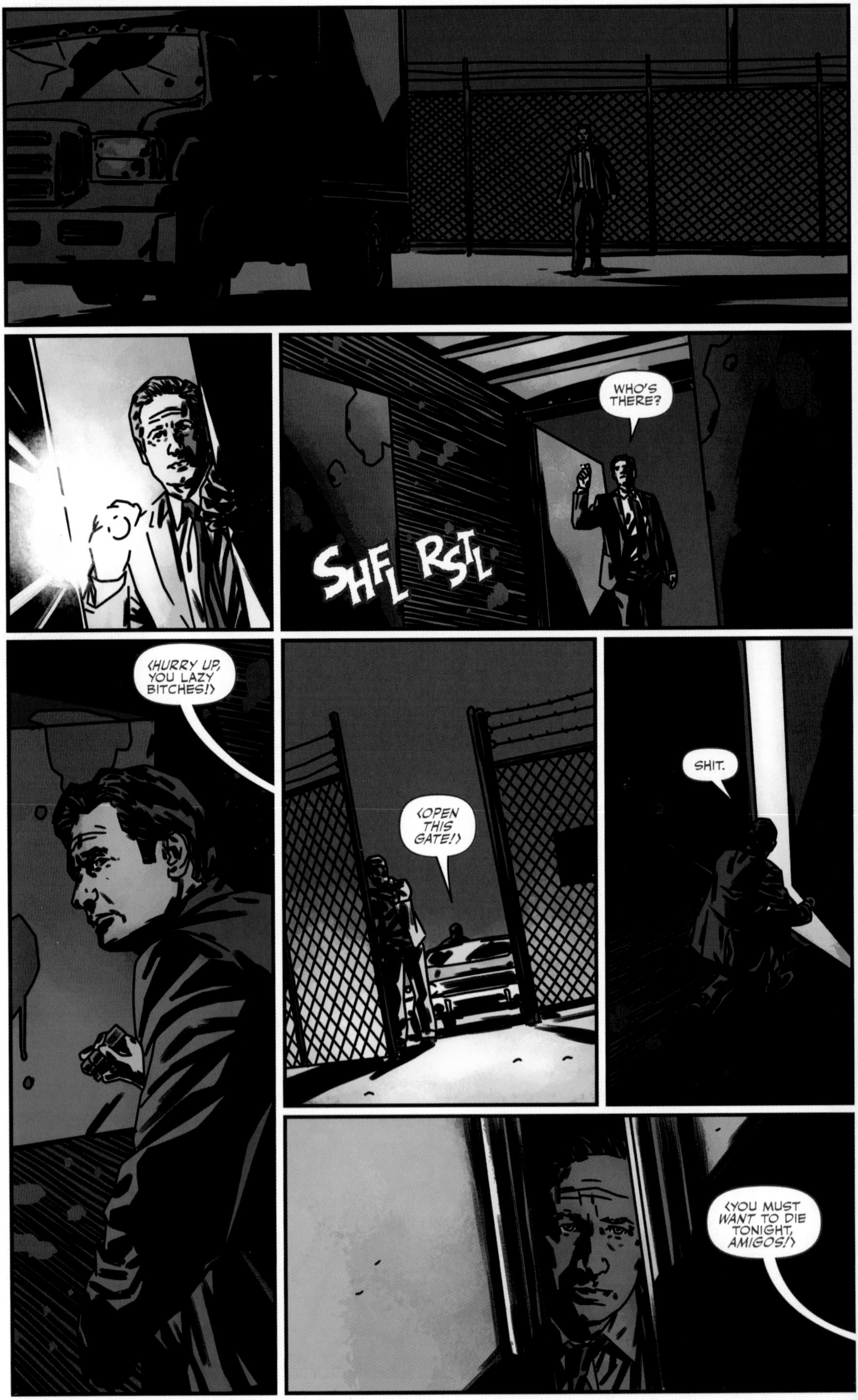
WHO'S THERE?
SHFL RSTL
‹HURRY UP, YOU LAZY BITCHES!›
‹OPEN THIS GATE!›
SHIT.
‹YOU MUST WANT TO DIE TONIGHT, AMIGOS!›

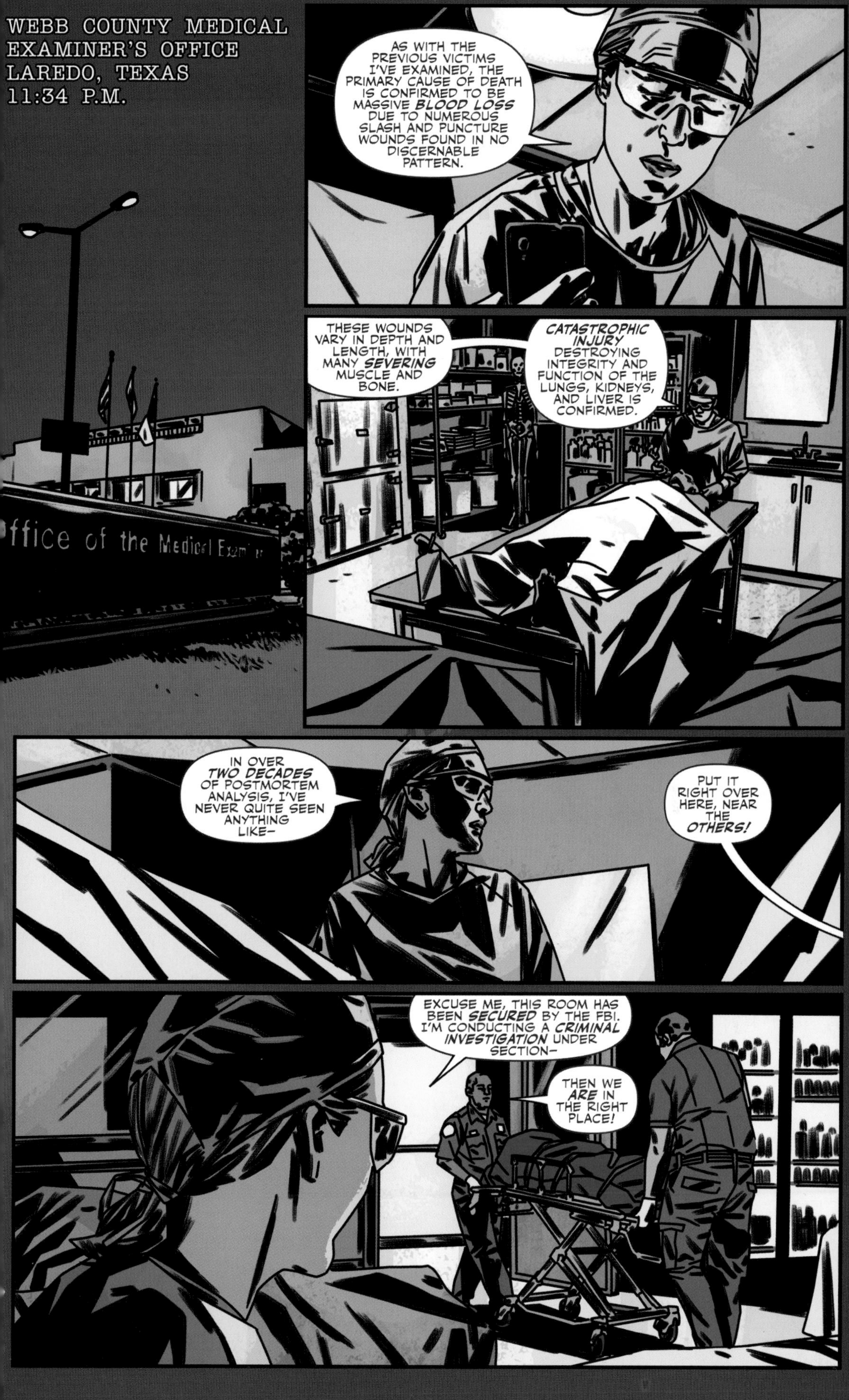
WEBB COUNTY MEDICAL EXAMINER'S OFFICE LAREDO, TEXAS 11:34 P.M.
AS WITH THE PREVIOUS VICTIMS I'VE EXAMINED, THE PRIMARY CAUSE OF DEATH IS CONFIRMED TO BE MASSIVE BLOOD LOSS DUE TO NUMEROUS SLASH AND PUNCTURE WOUNDS FOUND IN NO DISCERNABLE PATTERN.
Office of the Medical Examiner
THESE WOUNDS VARY IN DEPTH AND LENGTH, WITH MANY SEVERING MUSCLE AND BONE.
CATASTROPHIC INJURY DESTROYING INTEGRITY AND FUNCTION OF THE LUNGS, KIDNEYS, AND LIVER IS CONFIRMED.
IN OVER TWO DECADES OF POSTMORTEM ANALYSIS, I'VE NEVER QUITE SEEN ANYTHING LIKE–
PUT IT RIGHT OVER HERE, NEAR THE OTHERS!
EXCUSE ME, THIS ROOM HAS BEEN SECURED BY THE FBI. I'M CONDUCTING A CRIMINAL INVESTIGATION UNDER SECTION–
THEN WE ARE IN THE RIGHT PLACE!

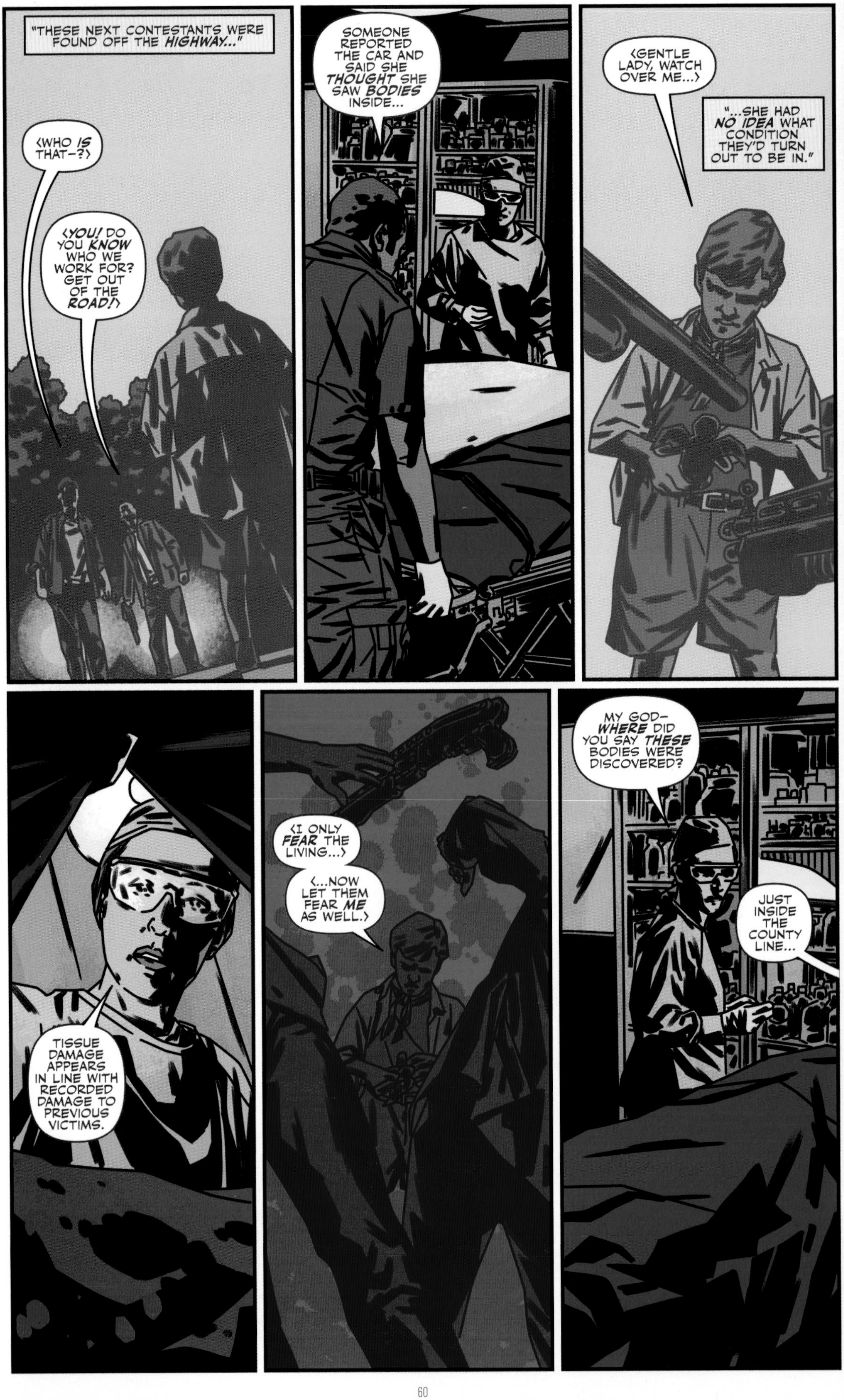
"THESE NEXT CONTESTANTS WERE FOUND OFF THE HIGHWAY..."
‹WHO IS THAT—?›
‹YOU! DO YOU KNOW WHO WE WORK FOR? GET OUT OF THE ROAD!›
SOMEONE REPORTED THE CAR AND SAID SHE THOUGHT SHE SAW BODIES INSIDE...
‹GENTLE LADY, WATCH OVER ME...›
"...SHE HAD NO IDEA WHAT CONDITION THEY'D TURN OUT TO BE IN."
TISSUE DAMAGE APPEARS IN LINE WITH RECORDED DAMAGE TO PREVIOUS VICTIMS.
‹I ONLY FEAR THE LIVING...›
‹...NOW LET THEM FEAR ME AS WELL.›
MY GOD— WHERE DID YOU SAY THESE BODIES WERE DISCOVERED?
JUST INSIDE THE COUNTY LINE...

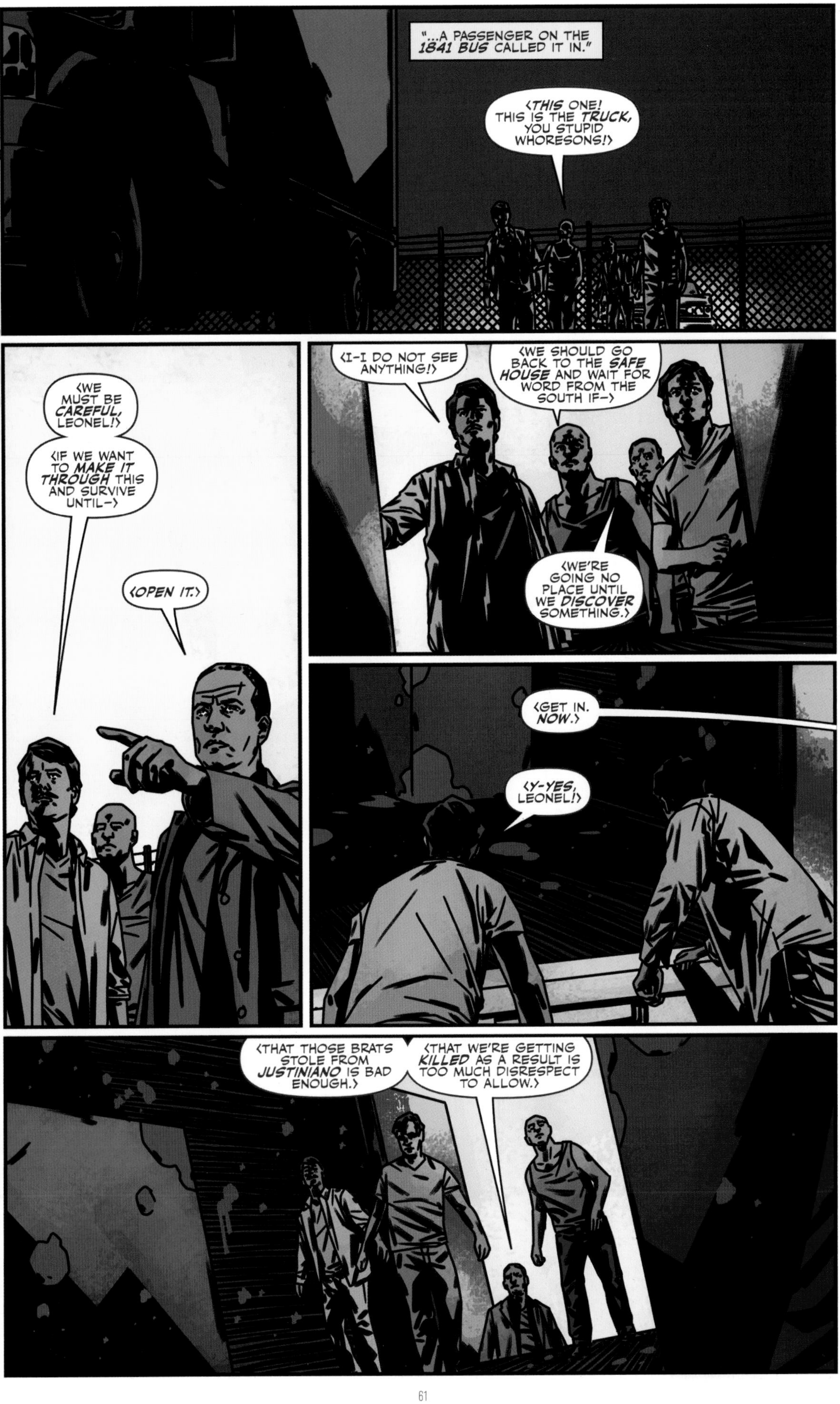
"...A PASSENGER ON THE 1841 BUS CALLED IT IN."
‹THIS ONE! THIS IS THE TRUCK, YOU STUPID WHORESONS!›
‹WE MUST BE CAREFUL, LEONEL!›
‹IF WE WANT TO MAKE IT THROUGH THIS AND SURVIVE UNTIL–›
‹OPEN IT.›
‹I-I DO NOT SEE ANYTHING!›
‹WE SHOULD GO BACK TO THE SAFE HOUSE AND WAIT FOR WORD FROM THE SOUTH IF–›
‹WE'RE GOING NO PLACE UNTIL WE DISCOVER SOMETHING.›
‹GET IN. NOW.›
‹Y-YES, LEONEL!›
‹THAT THOSE BRATS STOLE FROM JUSTINIANO IS BAD ENOUGH.›
‹THAT WE'RE GETTING KILLED AS A RESULT IS TOO MUCH DISRESPECT TO ALLOW.›

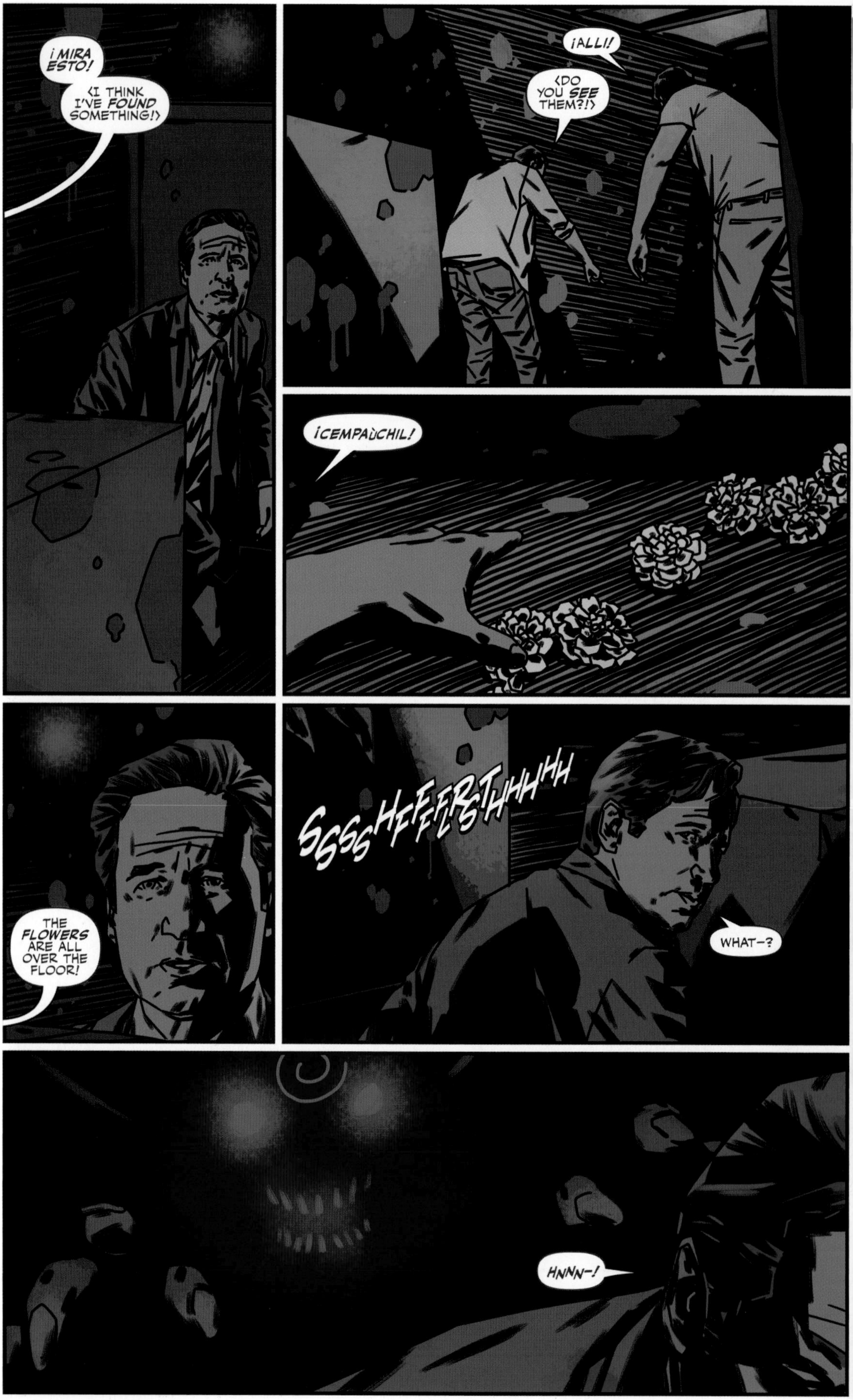

¡MIRA ESTO!
<I THINK I'VE FOUND SOMETHING!>
¡ALLI!
<DO YOU SEE THEM?!>
¡CEMPAÚCHIL!
THE FLOWERS ARE ALL OVER THE FLOOR!
SSSSHFFFFRSTHHHHH
WHAT-?
HNNN-!

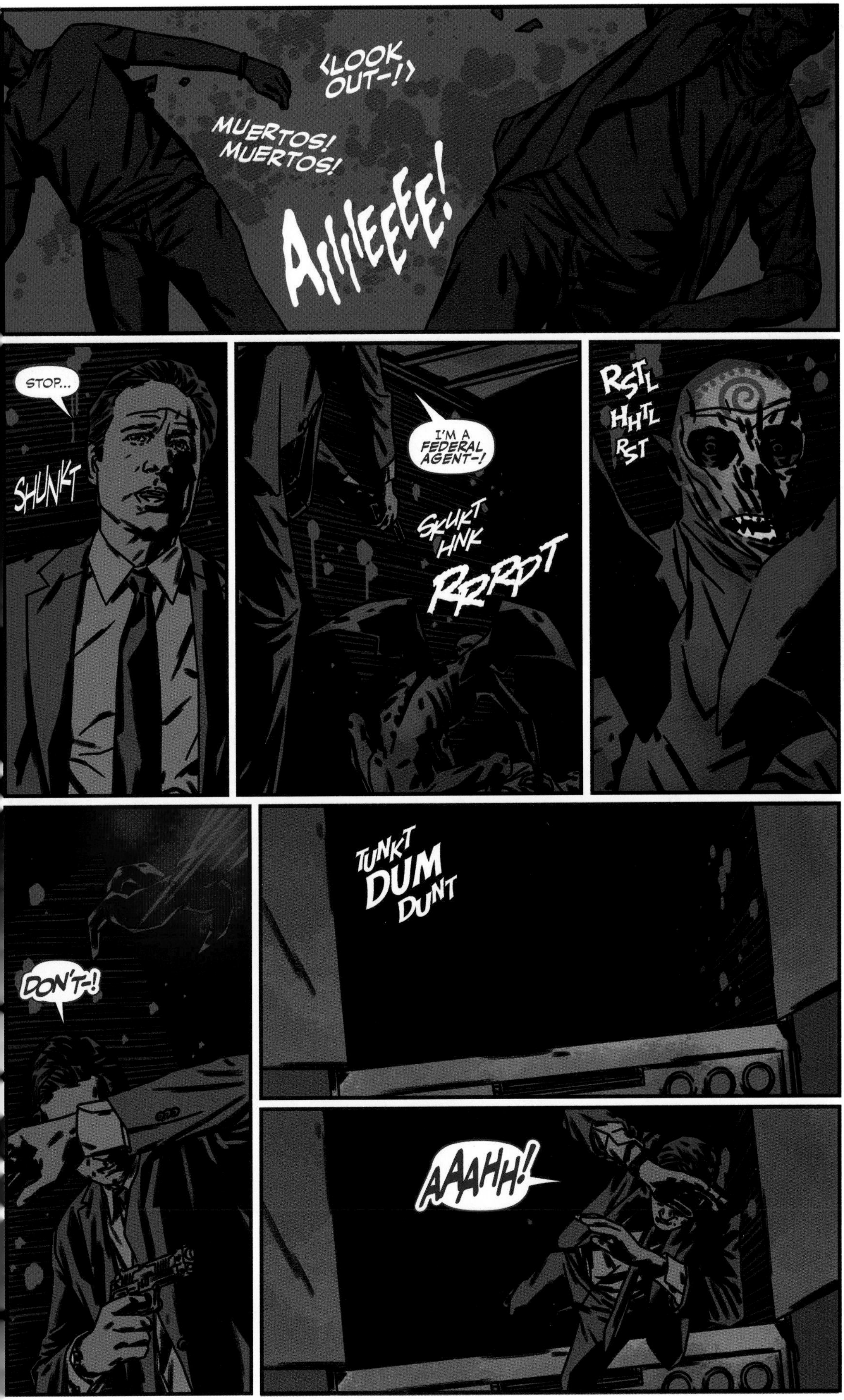
‹LOOK OUT-!›
MUERTOS! MUERTOS!
AIIIIEEEE!
STOP...
SHUNKT
I'M A FEDERAL AGENT-!
SKUKT HNK
RRRPT
RSTL HHTL RST
DON'T-!
TUNKT DUM DUNT
AAAHH!

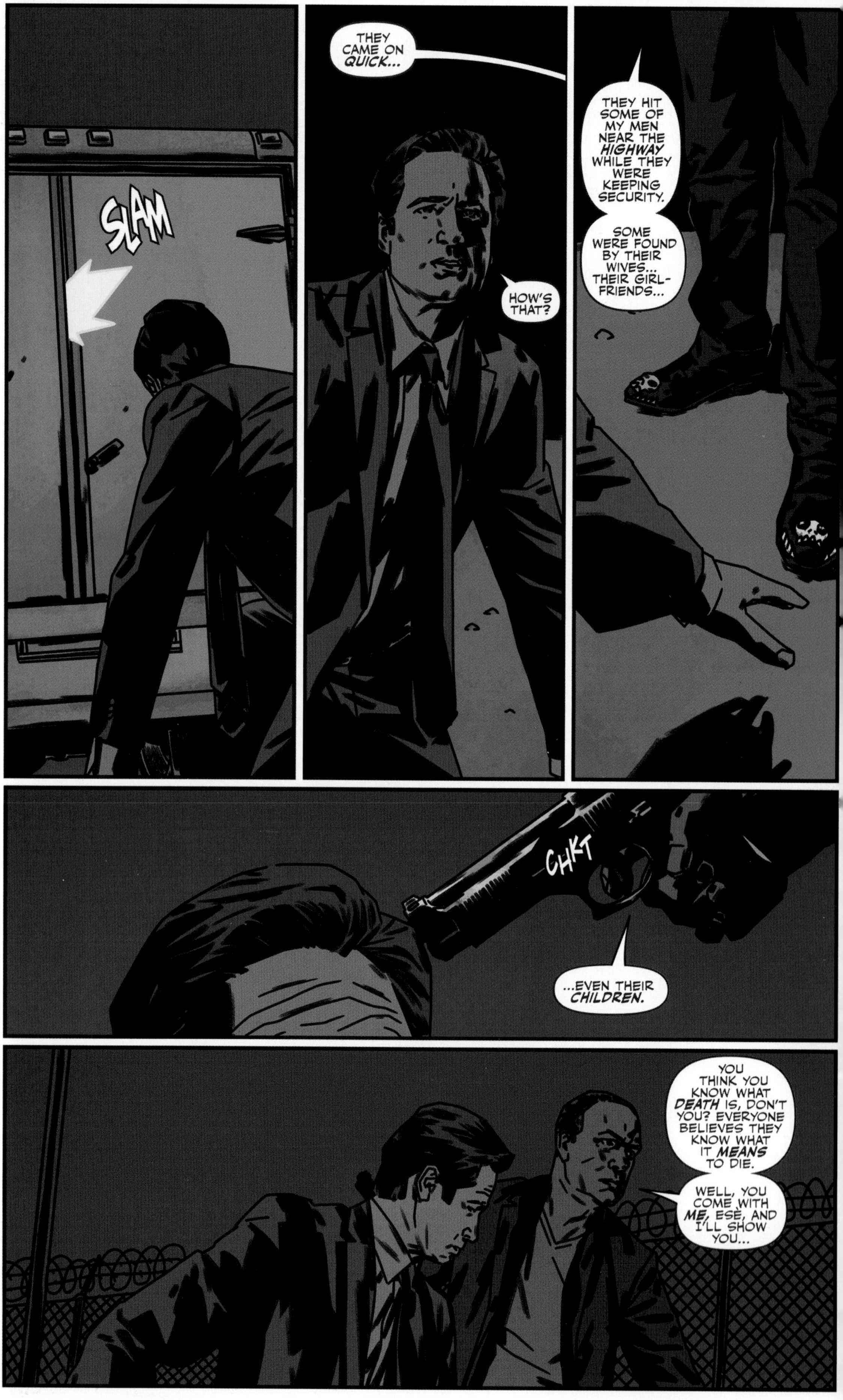
SLAM
THEY CAME ON QUICK...
HOW'S THAT?
THEY HIT SOME OF MY MEN NEAR THE HIGHWAY WHILE THEY WERE KEEPING SECURITY.
SOME WERE FOUND BY THEIR WIVES... THEIR GIRL-FRIENDS...
CHKT
...EVEN THEIR CHILDREN.
YOU THINK YOU KNOW WHAT DEATH IS, DON'T YOU? EVERYONE BELIEVES THEY KNOW WHAT IT MEANS TO DIE.
WELL, YOU COME WITH ME, ESE, AND I'LL SHOW YOU...

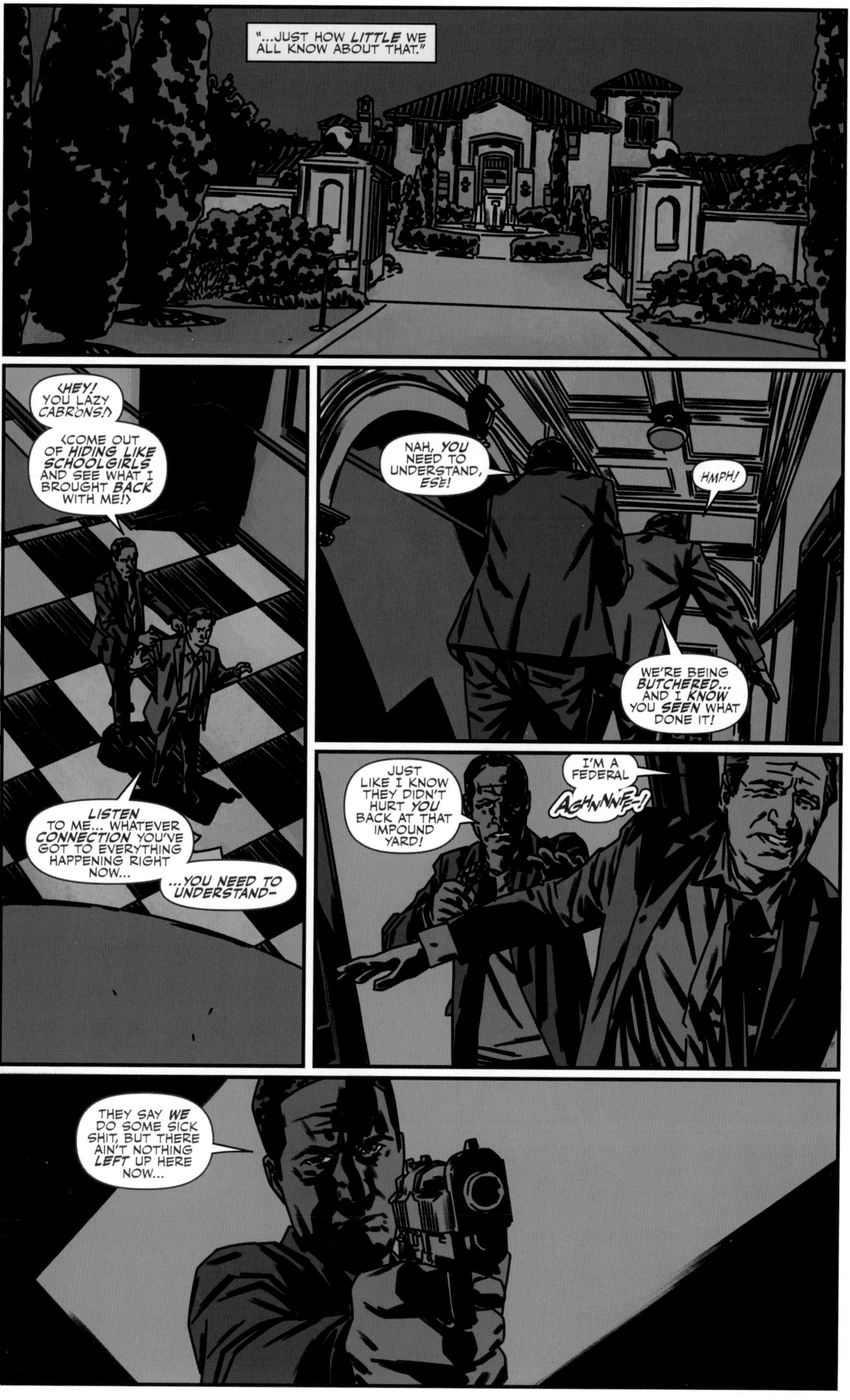
"...JUST HOW LITTLE WE ALL KNOW ABOUT THAT."
‹HEY! YOU LAZY CABRONS!›
‹COME OUT OF HIDING LIKE SCHOOLGIRLS AND SEE WHAT I BROUGHT BACK WITH ME!›
LISTEN TO ME... WHATEVER CONNECTION YOU'VE GOT TO EVERYTHING HAPPENING RIGHT NOW...
...YOU NEED TO UNDERSTAND–
NAH, YOU NEED TO UNDERSTAND, ESE!
HMPH!
WE'RE BEING BUTCHERED... AND I KNOW YOU SEEN WHAT DONE IT!
JUST LIKE I KNOW THEY DIDN'T HURT YOU BACK AT THAT IMPOUND YARD!
I'M A FEDERAL
AGHNNNF–!
THEY SAY WE DO SOME SICK SHIT, BUT THERE AIN'T NOTHING LEFT UP HERE NOW...

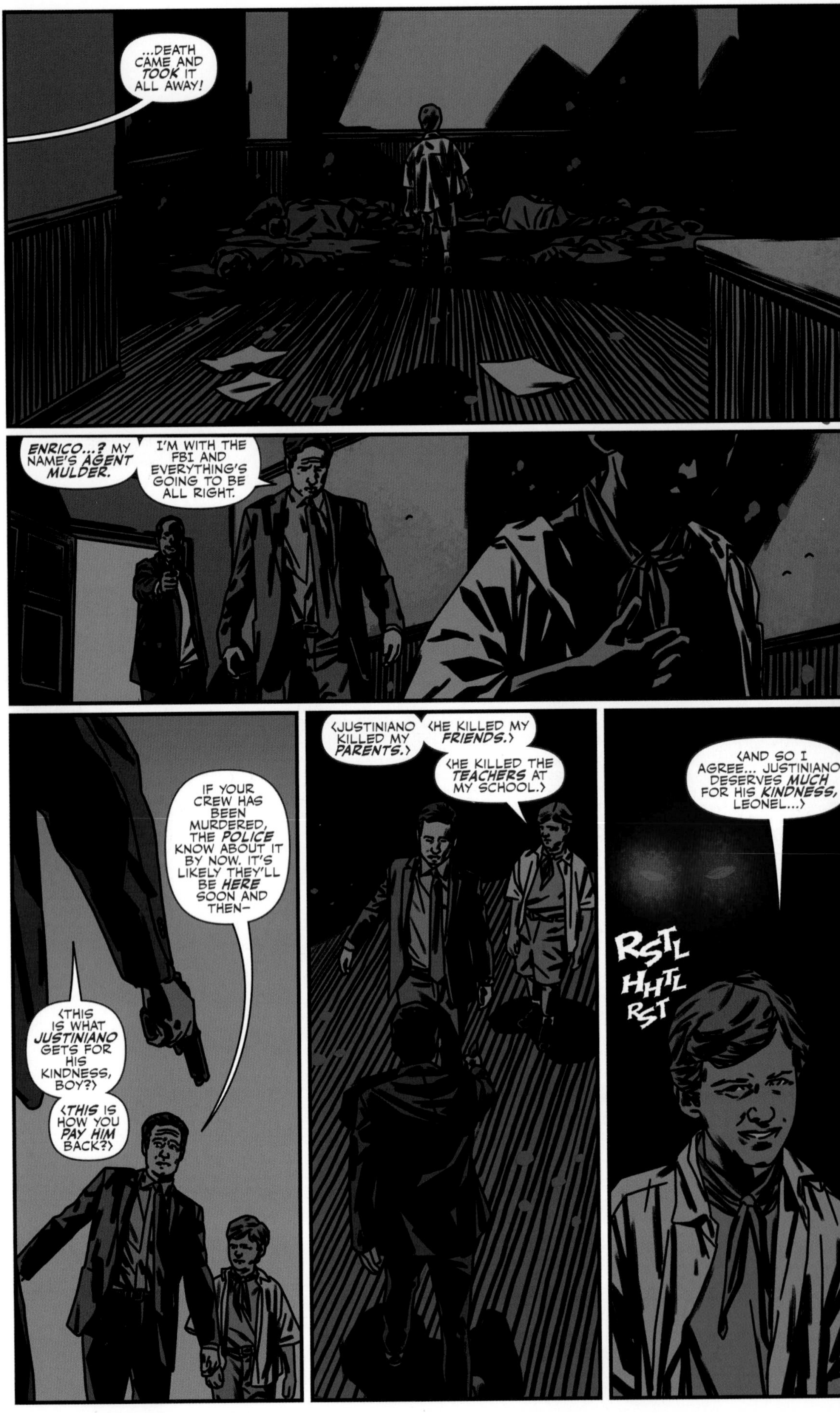
...DEATH CAME AND TOOK IT ALL AWAY!
ENRICO...? MY NAME'S AGENT MULDER.
I'M WITH THE FBI AND EVERYTHING'S GOING TO BE ALL RIGHT.
IF YOUR CREW HAS BEEN MURDERED, THE POLICE KNOW ABOUT IT BY NOW. IT'S LIKELY THEY'LL BE HERE SOON AND THEN–
<THIS IS WHAT JUSTINIANO GETS FOR HIS KINDNESS, BOY?>
<THIS IS HOW YOU PAY HIM BACK?>
<JUSTINIANO KILLED MY PARENTS.>
<HE KILLED MY FRIENDS.>
<HE KILLED THE TEACHERS AT MY SCHOOL.>
<AND SO I AGREE... JUSTINIANO DESERVES MUCH FOR HIS KINDNESS, LEONEL...>
RSTL
HHTL
RST

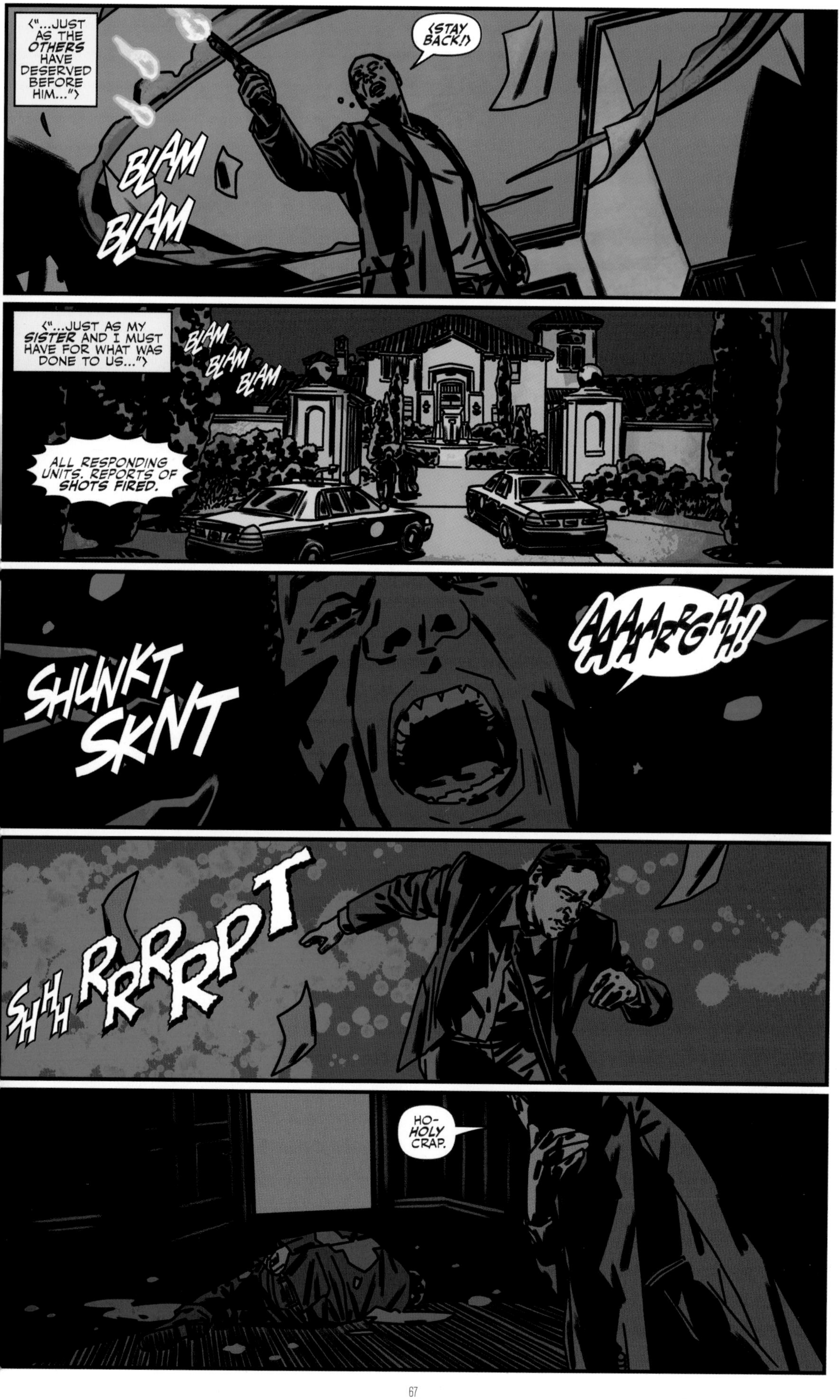

<"...JUST AS THE OTHERS HAVE DESERVED BEFORE HIM...">
<STAY BACK!>
BLAM
BLAM
<"...JUST AS MY SISTER AND I MUST HAVE FOR WHAT WAS DONE TO US...">
BLAM
BLAM
BLAM
ALL RESPONDING UNITS. REPORTS OF SHOTS FIRED.
SHUNKT
SKNT
AAAAARRGHH!
SHHHRRRRPT
HO-HOLY CRAP.

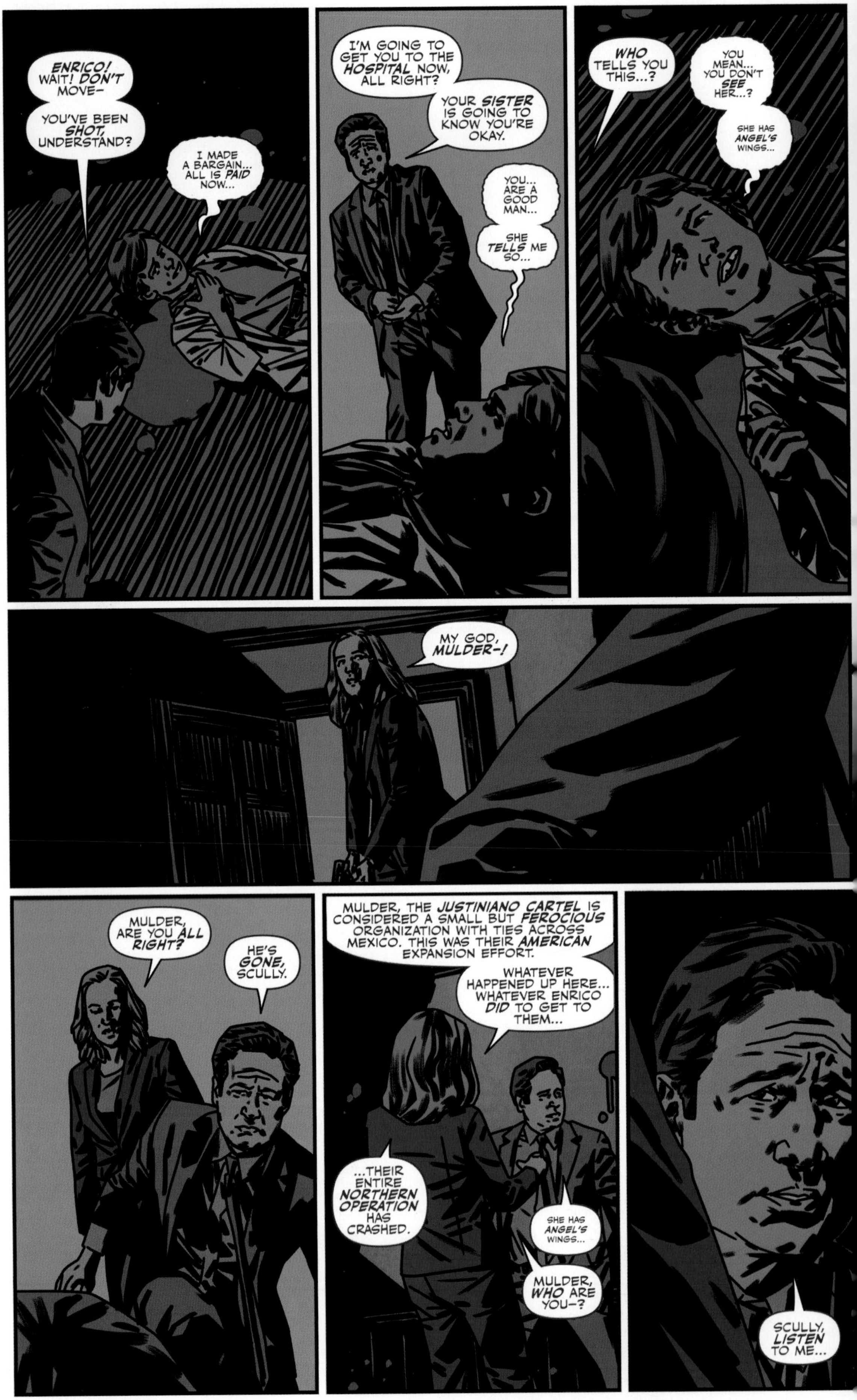

ENRICO! WAIT! DON'T MOVE–
YOU'VE BEEN SHOT, UNDERSTAND?
I MADE A BARGAIN... ALL IS PAID NOW...
I'M GOING TO GET YOU TO THE HOSPITAL NOW, ALL RIGHT?
YOUR SISTER IS GOING TO KNOW YOU'RE OKAY.
YOU... ARE A GOOD MAN...
SHE TELLS ME SO...
WHO TELLS YOU THIS...?
YOU MEAN... YOU DON'T SEE HER...?
SHE HAS ANGEL'S WINGS...
MY GOD, MULDER–!
MULDER, ARE YOU ALL RIGHT?
HE'S GONE, SCULLY.
MULDER, THE JUSTINIANO CARTEL IS CONSIDERED A SMALL BUT FEROCIOUS ORGANIZATION WITH TIES ACROSS MEXICO. THIS WAS THEIR AMERICAN EXPANSION EFFORT.
WHATEVER HAPPENED UP HERE... WHATEVER ENRICO DID TO GET TO THEM...
...THEIR ENTIRE NORTHERN OPERATION HAS CRASHED.
SHE HAS ANGEL'S WINGS...
MULDER, WHO ARE YOU–?
SCULLY, LISTEN TO ME...

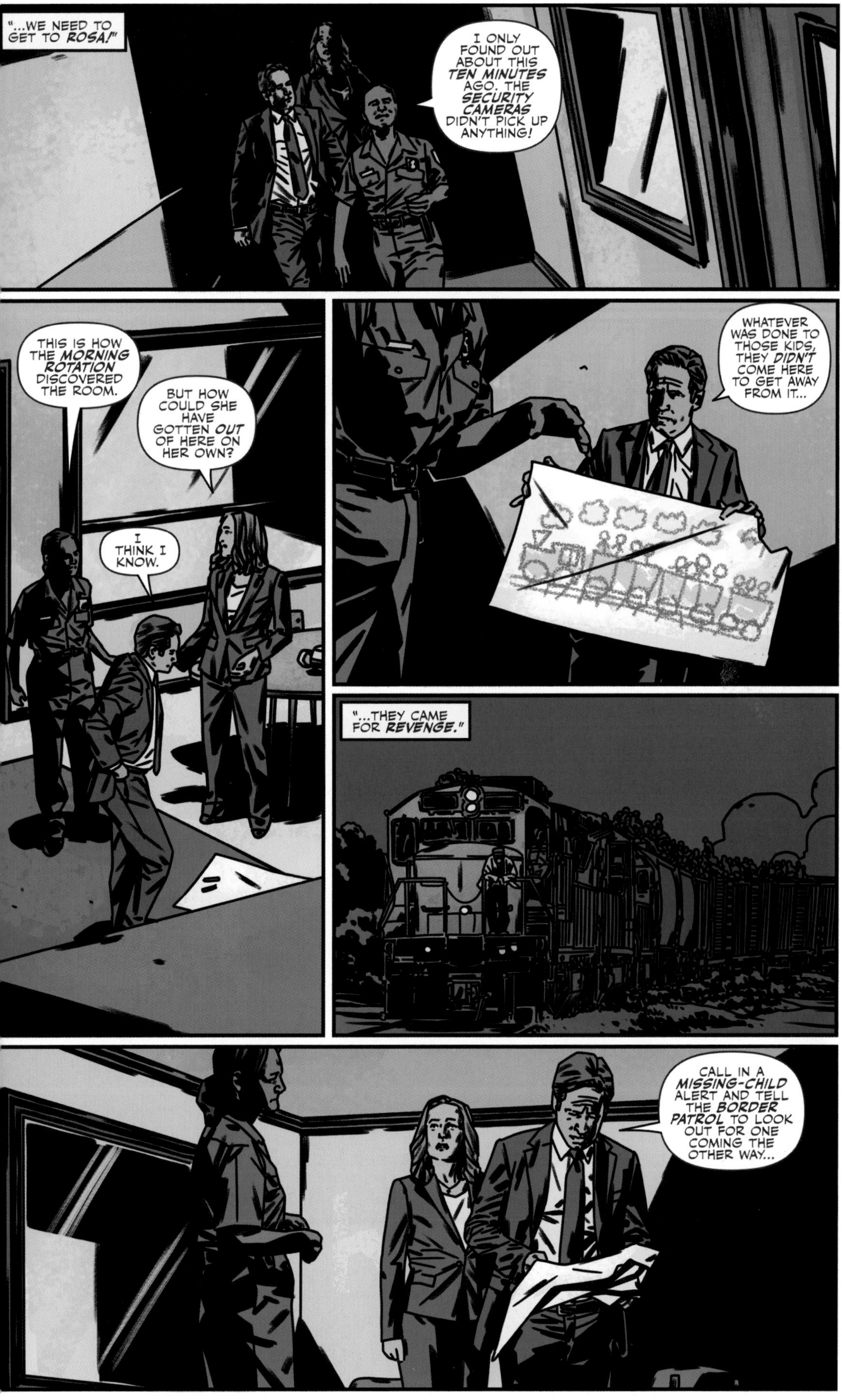
"...WE NEED TO GET TO ROSA!"
I ONLY FOUND OUT ABOUT THIS TEN MINUTES AGO. THE SECURITY CAMERAS DIDN'T PICK UP ANYTHING!
THIS IS HOW THE MORNING ROTATION DISCOVERED THE ROOM.
BUT HOW COULD SHE HAVE GOTTEN OUT OF HERE ON HER OWN?
I THINK I KNOW.
WHATEVER WAS DONE TO THOSE KIDS, THEY DIDN'T COME HERE TO GET AWAY FROM IT...
"...THEY CAME FOR REVENGE."
CALL IN A MISSING-CHILD ALERT AND TELL THE BORDER PATROL TO LOOK OUT FOR ONE COMING THE OTHER WAY...

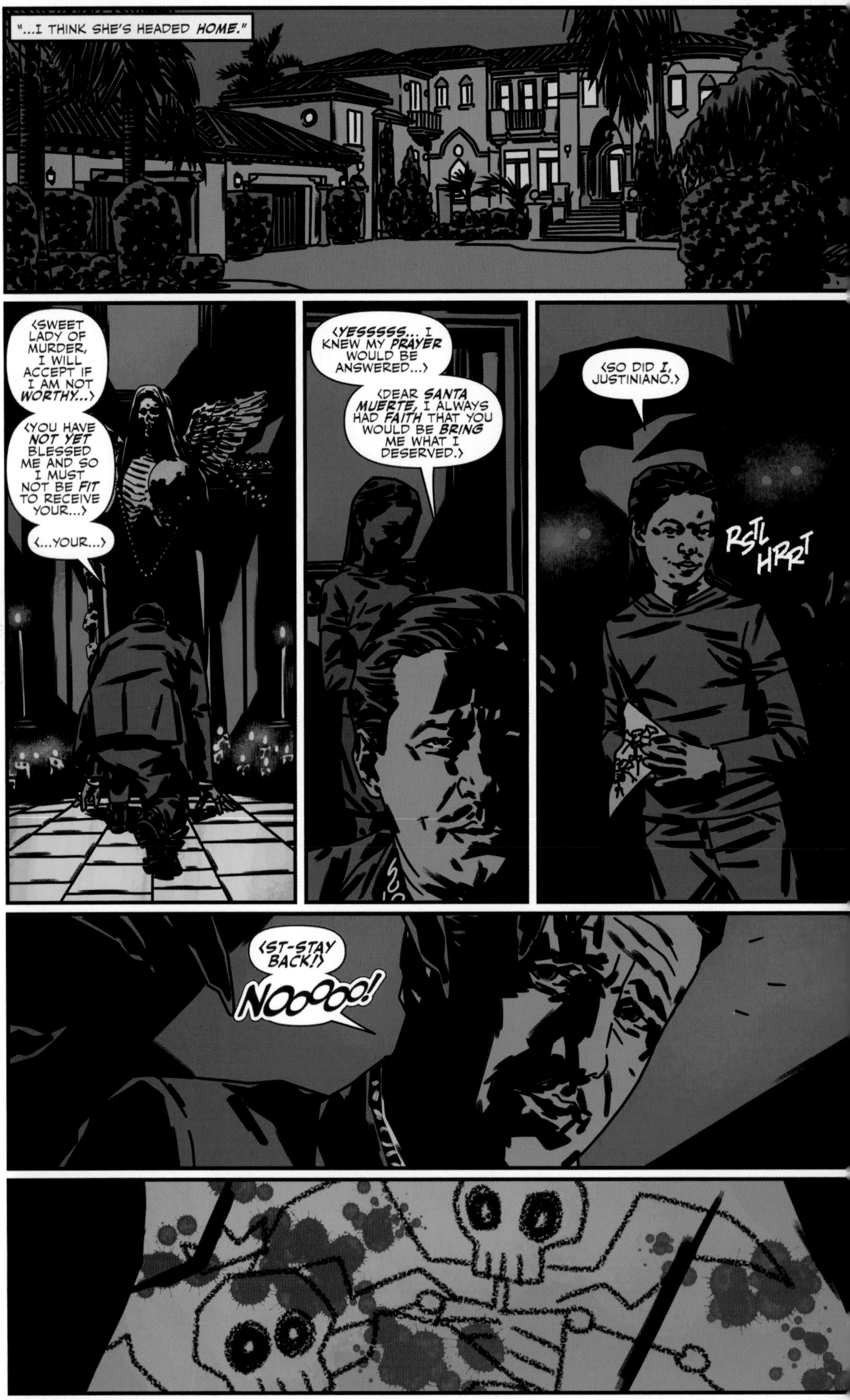
"...I THINK SHE'S HEADED HOME."
<SWEET LADY OF MURDER, I WILL ACCEPT IF I AM NOT WORTHY...>
<YOU HAVE NOT YET BLESSED ME AND SO I MUST NOT BE FIT TO RECEIVE YOUR...>
<...YOUR...>
<YESSSSS... I KNEW MY PRAYER WOULD BE ANSWERED...>
<DEAR SANTA MUERTE, I ALWAYS HAD FAITH THAT YOU WOULD BE BRING ME WHAT I DESERVED.>
<SO DID I, JUSTINIANO.>
RSTL HRRT
<ST-STAY BACK!>
NOOOOO!

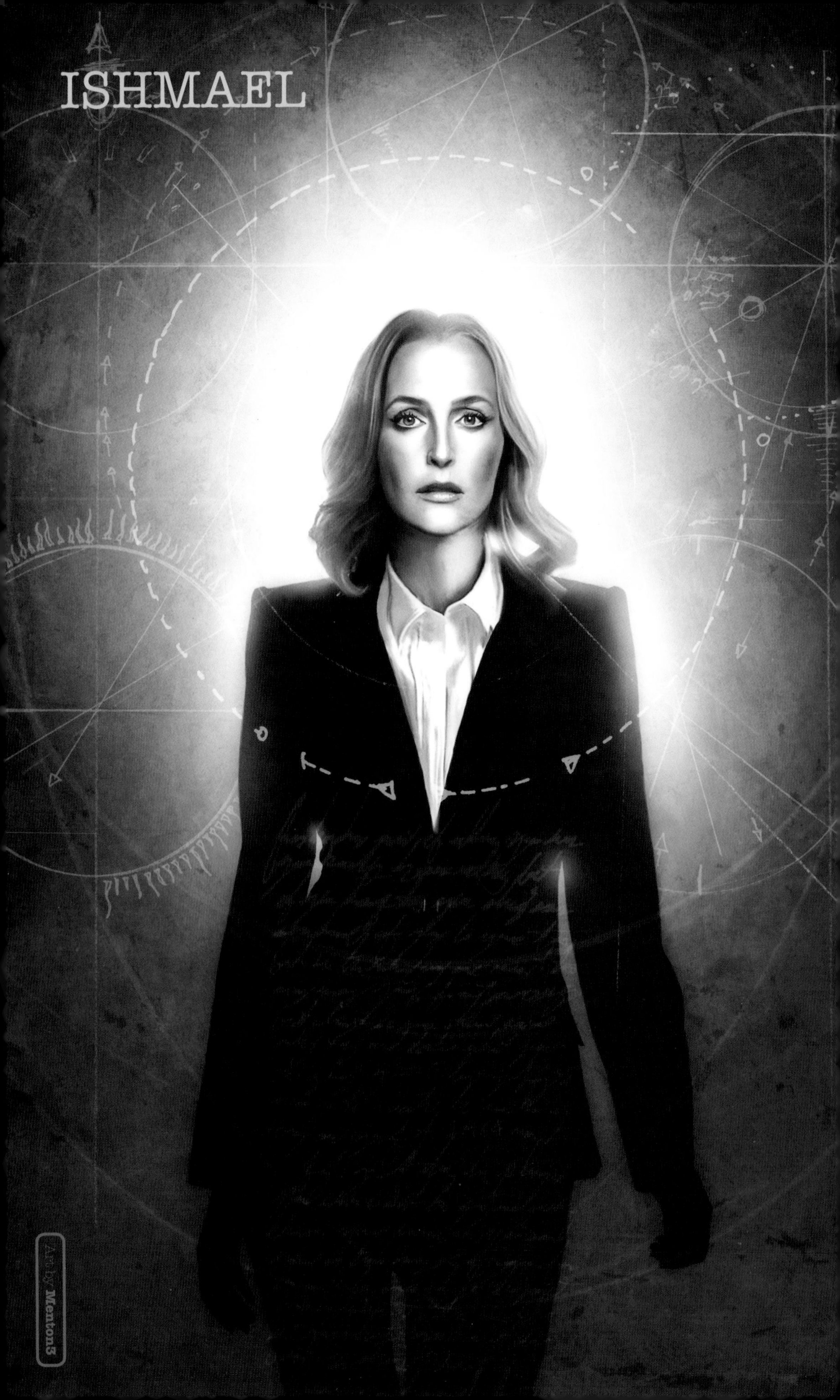

ISHMAEL
Art by Menton3

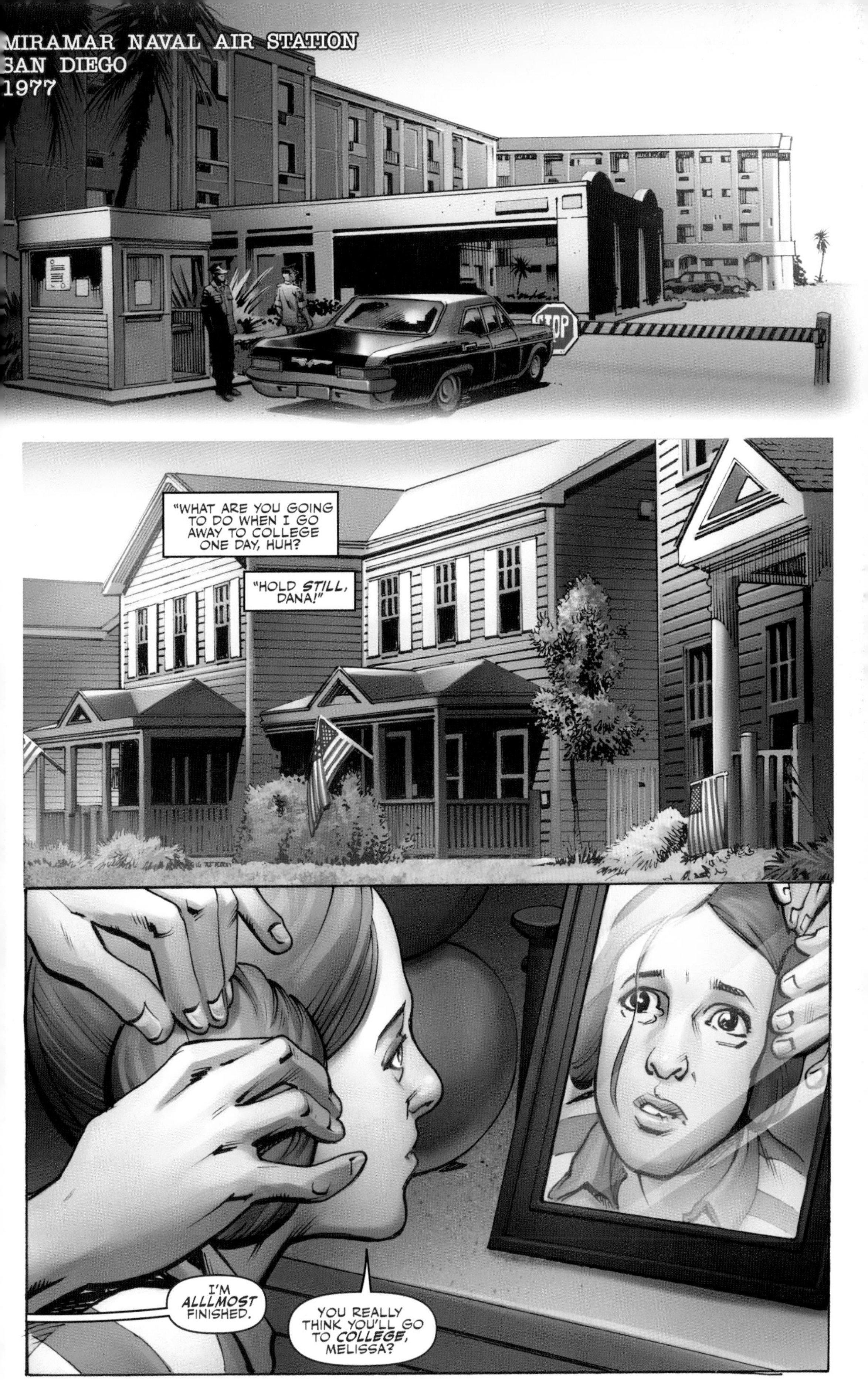
MIRAMAR NAVAL AIR STATION
SAN DIEGO
1977
STOP
"WHAT ARE YOU GOING TO DO WHEN I GO AWAY TO COLLEGE ONE DAY, HUH?
"HOLD STILL, DANA!"
I'M ALLLMOST FINISHED.
YOU REALLY THINK YOU'LL GO TO COLLEGE, MELISSA?

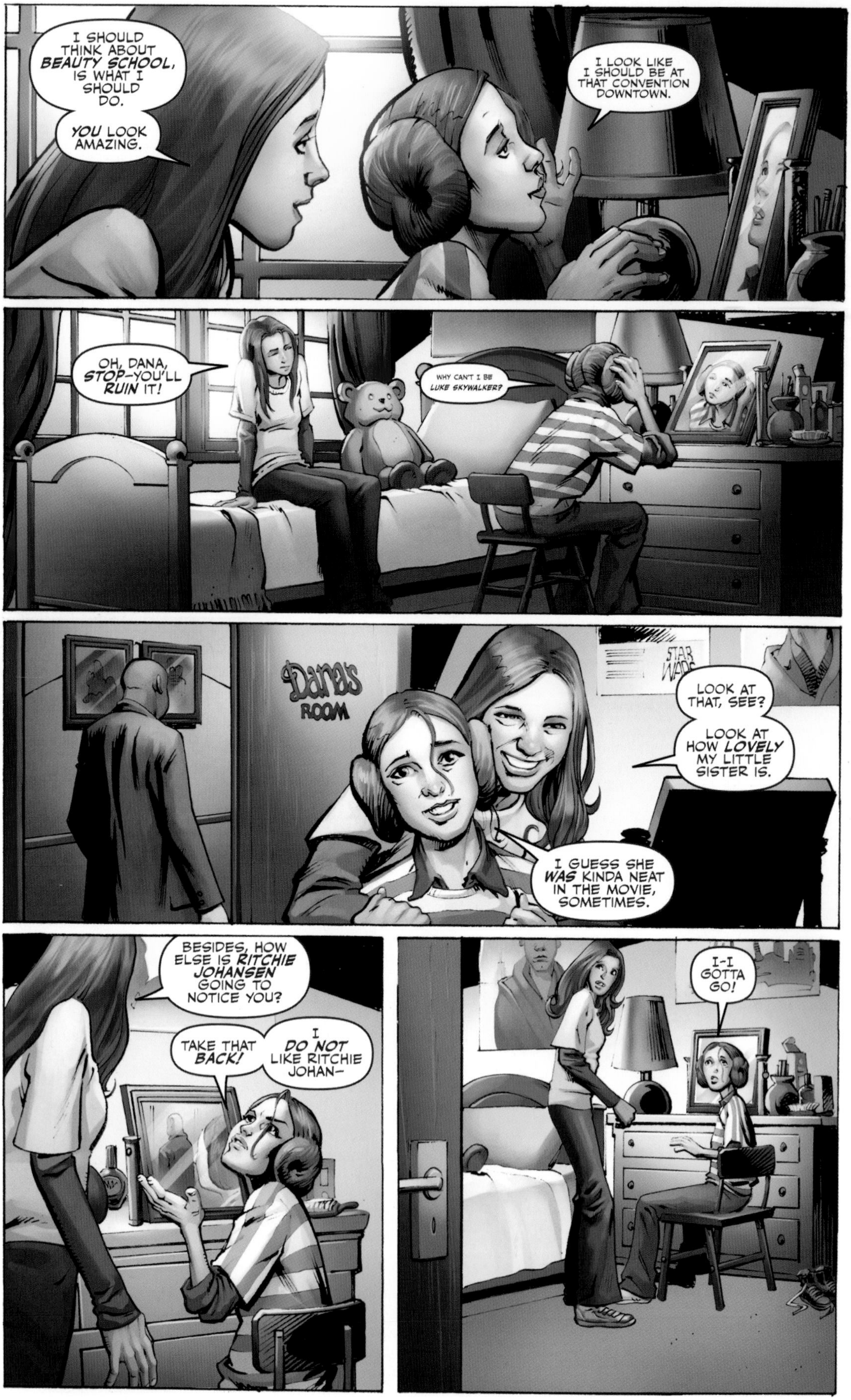

I SHOULD THINK ABOUT *BEAUTY SCHOOL,* IS WHAT I SHOULD DO.
YOU LOOK AMAZING.
I LOOK LIKE I SHOULD BE AT THAT CONVENTION DOWNTOWN.
OH, DANA, *STOP*—YOU'LL *RUIN* IT!
WHY CAN'T I BE *LUKE SKYWALKER?*
DANA'S ROOM
STAR WARS
LOOK AT THAT, SEE?
LOOK AT HOW *LOVELY* MY LITTLE SISTER IS.
I GUESS SHE *WAS* KINDA NEAT IN THE MOVIE, SOMETIMES.
BESIDES, HOW ELSE IS *RITCHIE JOHANSEN* GOING TO NOTICE YOU?
I *DO NOT* LIKE RITCHIE JOHAN–
TAKE THAT *BACK!*
I-I GOTTA GO!

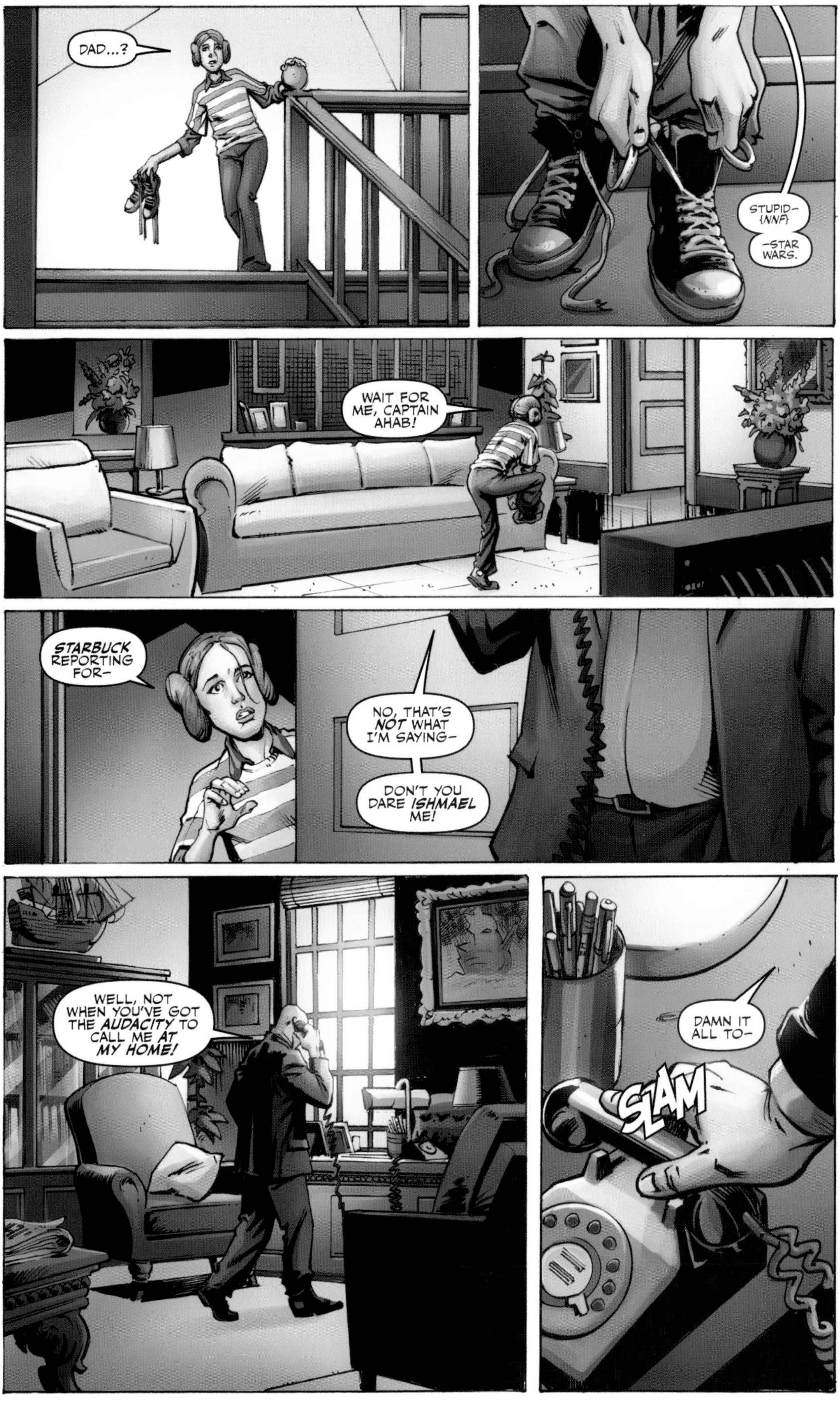
DAD...?
STUPID-{NNF}
-STAR WARS.
WAIT FOR ME, CAPTAIN AHAB!
STARBUCK REPORTING FOR-
NO, THAT'S *NOT* WHAT I'M SAYING-
DON'T YOU DARE *ISHMAEL* ME!
WELL, NOT WHEN YOU'VE GOT THE *AUDACITY* TO CALL ME *AT MY HOME!*
DAMN IT ALL TO-
SLAM

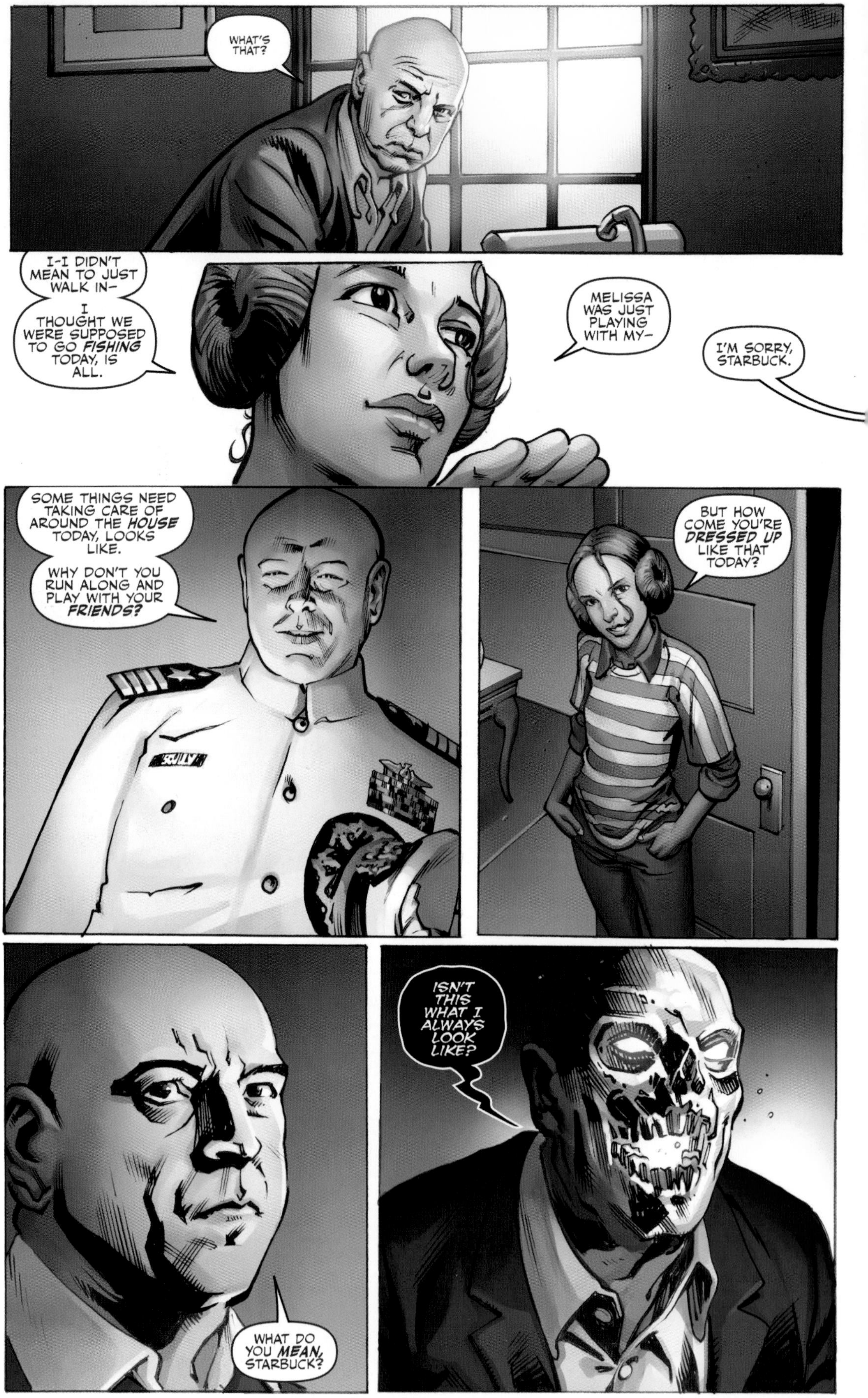
WHAT'S THAT?
I-I DIDN'T MEAN TO JUST WALK IN-
I THOUGHT WE WERE SUPPOSED TO GO FISHING TODAY, IS ALL.
MELISSA WAS JUST PLAYING WITH MY-
I'M SORRY, STARBUCK.
SOME THINGS NEED TAKING CARE OF AROUND THE HOUSE TODAY, LOOKS LIKE.
WHY DON'T YOU RUN ALONG AND PLAY WITH YOUR FRIENDS?
SCULLY
BUT HOW COME YOU'RE DRESSED UP LIKE THAT TODAY?
WHAT DO YOU MEAN, STARBUCK?
ISN'T THIS WHAT I ALWAYS LOOK LIKE?

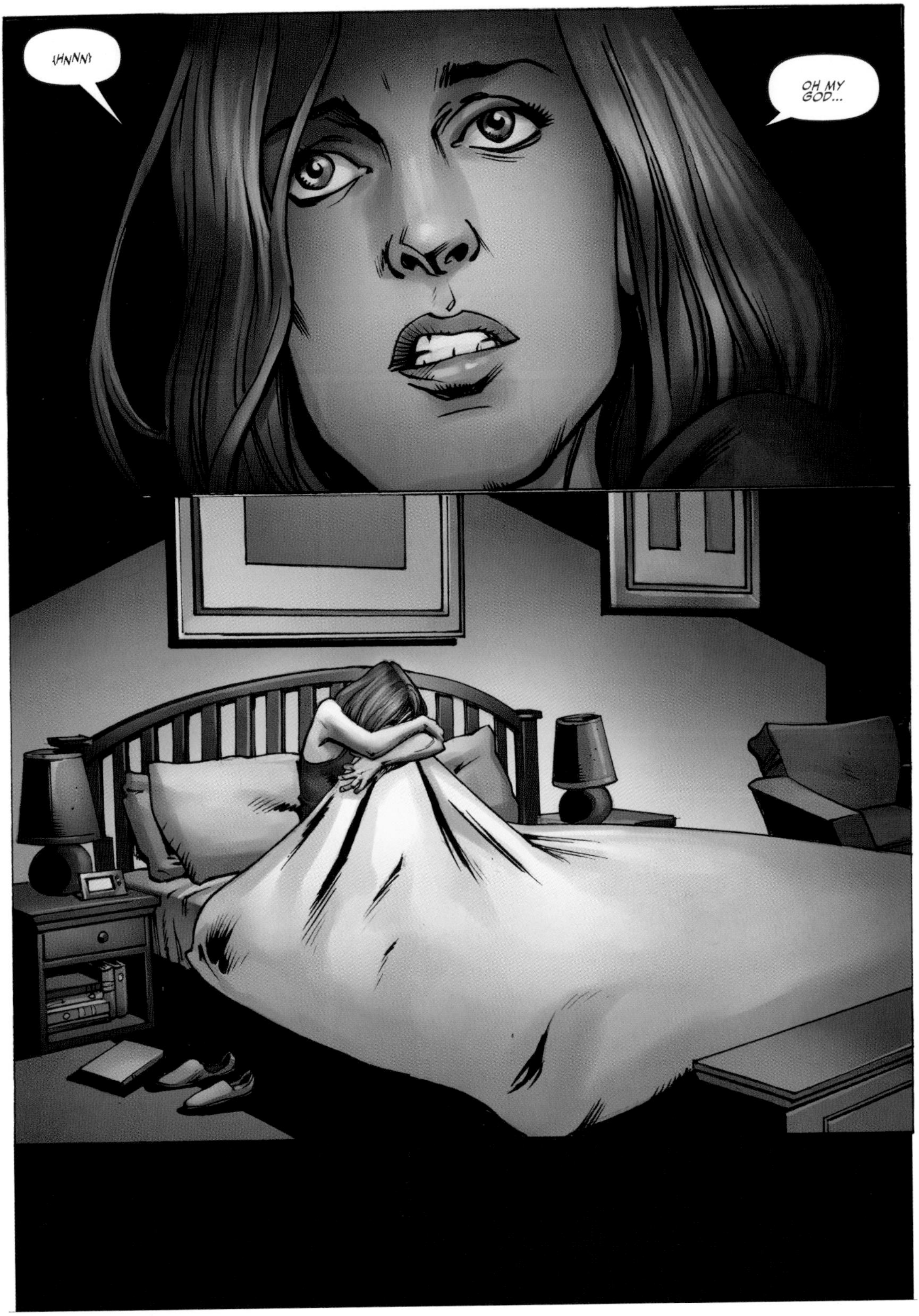
{HNNN}
OH MY GOD...

THE X FILES™

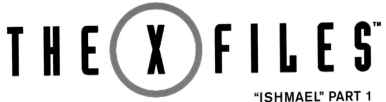

“ISHMAEL” PART 1

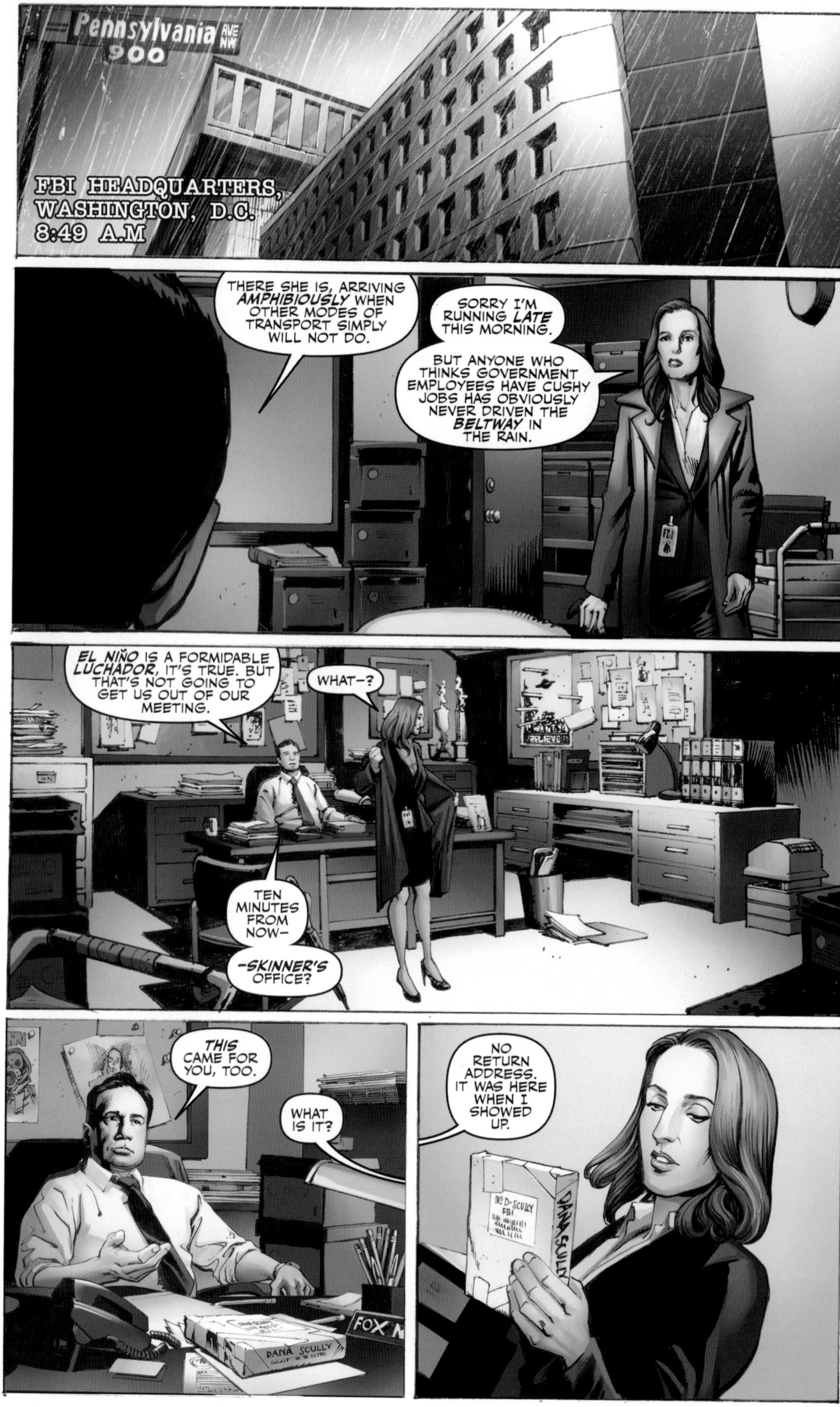
Pennsylvania AVE NW
900
FBI HEADQUARTERS, WASHINGTON, D.C. 8:49 A.M
THERE SHE IS, ARRIVING AMPHIBIOUSLY WHEN OTHER MODES OF TRANSPORT SIMPLY WILL NOT DO.
SORRY I'M RUNNING LATE THIS MORNING.
BUT ANYONE WHO THINKS GOVERNMENT EMPLOYEES HAVE CUSHY JOBS HAS OBVIOUSLY NEVER DRIVEN THE BELTWAY IN THE RAIN.
EL NIÑO IS A FORMIDABLE LUCHADOR, IT'S TRUE. BUT THAT'S NOT GOING TO GET US OUT OF OUR MEETING.
WHAT-?
TEN MINUTES FROM NOW-
-SKINNER'S OFFICE?
THIS CAME FOR YOU, TOO.
WHAT IS IT?
DANA SCULLY
NO RETURN ADDRESS. IT WAS HERE WHEN I SHOWED UP.
MS D. SCULLY
FBI
DANA SCULLY

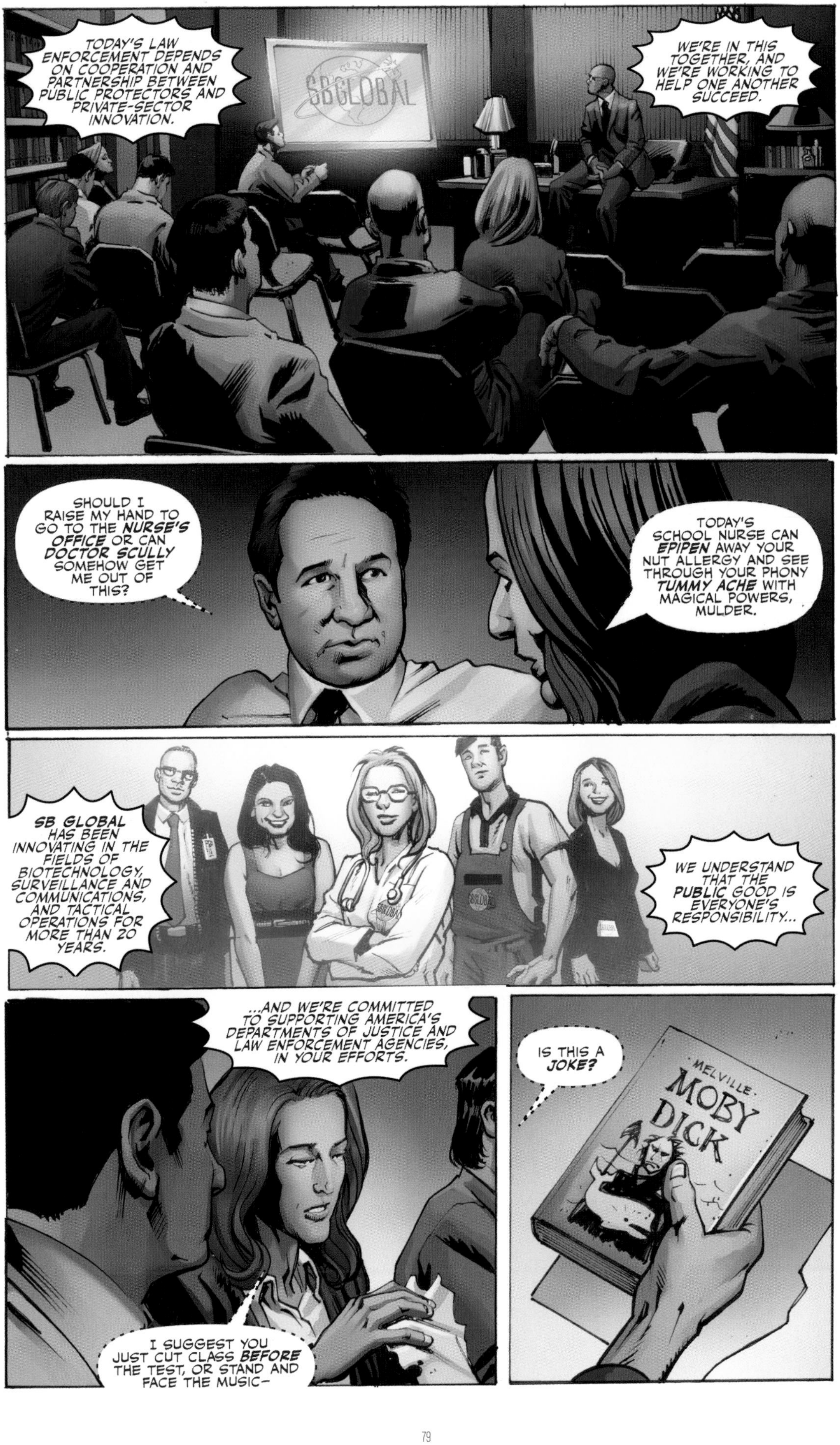
TODAY'S LAW ENFORCEMENT DEPENDS ON COOPERATION AND PARTNERSHIP BETWEEN PUBLIC PROTECTORS AND PRIVATE-SECTOR INNOVATION.
SBGLOBAL
WE'RE IN THIS TOGETHER, AND WE'RE WORKING TO HELP ONE ANOTHER SUCCEED.
SHOULD I RAISE MY HAND TO GO TO THE NURSE'S OFFICE OR CAN DOCTOR SCULLY SOMEHOW GET ME OUT OF THIS?
TODAY'S SCHOOL NURSE CAN EPIPEN AWAY YOUR NUT ALLERGY AND SEE THROUGH YOUR PHONY TUMMY ACHE WITH MAGICAL POWERS, MULDER.
SB GLOBAL HAS BEEN INNOVATING IN THE FIELDS OF BIOTECHNOLOGY, SURVEILLANCE AND COMMUNICATIONS, AND TACTICAL OPERATIONS FOR MORE THAN 20 YEARS.
WE UNDERSTAND THAT THE PUBLIC GOOD IS EVERYONE'S RESPONSIBILITY...
...AND WE'RE COMMITTED TO SUPPORTING AMERICA'S DEPARTMENTS OF JUSTICE AND LAW ENFORCEMENT AGENCIES, IN YOUR EFFORTS.
I SUGGEST YOU JUST CUT CLASS BEFORE THE TEST, OR STAND AND FACE THE MUSIC–
IS THIS A JOKE?
MELVILLE
MOBY DICK

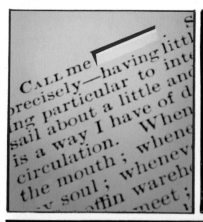

CALL me—having littl[e]
precisely—[havi]ng particular to inte[rest]
sail about a little and [se]
is a way I have of d[riving off the]
circulation. When[ever I find myself growing grim about]
the mouth; whene[ver it is a damp, drizzly November in]
[m]y soul; whenev[er...]
[c]offin wareh[ouse...]
meet;

CALL ME...

DON'T YOU DARE ISHMAEL ME!

EXCUSE ME. SORRY... I-I JUST NEED A MOMENT.

FROM HELPING TO ENFORCE THE LAW TO HELPING SECURE THE NATION'S INTERESTS, SB GLOBAL IS HERE TO SERVE.

CAN WE HAVE THE LIGHTS PLEASE?

I'LL BE BACK AND COLLECT, UM...

...AGENT SCULLY'S HOMEWORK SO SHE DOESN'T MISS ANYTHING.

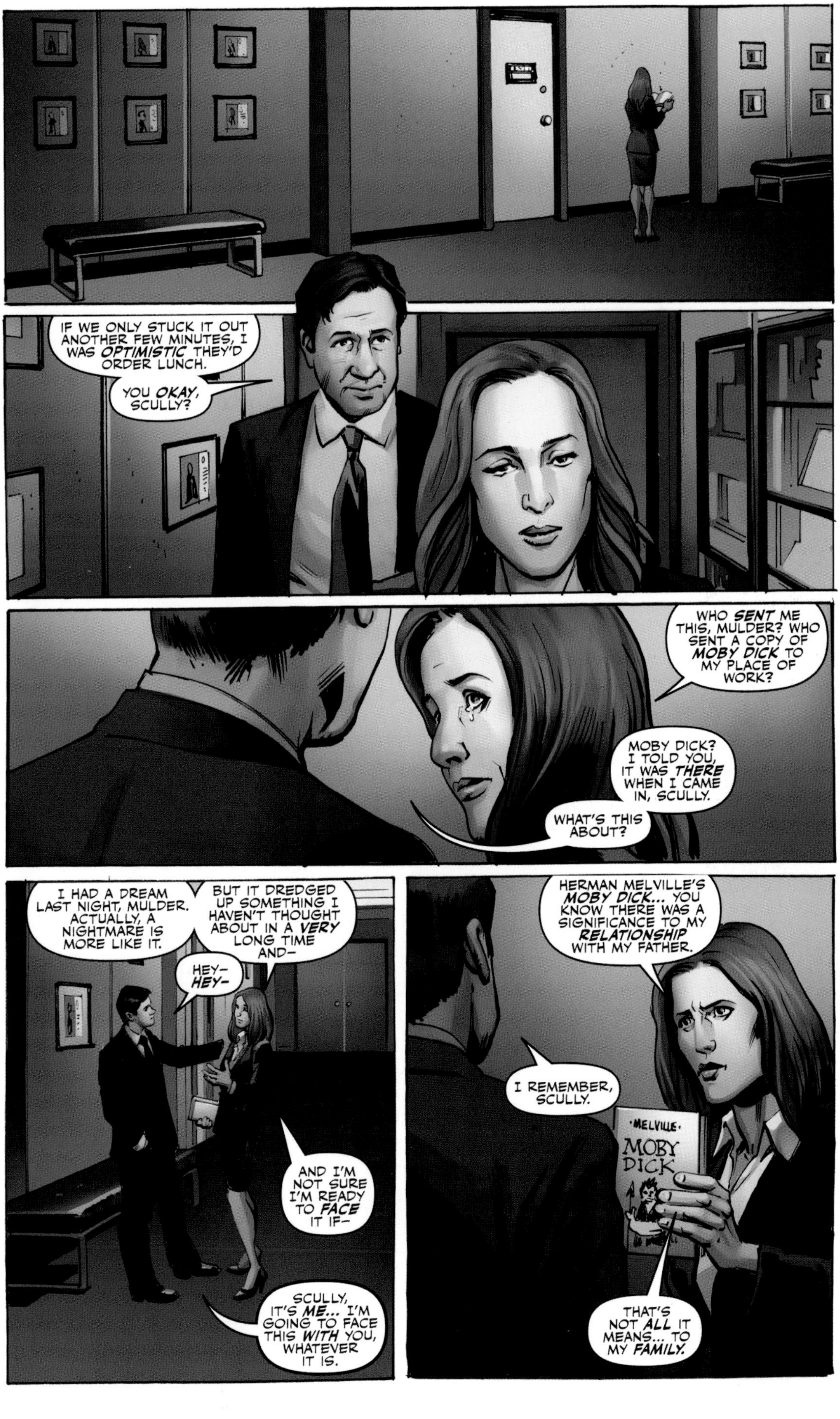
IF WE ONLY STUCK IT OUT ANOTHER FEW MINUTES, I WAS *OPTIMISTIC* THEY'D ORDER LUNCH.
YOU *OKAY*, SCULLY?
WHO *SENT* ME THIS, MULDER? WHO SENT A COPY OF *MOBY DICK* TO MY PLACE OF WORK?
MOBY DICK? I TOLD YOU, IT WAS *THERE* WHEN I CAME IN, SCULLY.
WHAT'S THIS ABOUT?
I HAD A DREAM LAST NIGHT, MULDER. ACTUALLY, A NIGHTMARE IS MORE LIKE IT.
BUT IT DREDGED UP SOMETHING I HAVEN'T THOUGHT ABOUT IN A *VERY* LONG TIME AND–
HEY– *HEY*–
AND I'M NOT SURE I'M READY TO *FACE* IT IF–
SCULLY, IT'S *ME*... I'M GOING TO FACE THIS *WITH* YOU, WHATEVER IT IS.
HERMAN MELVILLE'S *MOBY DICK*... YOU KNOW THERE WAS A SIGNIFICANCE TO MY *RELATIONSHIP* WITH MY FATHER.
I REMEMBER, SCULLY.
·MELVILLE·
MOBY DICK
THAT'S NOT *ALL* IT MEANS... TO MY *FAMILY*.

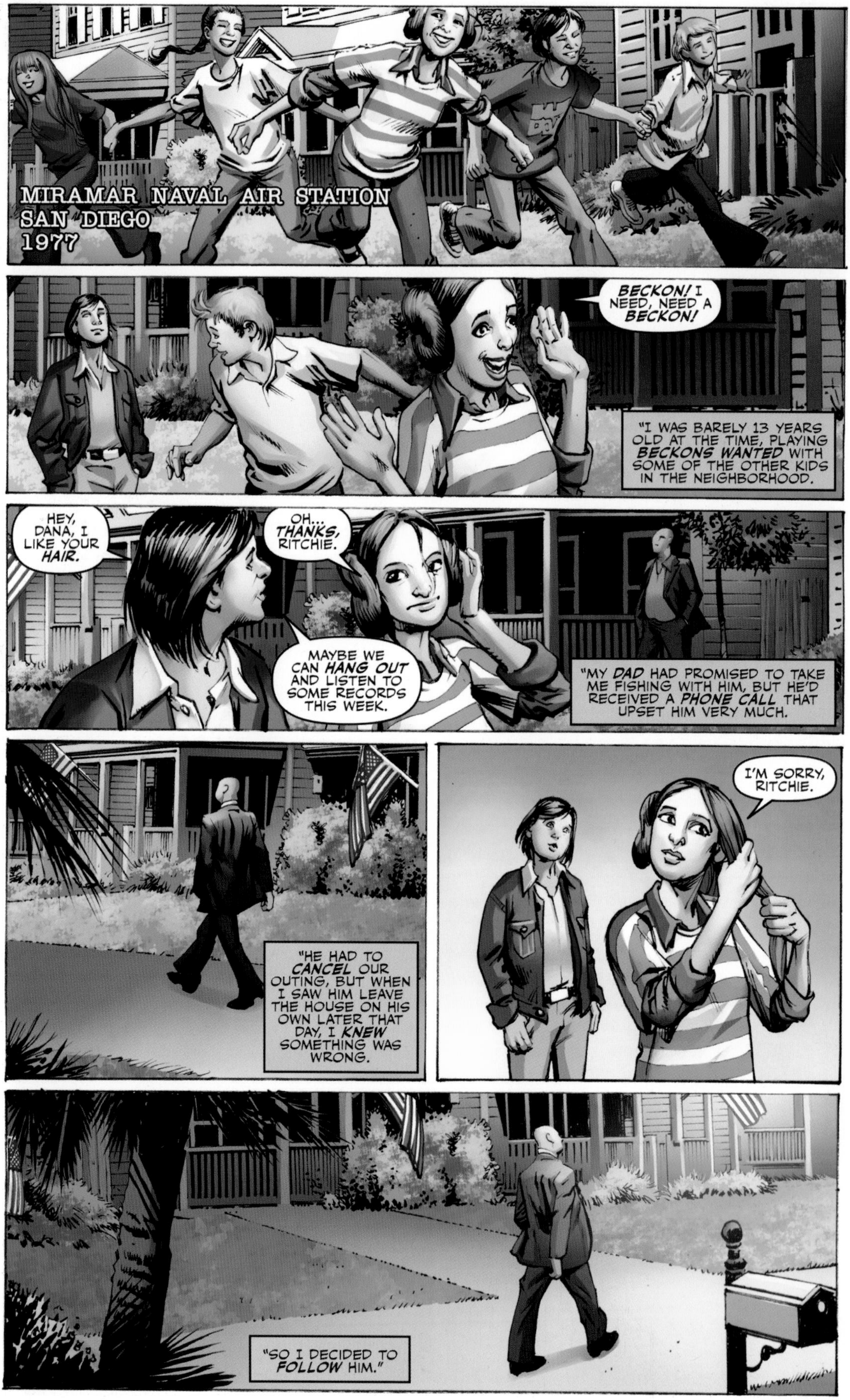
MIRAMAR NAVAL AIR STATION SAN DIEGO 1977
BECKON! I NEED, NEED A BECKON!
"I WAS BARELY 13 YEARS OLD AT THE TIME, PLAYING BECKONS WANTED WITH SOME OF THE OTHER KIDS IN THE NEIGHBORHOOD.
HEY, DANA, I LIKE YOUR HAIR.
OH... THANKS, RITCHIE.
MAYBE WE CAN HANG OUT AND LISTEN TO SOME RECORDS THIS WEEK.
"MY DAD HAD PROMISED TO TAKE ME FISHING WITH HIM, BUT HE'D RECEIVED A PHONE CALL THAT UPSET HIM VERY MUCH.
"HE HAD TO CANCEL OUR OUTING, BUT WHEN I SAW HIM LEAVE THE HOUSE ON HIS OWN LATER THAT DAY, I KNEW SOMETHING WAS WRONG.
I'M SORRY, RITCHIE.
"SO I DECIDED TO FOLLOW HIM."

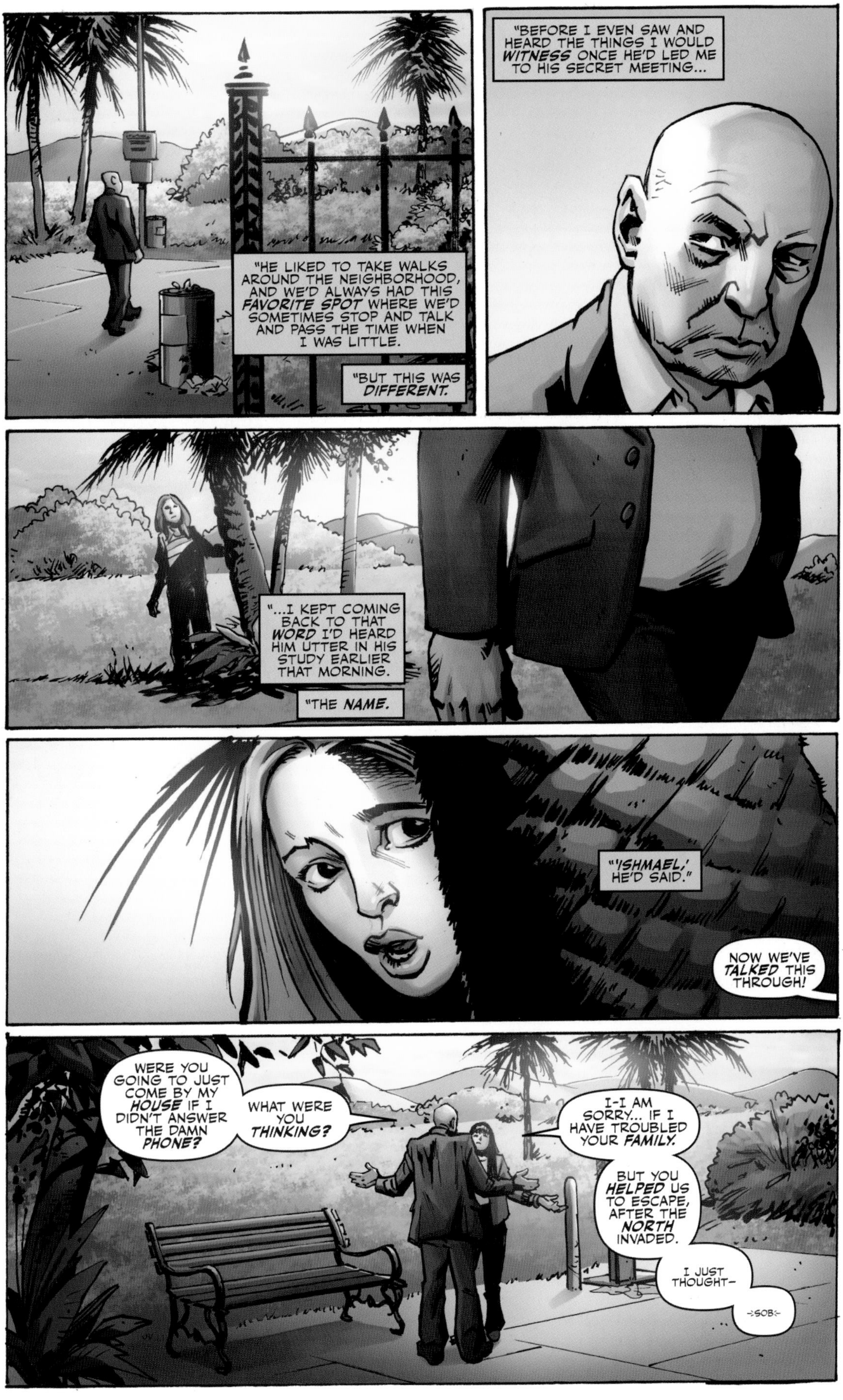
"HE LIKED TO TAKE WALKS AROUND THE NEIGHBORHOOD, AND WE'D ALWAYS HAD THIS FAVORITE SPOT WHERE WE'D SOMETIMES STOP AND TALK AND PASS THE TIME WHEN I WAS LITTLE.
"BUT THIS WAS DIFFERENT.
"BEFORE I EVEN SAW AND HEARD THE THINGS I WOULD WITNESS ONCE HE'D LED ME TO HIS SECRET MEETING...
"...I KEPT COMING BACK TO THAT WORD I'D HEARD HIM UTTER IN HIS STUDY EARLIER THAT MORNING.
"THE NAME.
"'ISHMAEL,' HE'D SAID."
NOW WE'VE TALKED THIS THROUGH!
WERE YOU GOING TO JUST COME BY MY HOUSE IF I DIDN'T ANSWER THE DAMN PHONE?
WHAT WERE YOU THINKING?
I-I AM SORRY... IF I HAVE TROUBLED YOUR FAMILY.
BUT YOU HELPED US TO ESCAPE, AFTER THE NORTH INVADED.
I JUST THOUGHT–
SOB

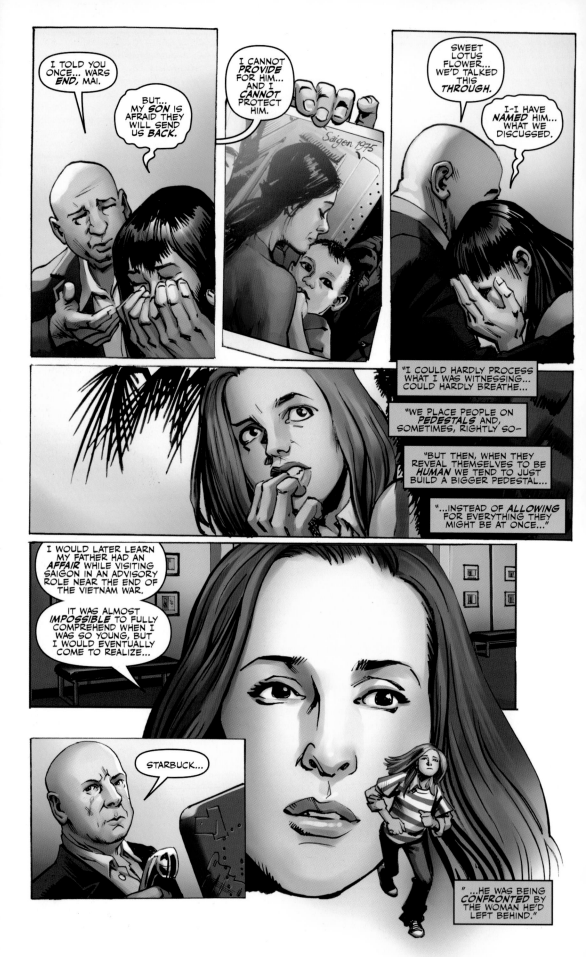

I TOLD YOU ONCE... WARS *END*, MAI.

BUT... MY *SON* IS AFRAID THEY WILL SEND US *BACK*.

I CANNOT *PROVIDE* FOR HIM... AND I *CANNOT* PROTECT HIM.

Saigon 1975

SWEET LOTUS FLOWER... WE'D TALKED THIS *THROUGH*.

I-I HAVE *NAMED* HIM... WHAT WE DISCUSSED.

"I COULD HARDLY PROCESS WHAT I WAS WITNESSING... COULD HARDLY BREATHE...

"WE PLACE PEOPLE ON *PEDESTALS* AND, SOMETIMES, RIGHTLY SO—

"BUT THEN, WHEN THEY REVEAL THEMSELVES TO BE *HUMAN* WE TEND TO JUST BUILD A BIGGER PEDESTAL...

"...INSTEAD OF *ALLOWING* FOR EVERYTHING THEY MIGHT BE AT ONCE..."

I WOULD LATER LEARN MY FATHER HAD AN *AFFAIR* WHILE VISITING SAIGON IN AN ADVISORY ROLE NEAR THE END OF THE VIETNAM WAR.

IT WAS ALMOST *IMPOSSIBLE* TO FULLY COMPREHEND WHEN I WAS SO YOUNG, BUT I WOULD EVENTUALLY COME TO REALIZE...

STARBUCK...

"...HE WAS BEING *CONFRONTED* BY THE WOMAN HE'D LEFT BEHIND."

I KNOW YOU USED TO CALL YOUR FATHER AHAB, AND THAT HIS PET NAME FOR YOU WAS *STARBUCK.*

BUT WHAT'S WITH—?

ISHMAEL IS THE *NARRATOR* OF THE STORY. HIS NAME ONLY APPEARS A *HANDFUL* OF TIMES IN THE ENTIRE BOOK.

BUT YOU *SEE?*

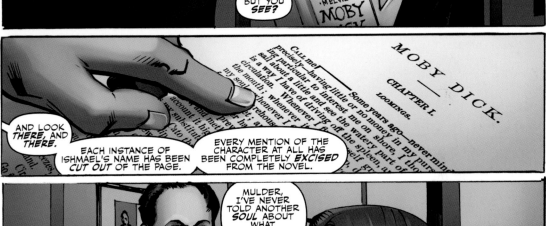

AND LOOK *THERE,* AND *THERE.*

EACH INSTANCE OF ISHMAEL'S NAME HAS BEEN *CUT OUT* OF THE PAGE.

EVERY MENTION OF THE CHARACTER AT ALL HAS BEEN COMPLETELY *EXCISED* FROM THE NOVEL.

MOBY DICK.

CHAPTER I.

LOOMINGS.

MULDER, I'VE NEVER TOLD ANOTHER *SOUL* ABOUT WHAT HAPPENED THAT DAY...

SCULLY, IF YOU REALLY THINK YOU'RE BEING *BLACKMAILED...*

...OR *STALKED* FOR SOME REASON—

MULDER, PLEASE...

WE NEED TO TELL *SKINNER.*

NO.

MULDER... I *WILL NOT* SEE MY FATHER'S MEMORY DISHONORED.

THERE'S A LOT I WOULD DO *BEFORE* I ALLOWED THAT.

SO, WHAT *ARE* YOU GOING TO DO?

SCULLY?

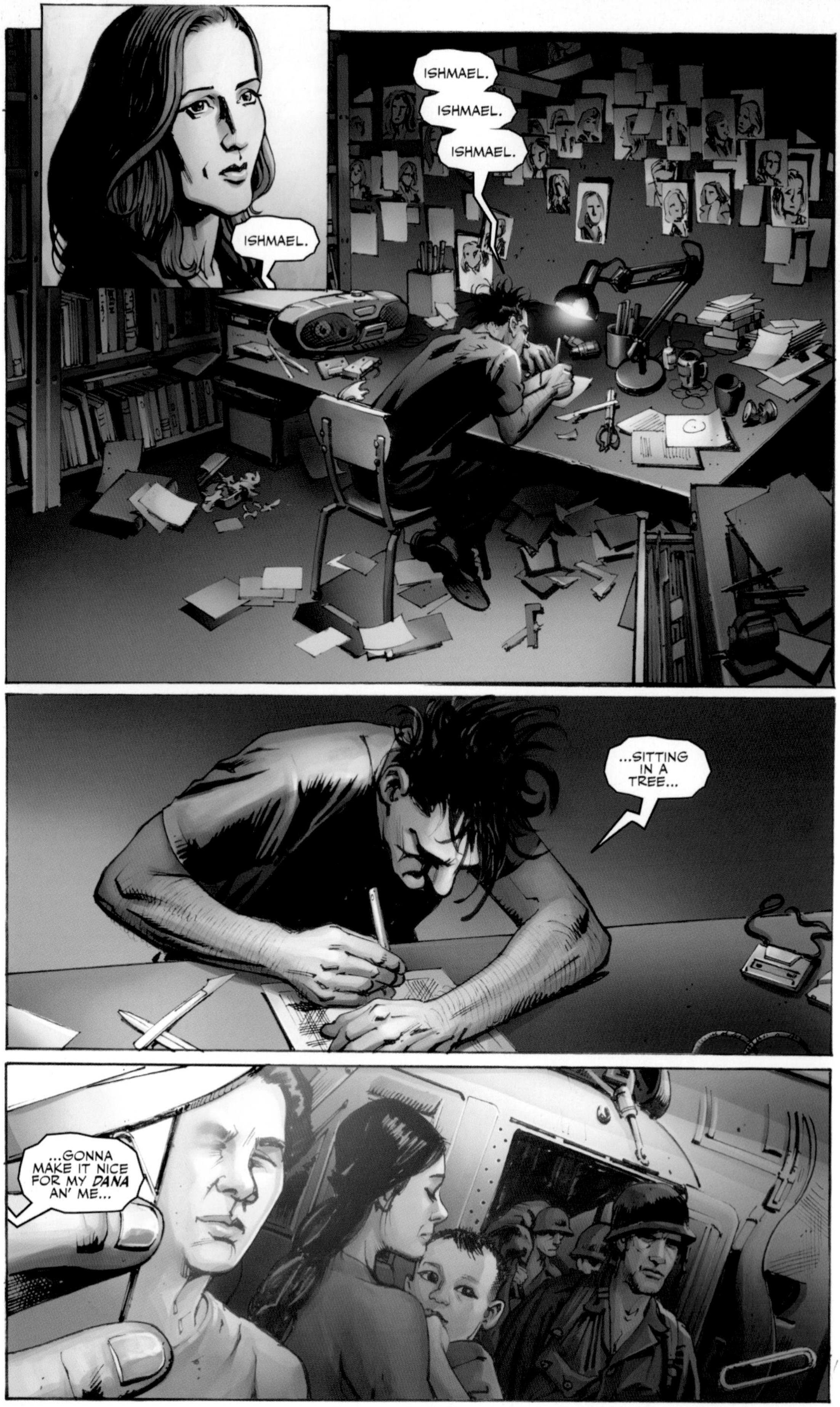
ISHMAEL.
ISHMAEL.
ISHMAEL.
ISHMAEL.
...SITTING IN A TREE...
...GONNA MAKE IT NICE FOR MY *DANA* AN' ME...

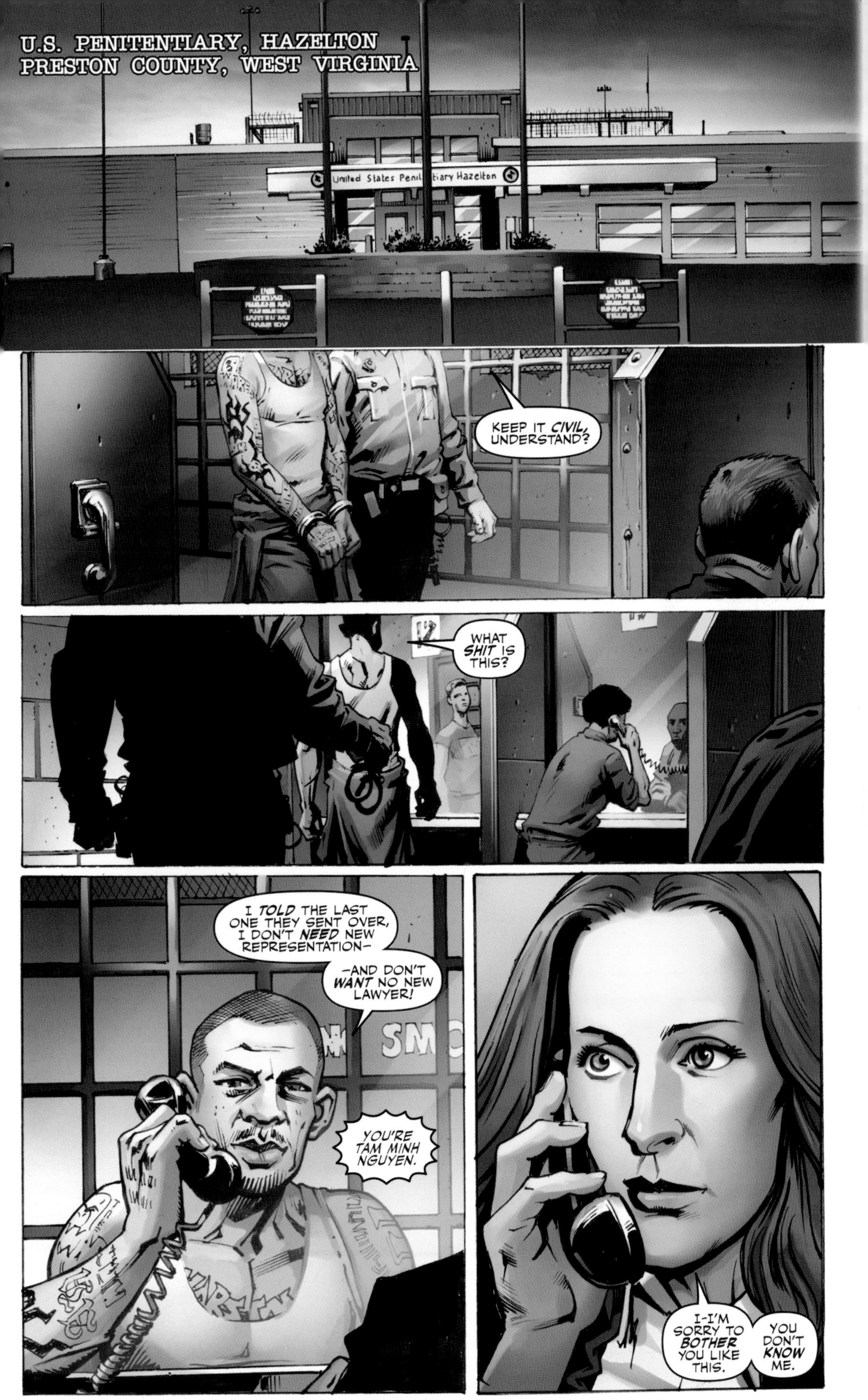
U.S. PENITENTIARY, HAZELTON
PRESTON COUNTY, WEST VIRGINIA
United States Penitentiary Hazelton
KEEP IT CIVIL, UNDERSTAND?
WHAT SHIT IS THIS?
I TOLD THE LAST ONE THEY SENT OVER, I DON'T NEED NEW REPRESENTATION–
–AND DON'T WANT NO NEW LAWYER!
YOU'RE TAM MINH NGUYEN.
I-I'M SORRY TO BOTHER YOU LIKE THIS.
YOU DON'T KNOW ME.

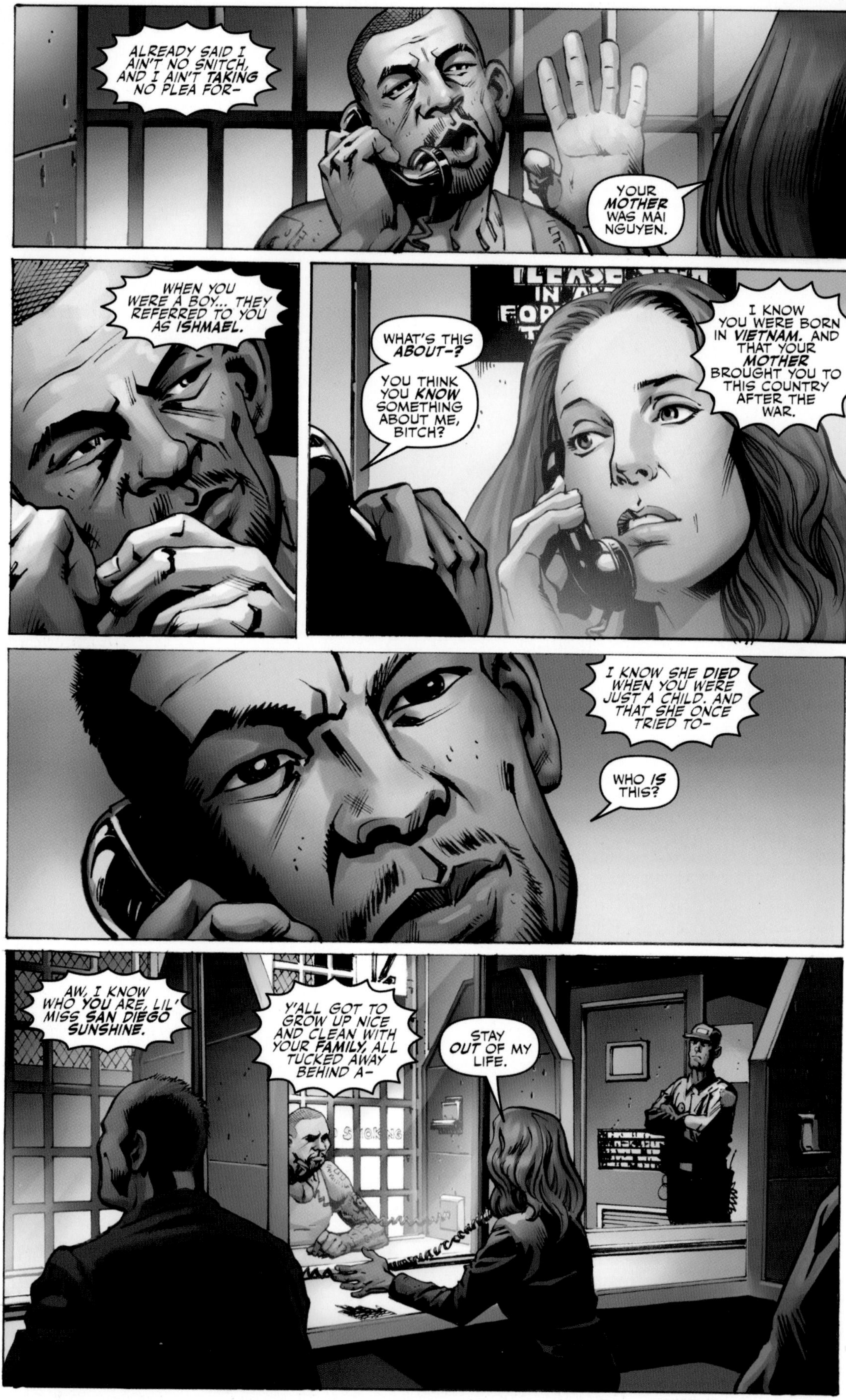

ALREADY SAID I AIN'T NO SNITCH, AND I AIN'T TAKING NO PLEA FOR-
YOUR MOTHER WAS MAI NGUYEN.
WHEN YOU WERE A BOY... THEY REFERRED TO YOU AS ISHMAEL.
WHAT'S THIS ABOUT-?
YOU THINK YOU KNOW SOMETHING ABOUT ME, BITCH?
I KNOW YOU WERE BORN IN VIETNAM. AND THAT YOUR MOTHER BROUGHT YOU TO THIS COUNTRY AFTER THE WAR.
I KNOW SHE DIED WHEN YOU WERE JUST A CHILD. AND THAT SHE ONCE TRIED TO-
WHO IS THIS?
AW, I KNOW WHO YOU ARE, LIL' MISS SAN DIEGO SUNSHINE.
Y'ALL GOT TO GROW UP NICE AND CLEAN WITH YOUR FAMILY, ALL TUCKED AWAY BEHIND A-
STAY OUT OF MY LIFE.

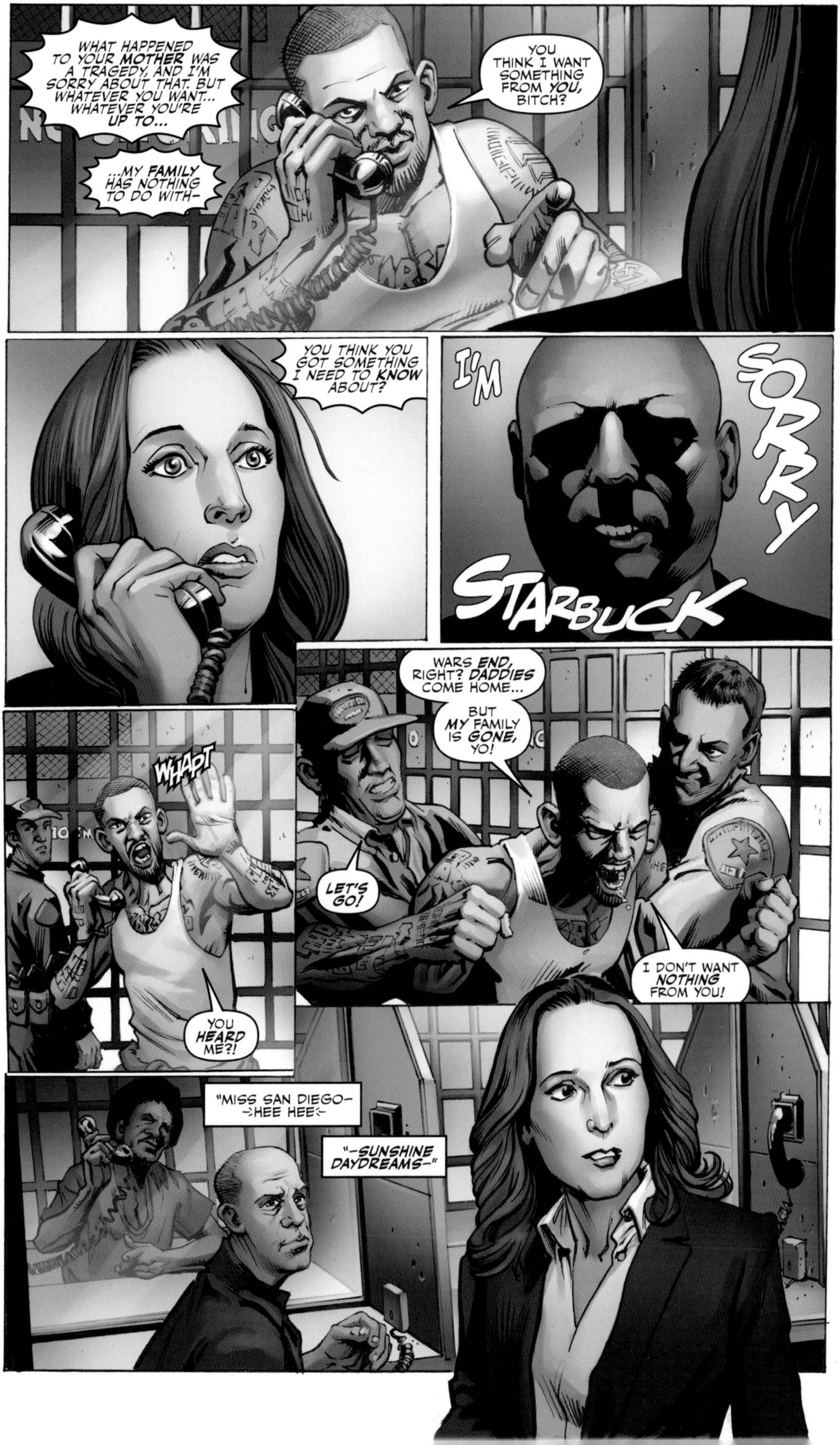
WHAT HAPPENED TO YOUR MOTHER WAS A TRAGEDY, AND I'M SORRY ABOUT THAT. BUT WHATEVER YOU WANT... WHATEVER YOU'RE UP TO...
...MY FAMILY HAS NOTHING TO DO WITH-
YOU THINK I WANT SOMETHING FROM YOU, BITCH?
YOU THINK YOU GOT SOMETHING I NEED TO KNOW ABOUT?
I'M SORRY STARBUCK
WHAPT
WARS END, RIGHT? DADDIES COME HOME...
BUT MY FAMILY IS GONE, YO!
LET'S GO!
I DON'T WANT NOTHING FROM YOU!
YOU HEARD ME?!
"MISS SAN DIEGO- ->HEE HEE<-
"-SUNSHINE DAYDREAMS-"

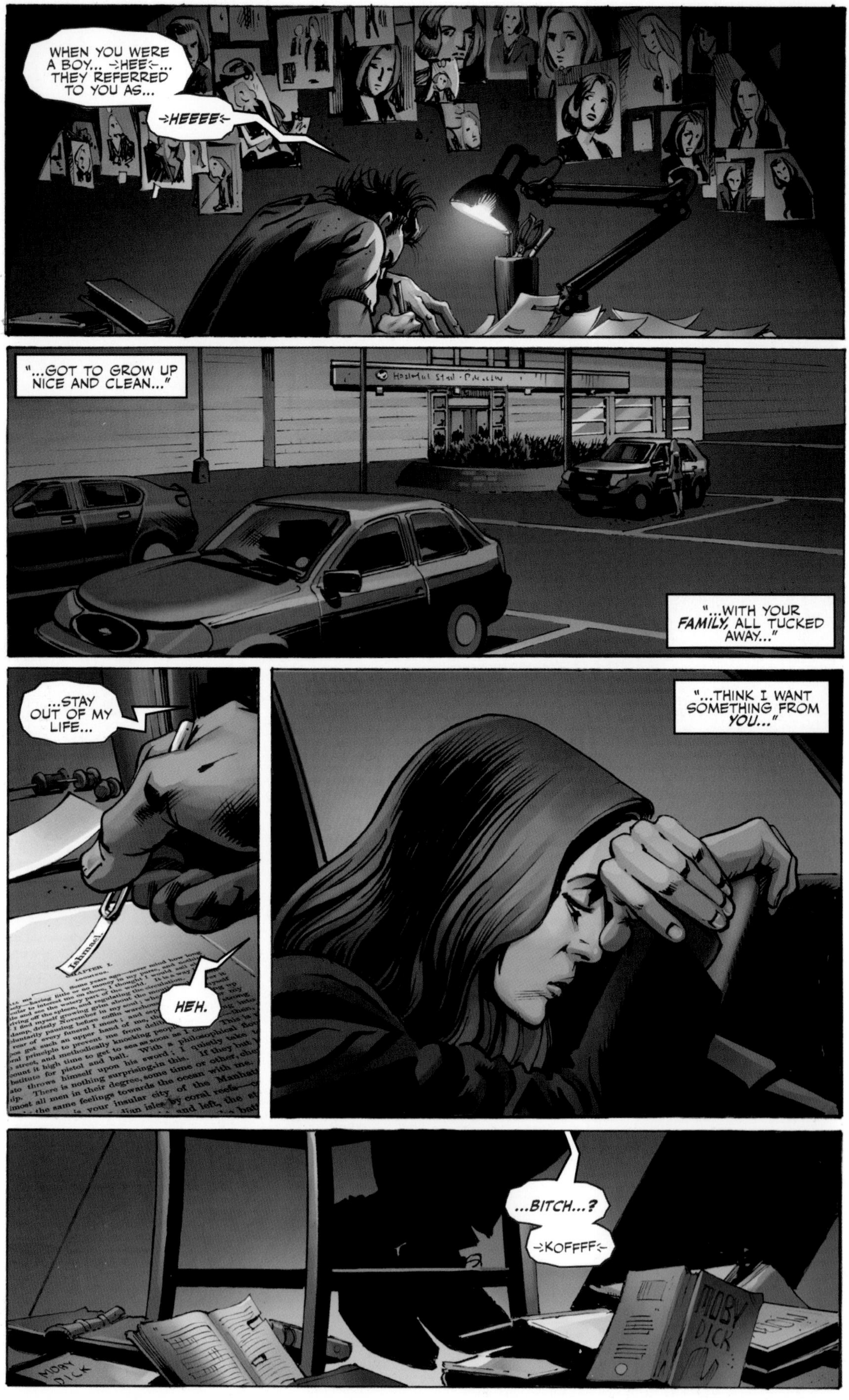

WHEN YOU WERE A BOY... ⇒HEE⇐... THEY REFERRED TO YOU AS...
⇒HEEEE⇐
"...GOT TO GROW UP NICE AND CLEAN..."
"...WITH YOUR FAMILY, ALL TUCKED AWAY..."
...STAY OUT OF MY LIFE...
HEH.
"...THINK I WANT SOMETHING FROM YOU..."
...BITCH...?
⇒KOFFFF⇐
MOBY DICK

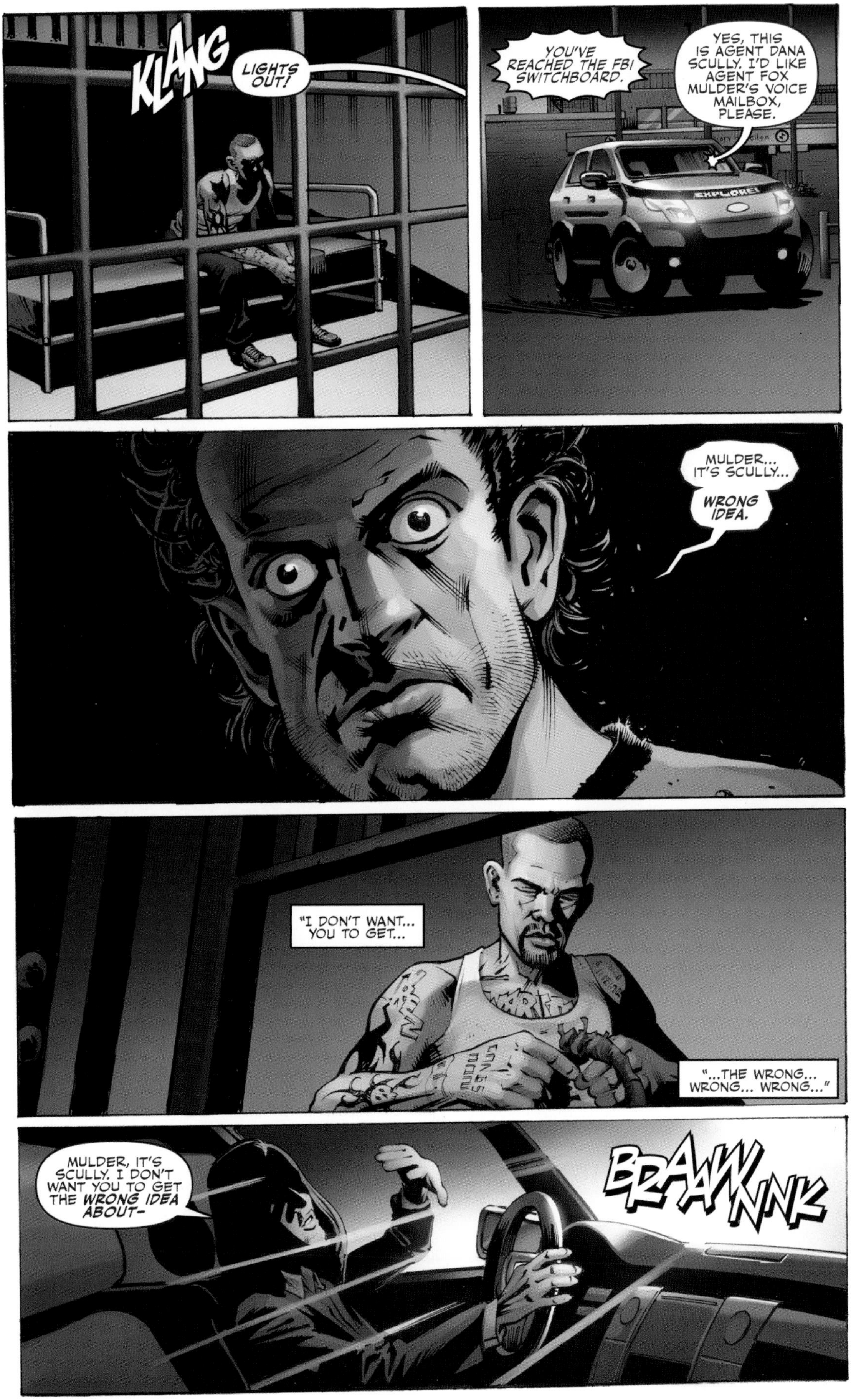
KLANG
LIGHTS OUT!
YOU'VE REACHED THE FBI SWITCHBOARD.
YES, THIS IS AGENT DANA SCULLY. I'D LIKE AGENT FOX MULDER'S VOICE MAILBOX, PLEASE.
EXPLORER
MULDER... IT'S SCULLY...
WRONG IDEA.
"I DON'T WANT... YOU TO GET...
"...THE WRONG... WRONG... WRONG..."
MULDER, IT'S SCULLY. I DON'T WANT YOU TO GET THE WRONG IDEA ABOUT-
BRAAWNNK

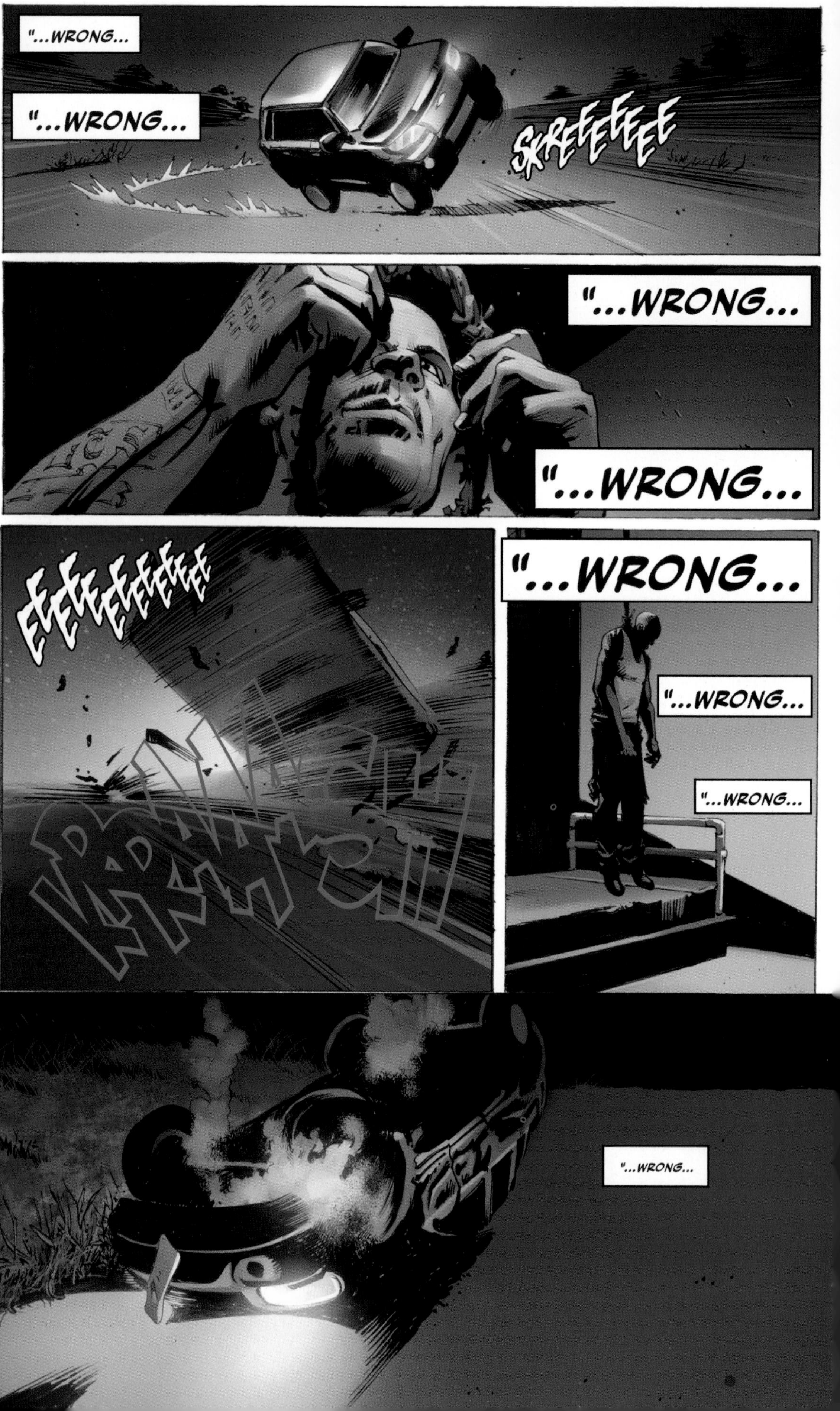

"...WRONG...
"...WRONG...
SKREEEEEEE
"...WRONG...
"...WRONG...
EEEEEEEEEEEE
"...WRONG...
"...WRONG...
"...WRONG...
"...WRONG...

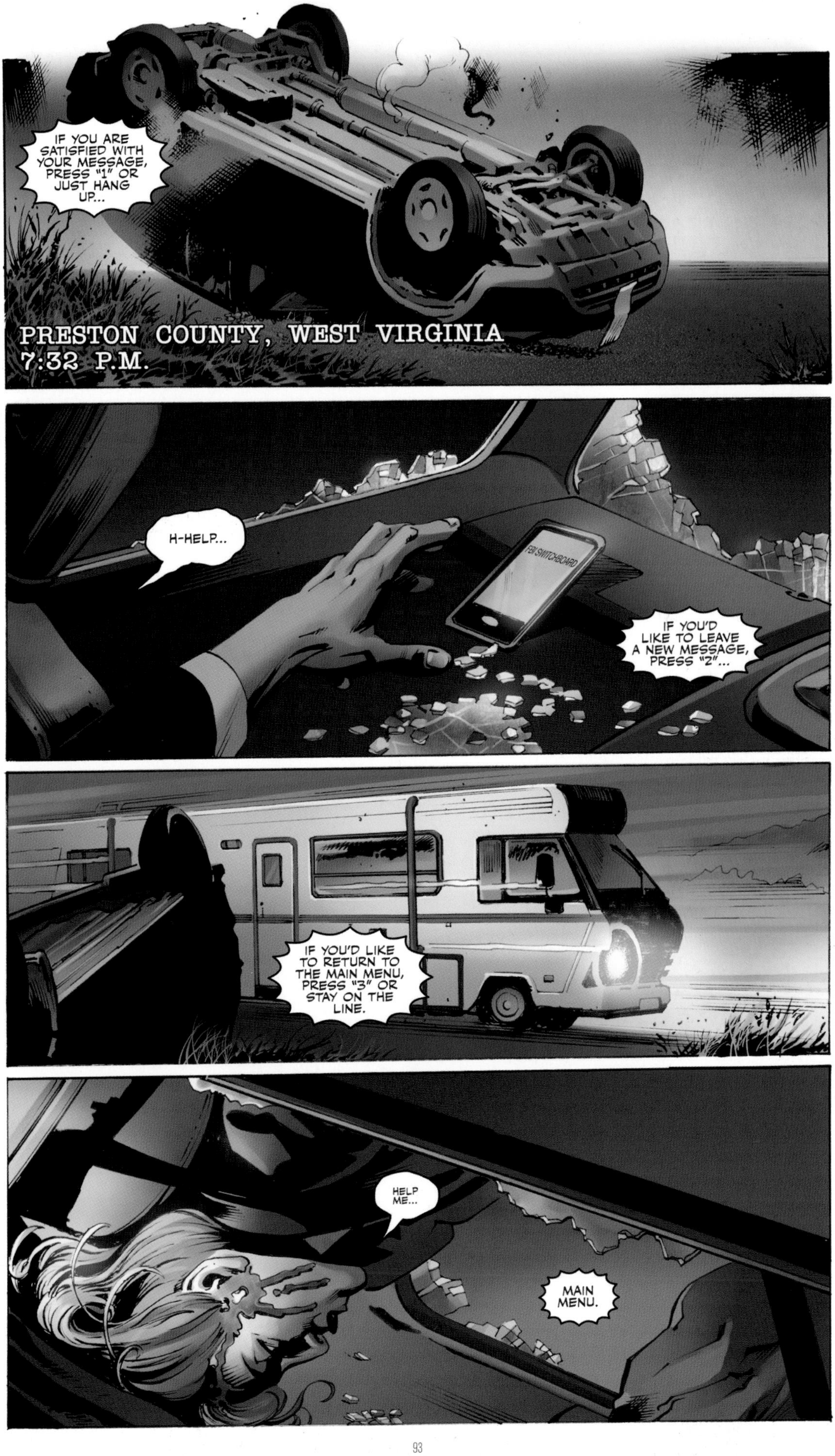
IF YOU ARE SATISFIED WITH YOUR MESSAGE, PRESS "1" OR JUST HANG UP...
PRESTON COUNTY, WEST VIRGINIA
7:32 P.M.
H-HELP...
FBI SWITCHBOARD
IF YOU'D LIKE TO LEAVE A NEW MESSAGE, PRESS "2"...
IF YOU'D LIKE TO RETURN TO THE MAIN MENU, PRESS "3" OR STAY ON THE LINE.
HELP ME...
MAIN MENU.

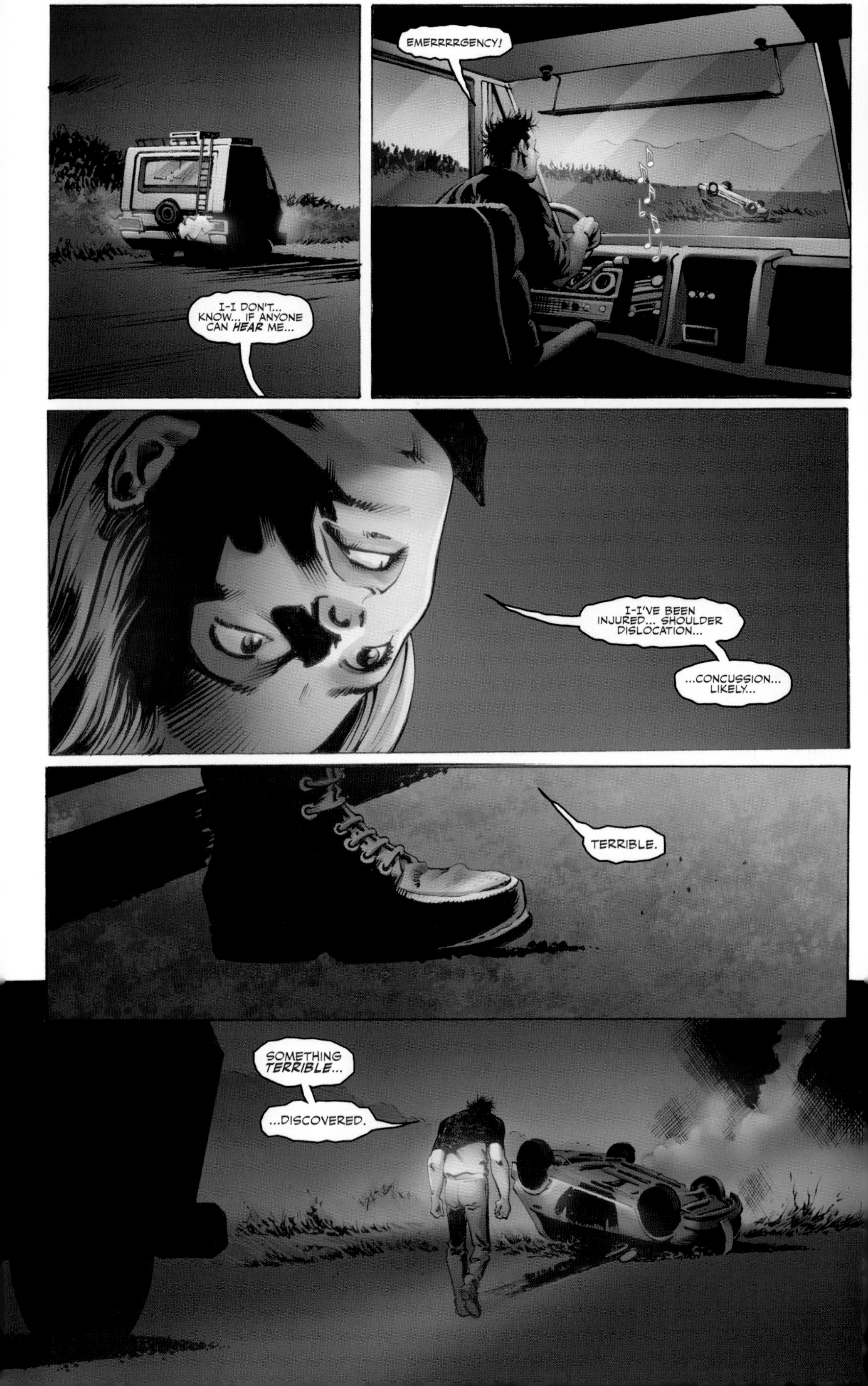
I-I DON'T... KNOW... IF ANYONE CAN HEAR ME...
EMERRRRGENCY!
I-I'VE BEEN INJURED... SHOULDER DISLOCATION...
...CONCUSSION... LIKELY...
TERRIBLE.
SOMETHING TERRIBLE...
...DISCOVERED.

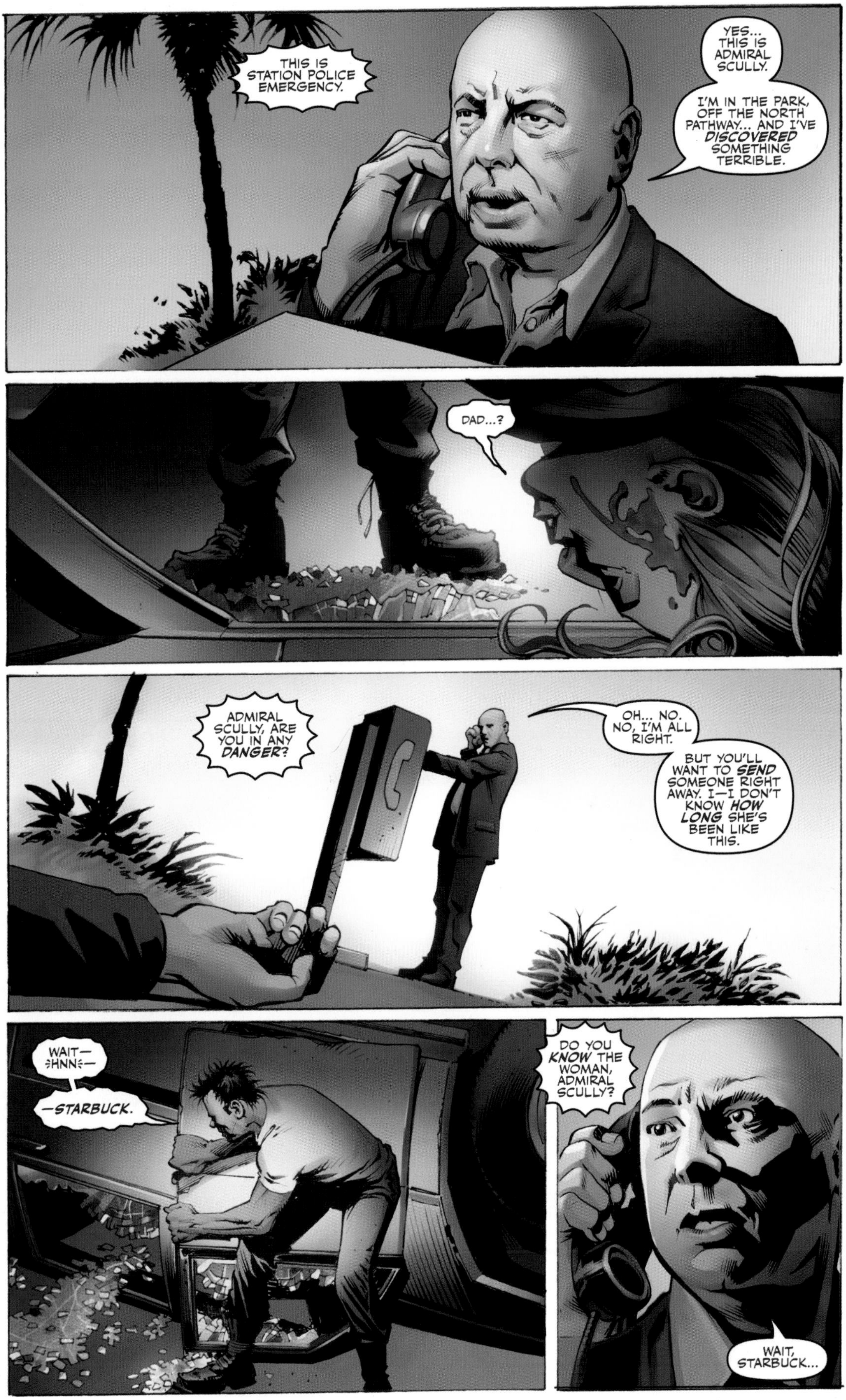
THIS IS STATION POLICE EMERGENCY.
YES... THIS IS ADMIRAL SCULLY.
I'M IN THE PARK, OFF THE NORTH PATHWAY... AND I'VE DISCOVERED SOMETHING TERRIBLE.
DAD...?
ADMIRAL SCULLY, ARE YOU IN ANY DANGER?
OH... NO. NO, I'M ALL RIGHT.
BUT YOU'LL WANT TO SEND SOMEONE RIGHT AWAY. I—I DON'T KNOW HOW LONG SHE'S BEEN LIKE THIS.
WAIT— HNN—
—STARBUCK.
DO YOU KNOW THE WOMAN, ADMIRAL SCULLY?
WAIT, STARBUCK...

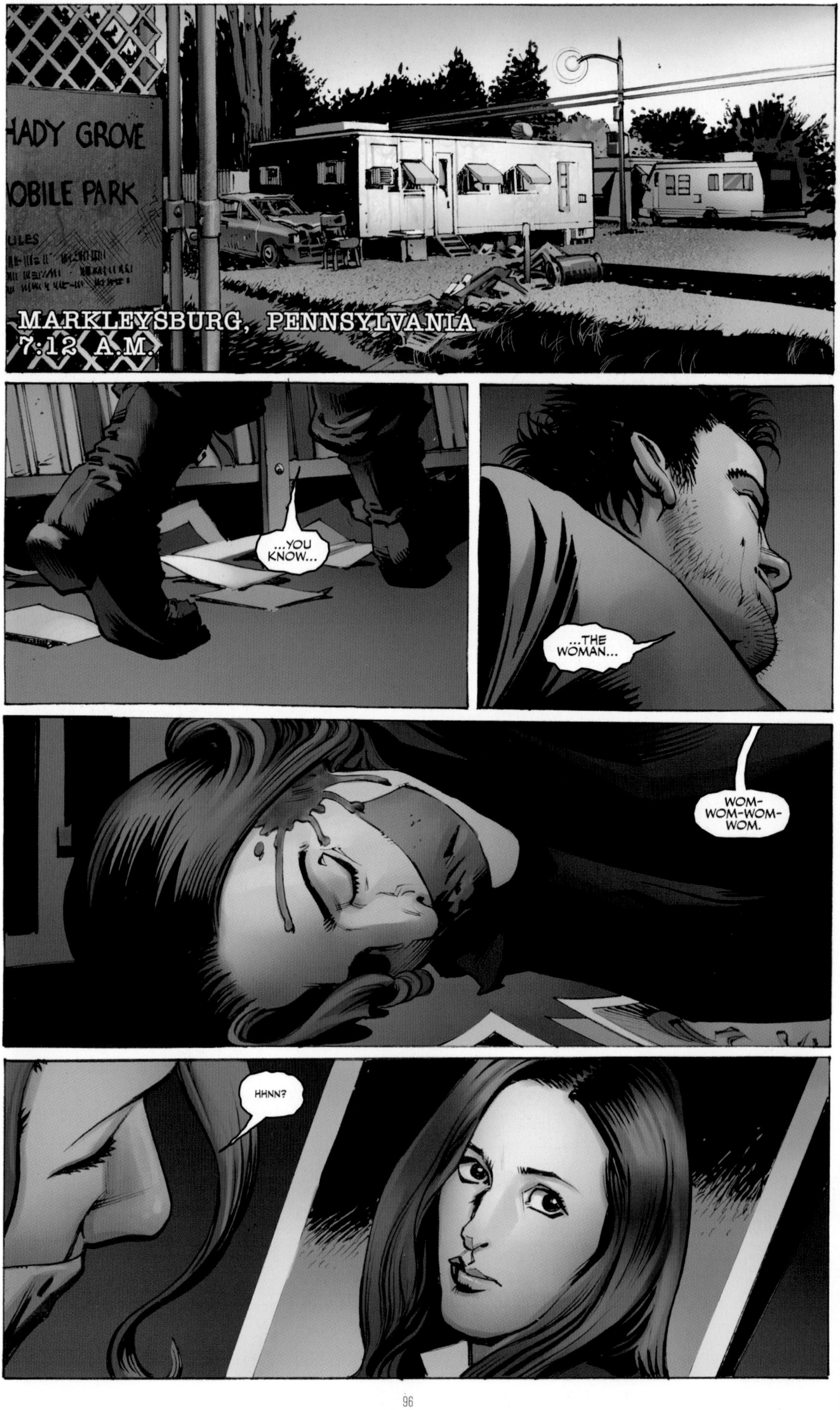
HADY GROVE
MOBILE PARK
MARKLEYSBURG, PENNSYLVANIA
7:12 A.M.
...YOU KNOW...
...THE WOMAN...
WOM-WOM-WOM-WOM.
HHNN?

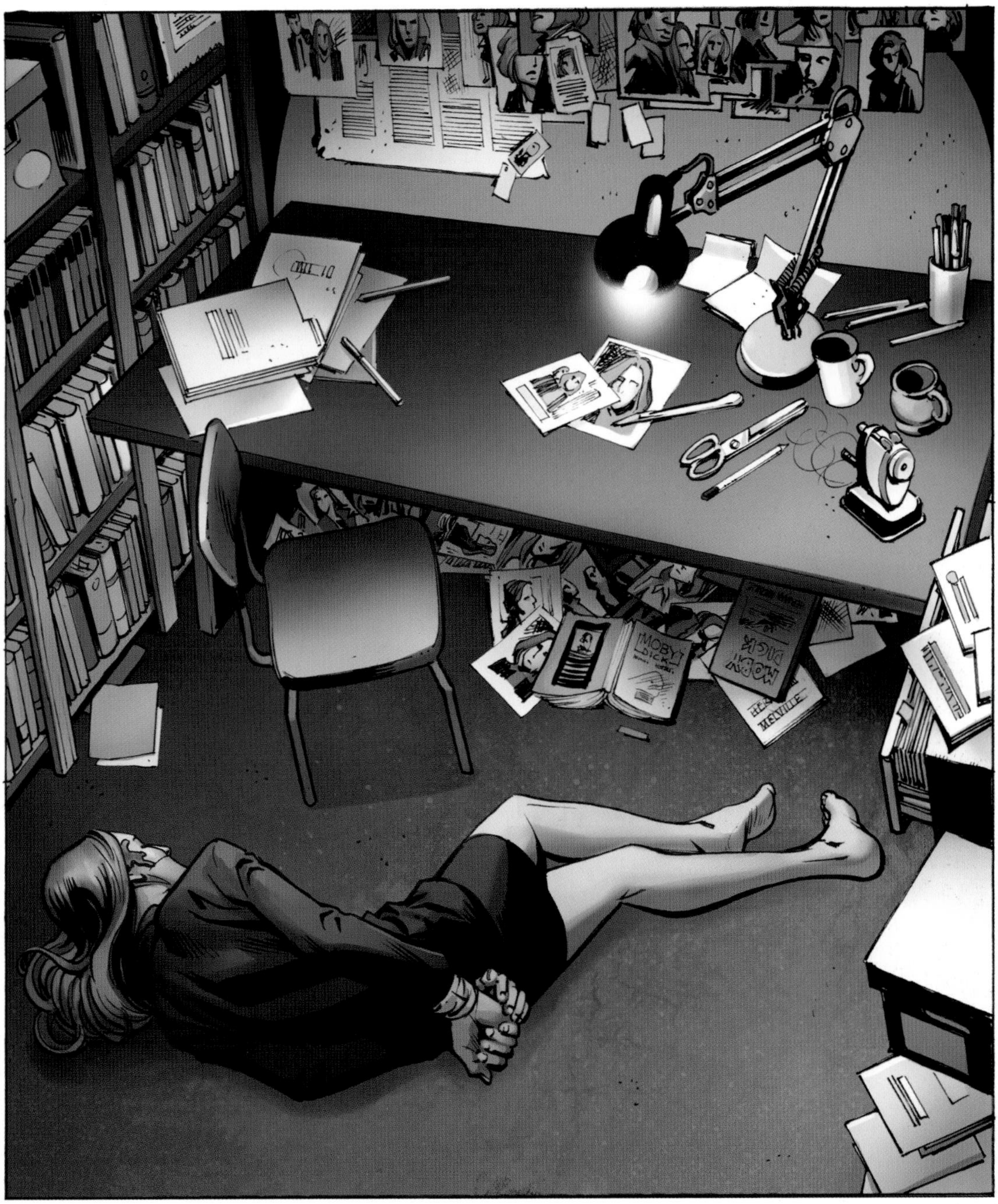
MOBY DICK
MOBY DICK
MELVILLE

THE X FILES™

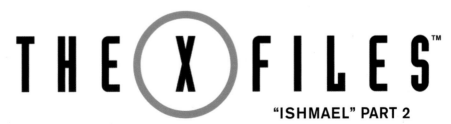

"ISHMAEL" PART 2

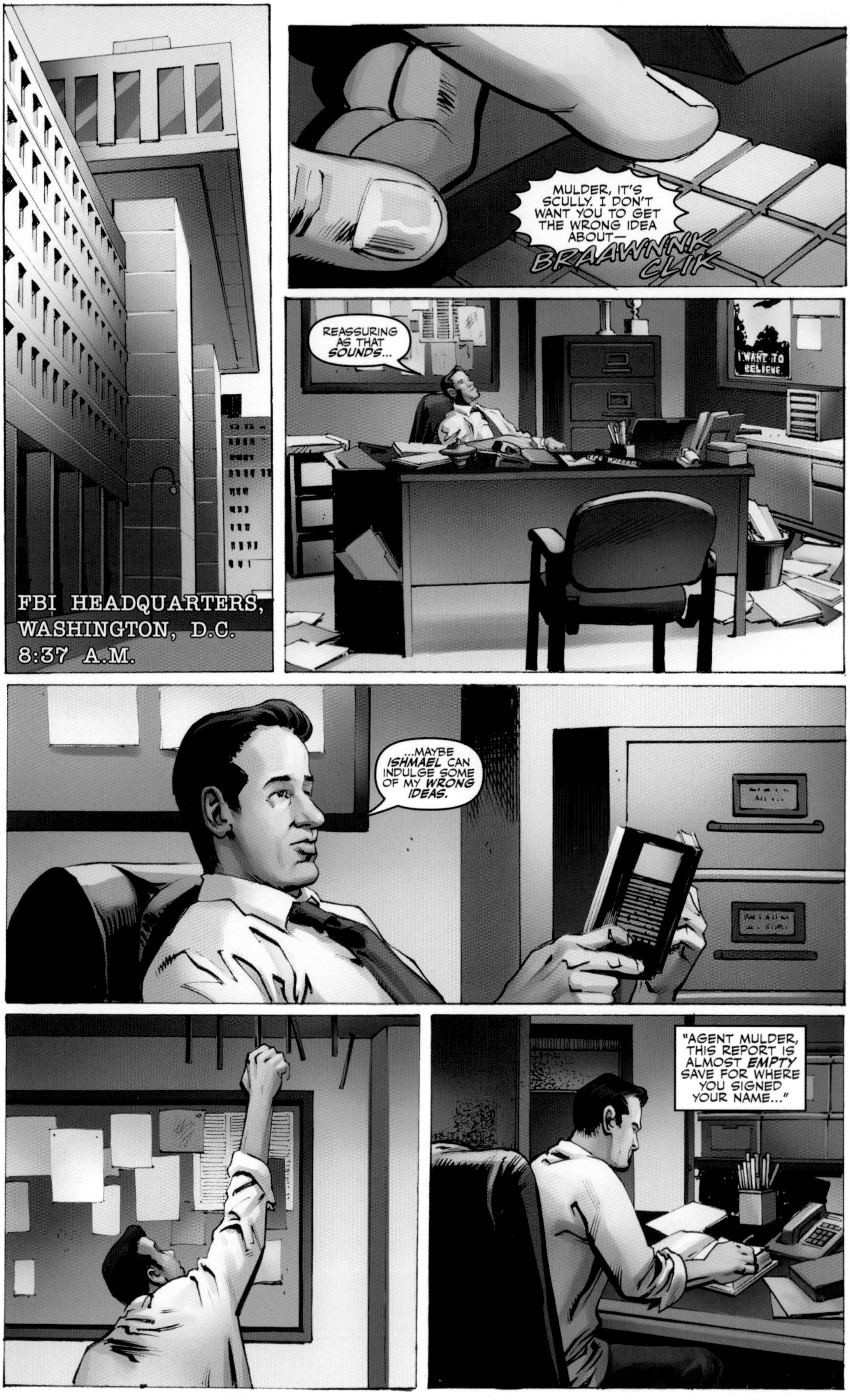
FBI HEADQUARTERS,
WASHINGTON, D.C.
8:37 A.M.
MULDER, IT'S SCULLY. I DON'T WANT YOU TO GET THE WRONG IDEA ABOUT—
BRAAWNNK CLIK
REASSURING AS THAT SOUNDS...
I WANT TO BELIEVE
...MAYBE ISHMAEL CAN INDULGE SOME OF MY WRONG IDEAS.
"AGENT MULDER, THIS REPORT IS ALMOST EMPTY SAVE FOR WHERE YOU SIGNED YOUR NAME..."

I JUST NEED ENOUGH FOR A *FEDERAL WARRANT*.

IF MY HUNCH IS *INCORRECT*, I'LL LET IT DROP.

AFTER I BACK UP YOUR FLIMSY ASSERTIONS BEFORE A *CIRCUIT JUDGE*, YOU THINK IT'LL *DROP*?

YOU WANT TO *INVESTIGATE* SOMEBODY, YOU CAN START BY TELLING ME *WHY*.

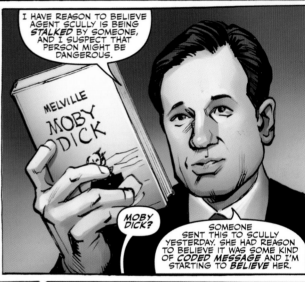

I HAVE REASON TO BELIEVE AGENT SCULLY IS BEING *STALKED* BY SOMEONE, AND I SUSPECT THAT PERSON MIGHT BE DANGEROUS.

MELVILLE
MOBY DICK

MOBY DICK?

SOMEONE SENT THIS TO SCULLY YESTERDAY. SHE HAD REASON TO BELIEVE IT WAS SOME KIND OF *CODED MESSAGE* AND I'M STARTING TO *BELIEVE* HER.

TO THE BEST OF *MY* KNOWLEDGE, SHE NEVER WENT HOME LAST NIGHT.

AND SHE HASN'T SHOWN UP FOR WORK YET THIS MORNING.

WHAT ABOUT THIS *NAME* ON YOUR WARRANT REQUISITION?

MARVIN KELLS.

THERE WAS NO *RETURN ADDRESS* ON THE PACKAGE SCULLY RECEIVED, BUT I NOTICED *IMPRESSIONS* IN THE BOOK'S BACK COVER...

I BELIEVE IT'S THE NAME OF A *TRAILER PARK* IN SOUTHERN PENNSYLVANIA.

SOMEBODY NAMED *MARVIN KELLS* RENTED A SPACE THERE LAST MONTH.

BUT THAT'S NOT ALL OF IT...

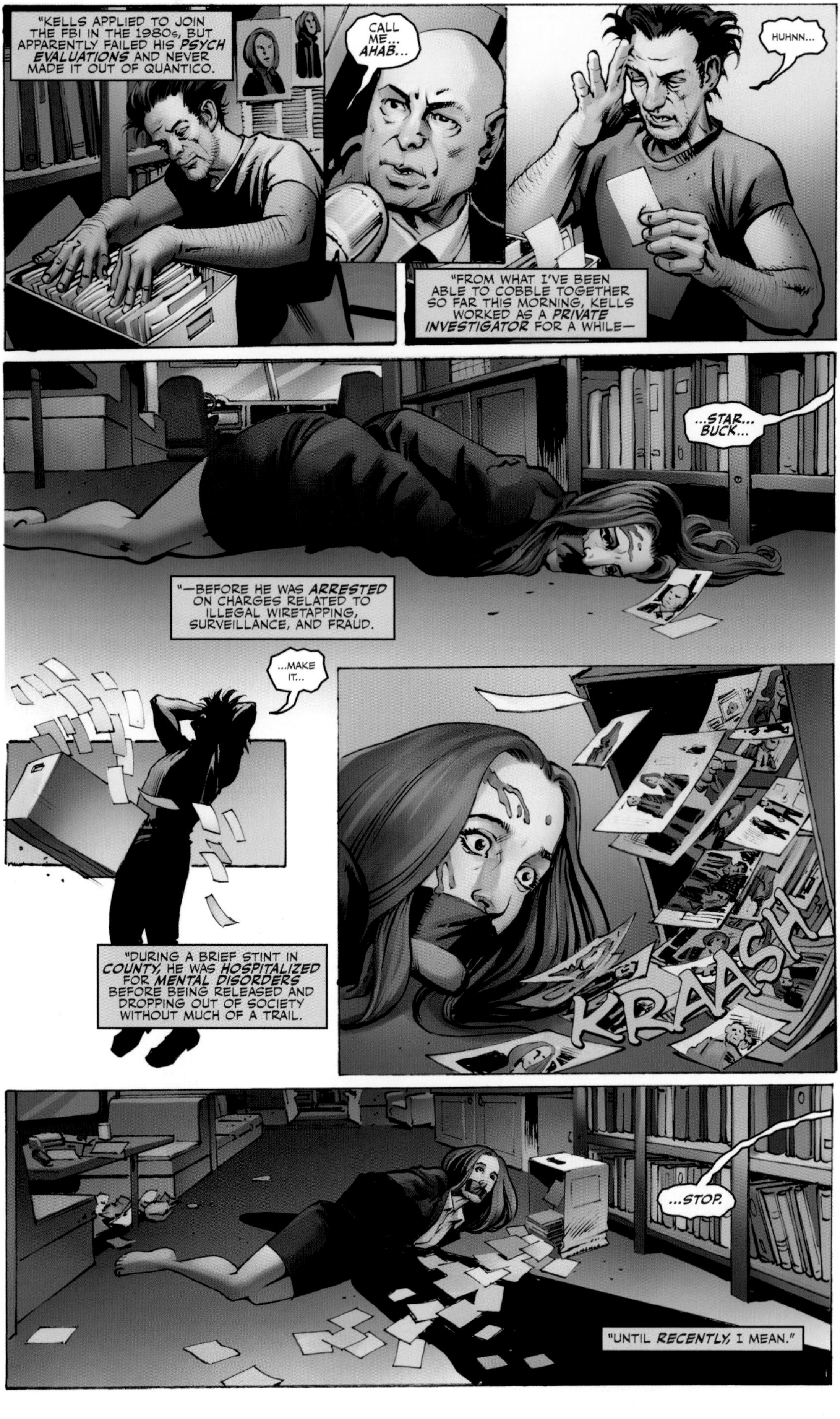
"KELLS APPLIED TO JOIN THE FBI IN THE 1980s, BUT APPARENTLY FAILED HIS PSYCH EVALUATIONS AND NEVER MADE IT OUT OF QUANTICO.
CALL ME... AHAB...
HUHNN...
"FROM WHAT I'VE BEEN ABLE TO COBBLE TOGETHER SO FAR THIS MORNING, KELLS WORKED AS A PRIVATE INVESTIGATOR FOR A WHILE—
...STAR... BUCK...
"—BEFORE HE WAS ARRESTED ON CHARGES RELATED TO ILLEGAL WIRETAPPING, SURVEILLANCE, AND FRAUD.
...MAKE IT...
"DURING A BRIEF STINT IN COUNTY, HE WAS HOSPITALIZED FOR MENTAL DISORDERS BEFORE BEING RELEASED AND DROPPING OUT OF SOCIETY WITHOUT MUCH OF A TRAIL.
KRAASH
...STOP.
"UNTIL RECENTLY, I MEAN."

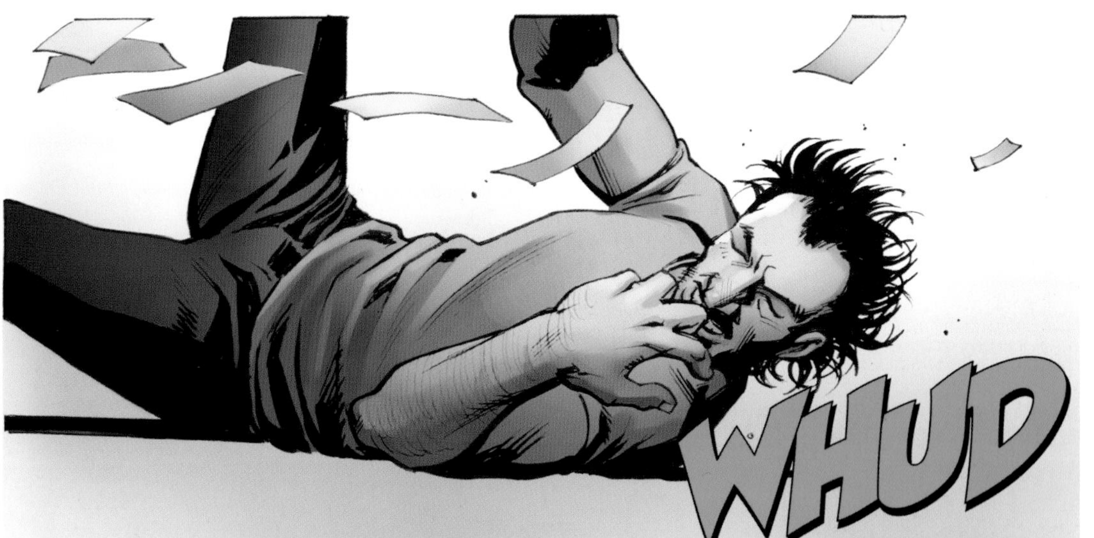
WHUD

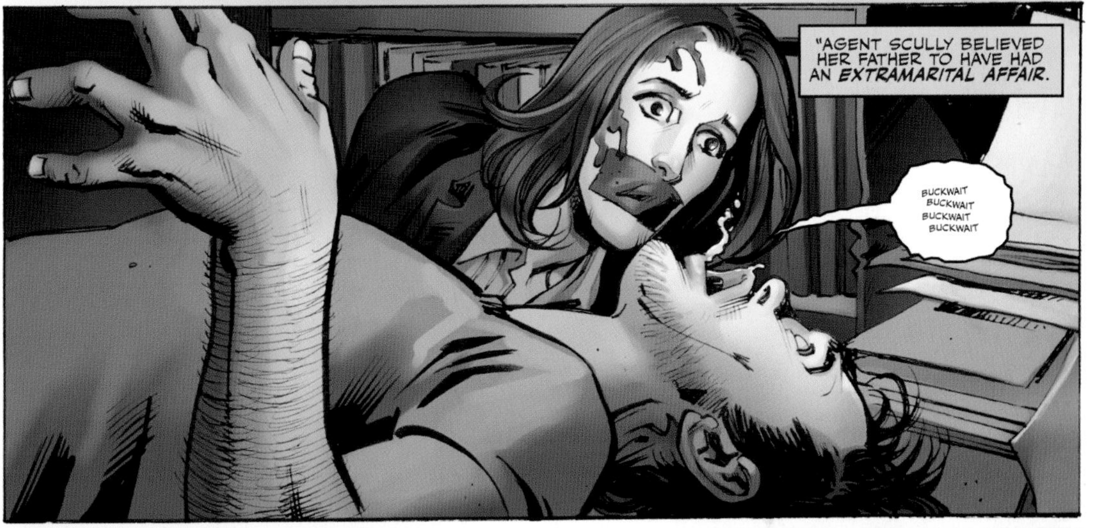
"AGENT SCULLY BELIEVED HER FATHER TO HAVE HAD AN EXTRAMARITAL AFFAIR.
BUCKWAIT BUCKWAIT BUCKWAIT BUCKWAIT

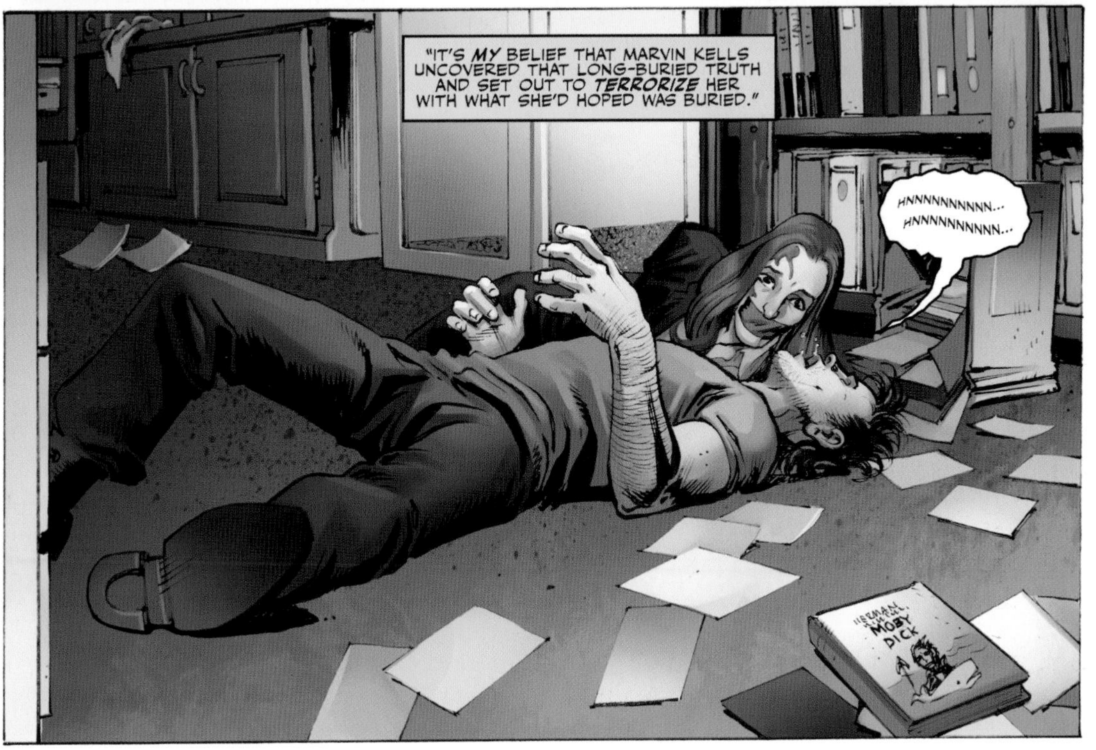
"IT'S MY BELIEF THAT MARVIN KELLS UNCOVERED THAT LONG-BURIED TRUTH AND SET OUT TO TERRORIZE HER WITH WHAT SHE'D HOPED WAS BURIED."
HNNNNNNNNNN... HNNNNNNNNNN...
MOBY DICK

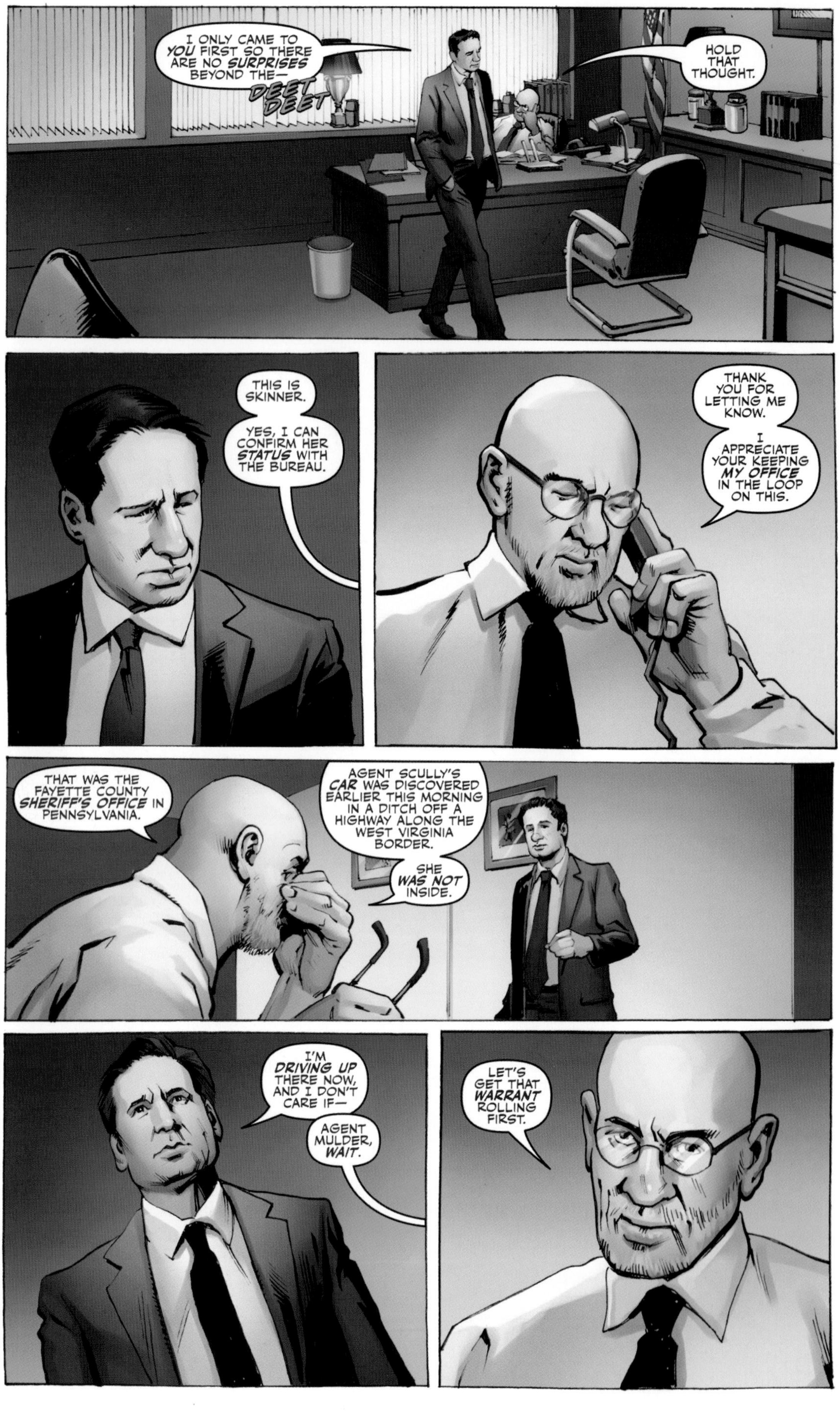

I ONLY CAME TO YOU FIRST SO THERE ARE NO SURPRISES BEYOND THE—
DEET DEET
HOLD THAT THOUGHT.
THIS IS SKINNER.
YES, I CAN CONFIRM HER STATUS WITH THE BUREAU.
THANK YOU FOR LETTING ME KNOW.
I APPRECIATE YOUR KEEPING MY OFFICE IN THE LOOP ON THIS.
THAT WAS THE FAYETTE COUNTY SHERIFF'S OFFICE IN PENNSYLVANIA.
AGENT SCULLY'S CAR WAS DISCOVERED EARLIER THIS MORNING IN A DITCH OFF A HIGHWAY ALONG THE WEST VIRGINIA BORDER.
SHE WAS NOT INSIDE.
I'M DRIVING UP THERE NOW, AND I DON'T CARE IF—
AGENT MULDER, WAIT.
LET'S GET THAT WARRANT ROLLING FIRST.

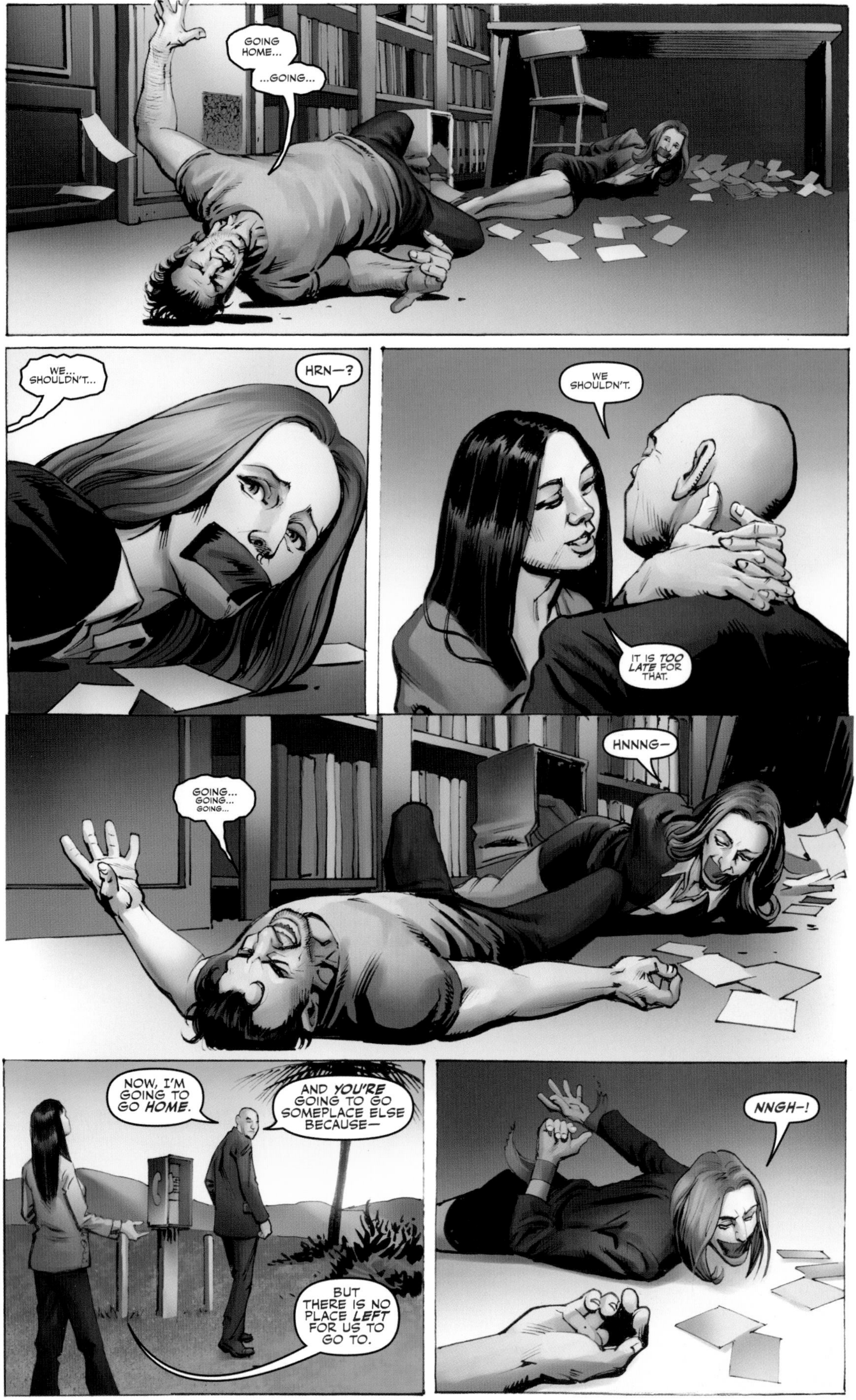
GOING HOME...
...GOING...
WE... SHOULDN'T...
HRN—?
WE SHOULDN'T.
IT IS TOO LATE FOR THAT.
GOING... GOING... GOING...
HNNNG—
NOW, I'M GOING TO GO HOME.
AND YOU'RE GOING TO GO SOMEPLACE ELSE BECAUSE—
BUT THERE IS NO PLACE LEFT FOR US TO GO TO.
NNGH—!

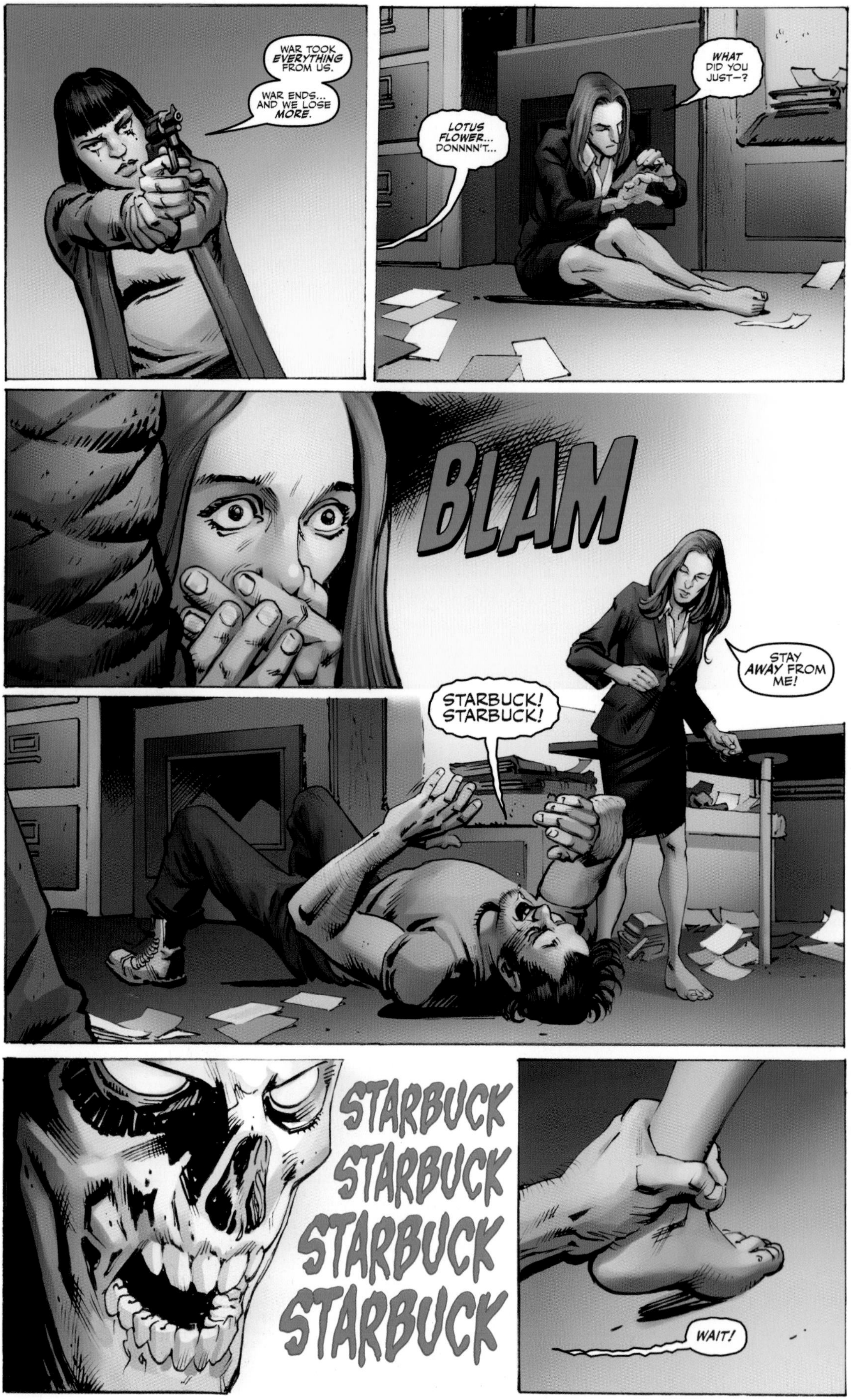

WAR TOOK EVERYTHING FROM US.
WAR ENDS... AND WE LOSE MORE.
LOTUS FLOWER... DONNNN'T...
WHAT DID YOU JUST—?
BLAM
STAY AWAY FROM ME!
STARBUCK! STARBUCK!
STARBUCK STARBUCK STARBUCK STARBUCK
WAIT!

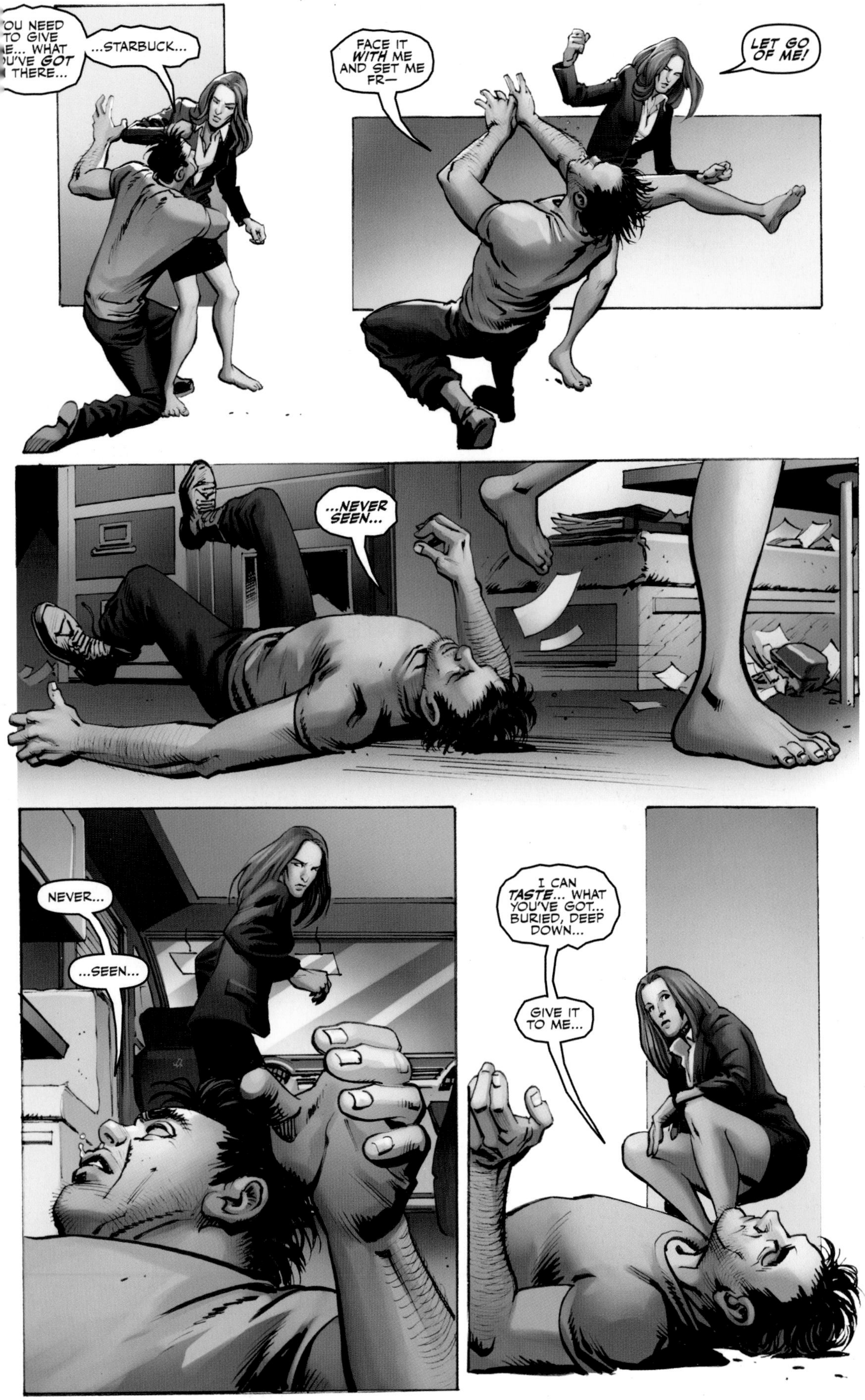

OU NEED TO GIVE E... WHAT U'VE GOT THERE...
...STARBUCK...
FACE IT WITH ME AND SET ME FR—
LET GO OF ME!
...NEVER SEEN...
NEVER...
...SEEN...
I CAN TASTE... WHAT YOU'VE GOT... BURIED, DEEP DOWN...
GIVE IT TO ME...

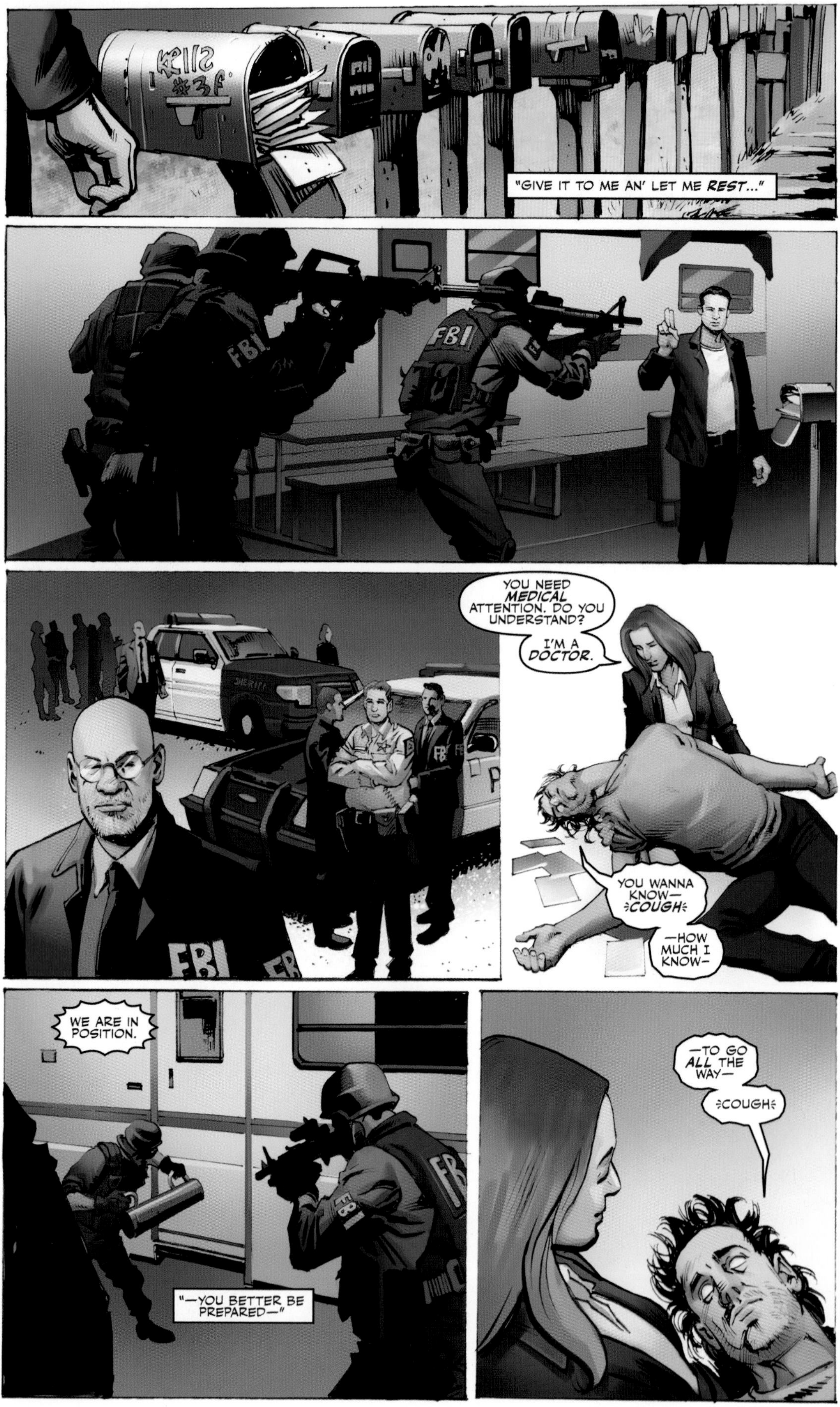
"GIVE IT TO ME AN' LET ME REST..."
YOU NEED MEDICAL ATTENTION. DO YOU UNDERSTAND?
I'M A DOCTOR.
YOU WANNA KNOW— ≑COUGH≑
—HOW MUCH I KNOW—
WE ARE IN POSITION.
"—YOU BETTER BE PREPARED—"
—TO GO ALL THE WAY—
≑COUGH≑

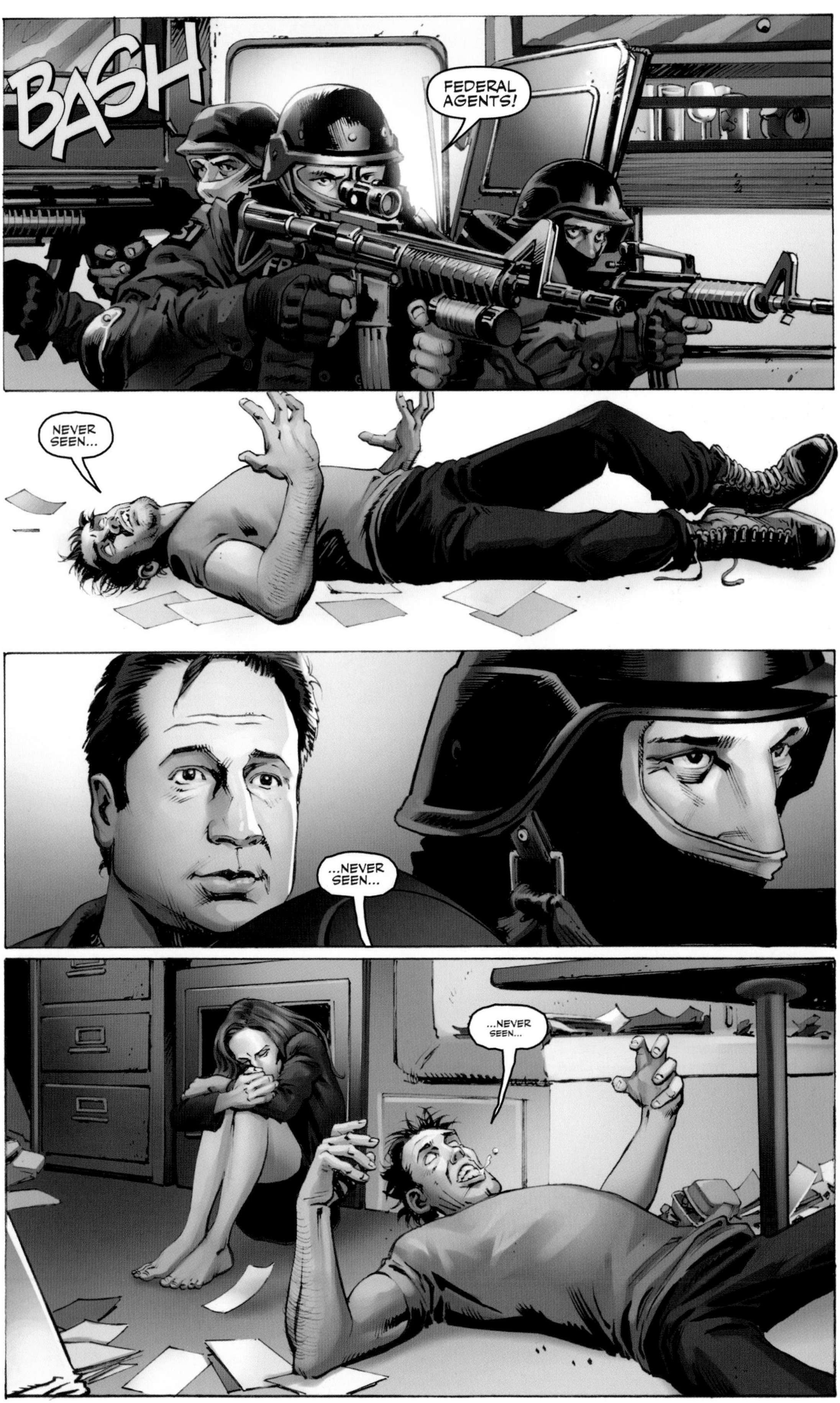
BASH
FEDERAL AGENTS!
NEVER SEEN...
...NEVER SEEN...
...NEVER SEEN...

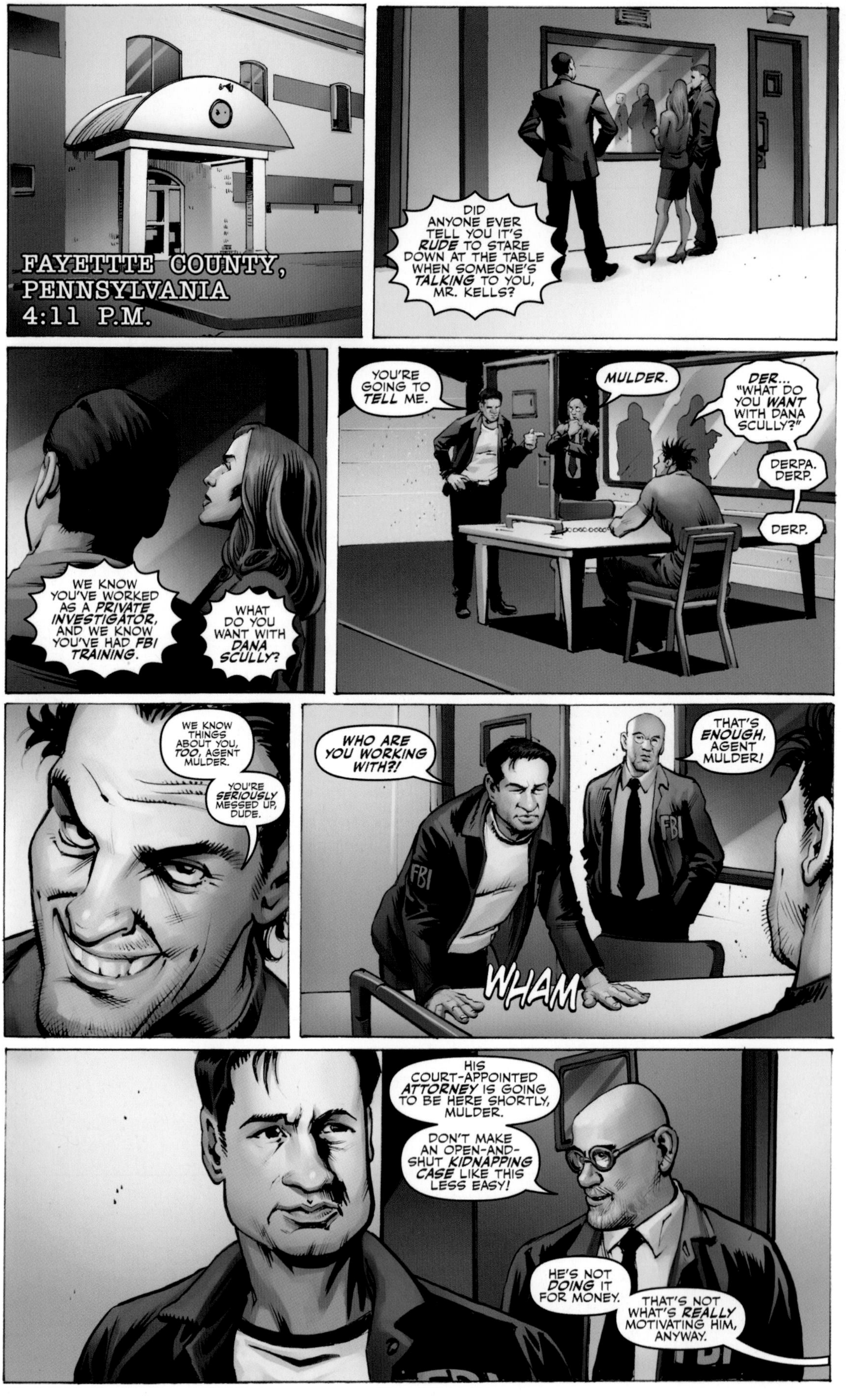
FAYETTTE COUNTY, PENNSYLVANIA 4:11 P.M.
DID ANYONE EVER TELL YOU IT'S RUDE TO STARE DOWN AT THE TABLE WHEN SOMEONE'S TALKING TO YOU, MR. KELLS?
WE KNOW YOU'VE WORKED AS A PRIVATE INVESTIGATOR, AND WE KNOW YOU'VE HAD FBI TRAINING.
WHAT DO YOU WANT WITH DANA SCULLY?
YOU'RE GOING TO TELL ME.
MULDER.
DER... "WHAT DO YOU WANT WITH DANA SCULLY?"
DERPA. DERP.
DERP.
WE KNOW THINGS ABOUT YOU, TOO, AGENT MULDER.
YOU'RE SERIOUSLY MESSED UP, DUDE.
WHO ARE YOU WORKING WITH?!
THAT'S ENOUGH, AGENT MULDER!
WHAM
HIS COURT-APPOINTED ATTORNEY IS GOING TO BE HERE SHORTLY, MULDER.
DON'T MAKE AN OPEN-AND-SHUT KIDNAPPING CASE LIKE THIS LESS EASY!
HE'S NOT DOING IT FOR MONEY.
THAT'S NOT WHAT'S REALLY MOTIVATING HIM, ANYWAY.

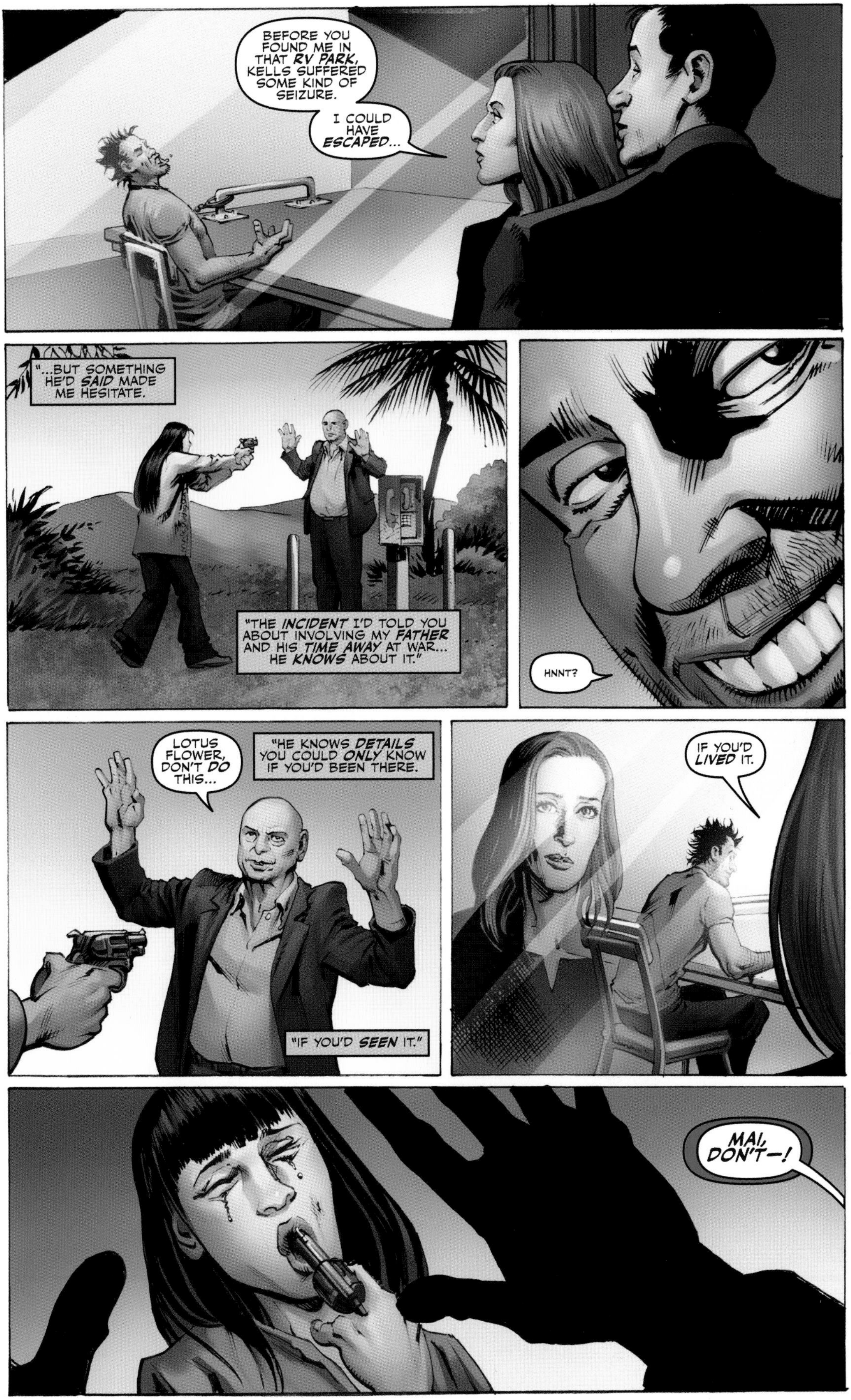
BEFORE YOU FOUND ME IN THAT RV PARK, KELLS SUFFERED SOME KIND OF SEIZURE.
I COULD HAVE ESCAPED...
"...BUT SOMETHING HE'D SAID MADE ME HESITATE.
"THE INCIDENT I'D TOLD YOU ABOUT INVOLVING MY FATHER AND HIS TIME AWAY AT WAR... HE KNOWS ABOUT IT."
HNNT?
LOTUS FLOWER, DON'T DO THIS...
"HE KNOWS DETAILS YOU COULD ONLY KNOW IF YOU'D BEEN THERE.
"IF YOU'D SEEN IT."
IF YOU'D LIVED IT.
MAI, DON'T—!

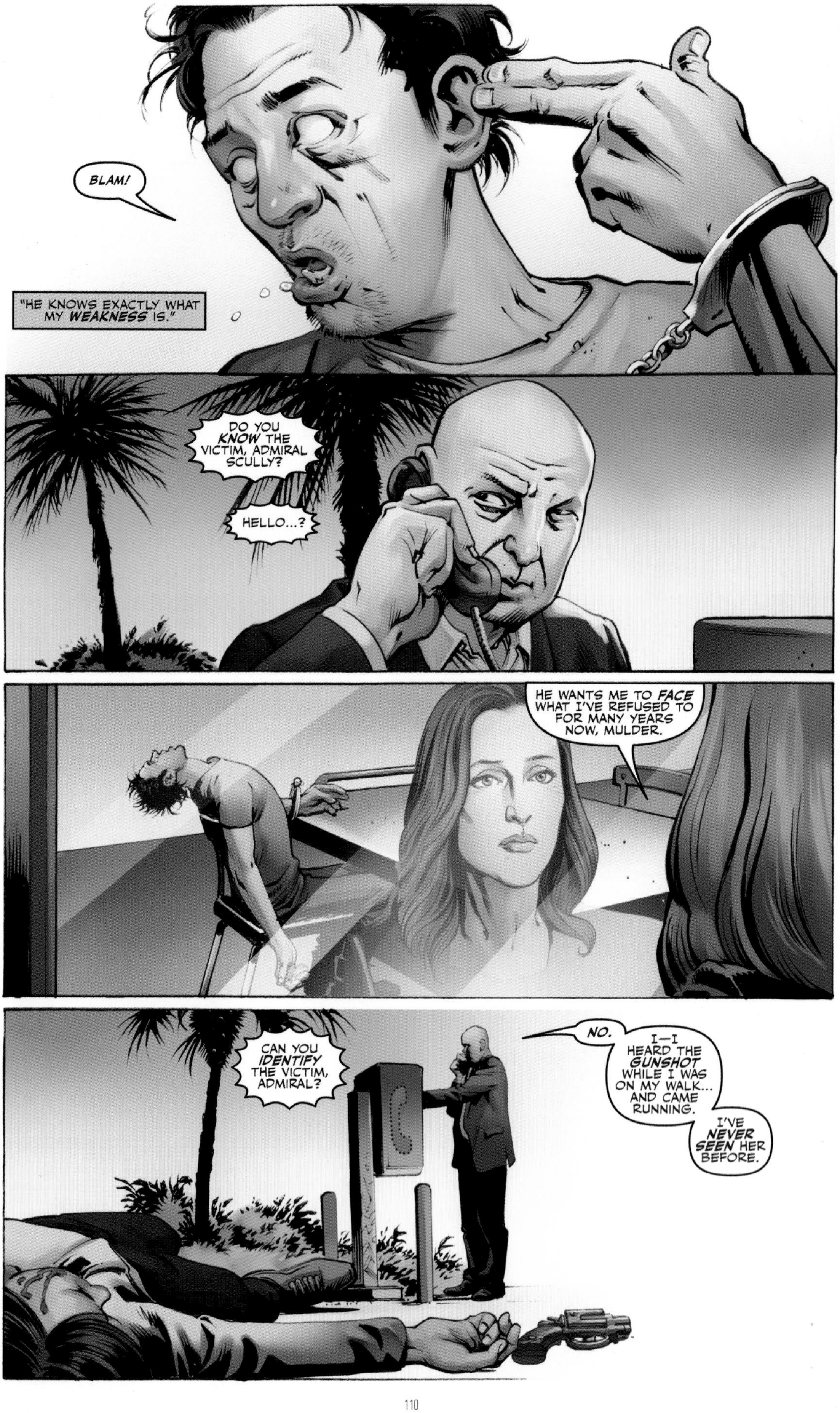

BLAM!
"HE KNOWS EXACTLY WHAT MY WEAKNESS IS."
DO YOU KNOW THE VICTIM, ADMIRAL SCULLY?
HELLO...?
HE WANTS ME TO FACE WHAT I'VE REFUSED TO FOR MANY YEARS NOW, MULDER.
CAN YOU IDENTIFY THE VICTIM, ADMIRAL?
NO.
I—I HEARD THE GUNSHOT WHILE I WAS ON MY WALK... AND CAME RUNNING.
I'VE NEVER SEEN HER BEFORE.

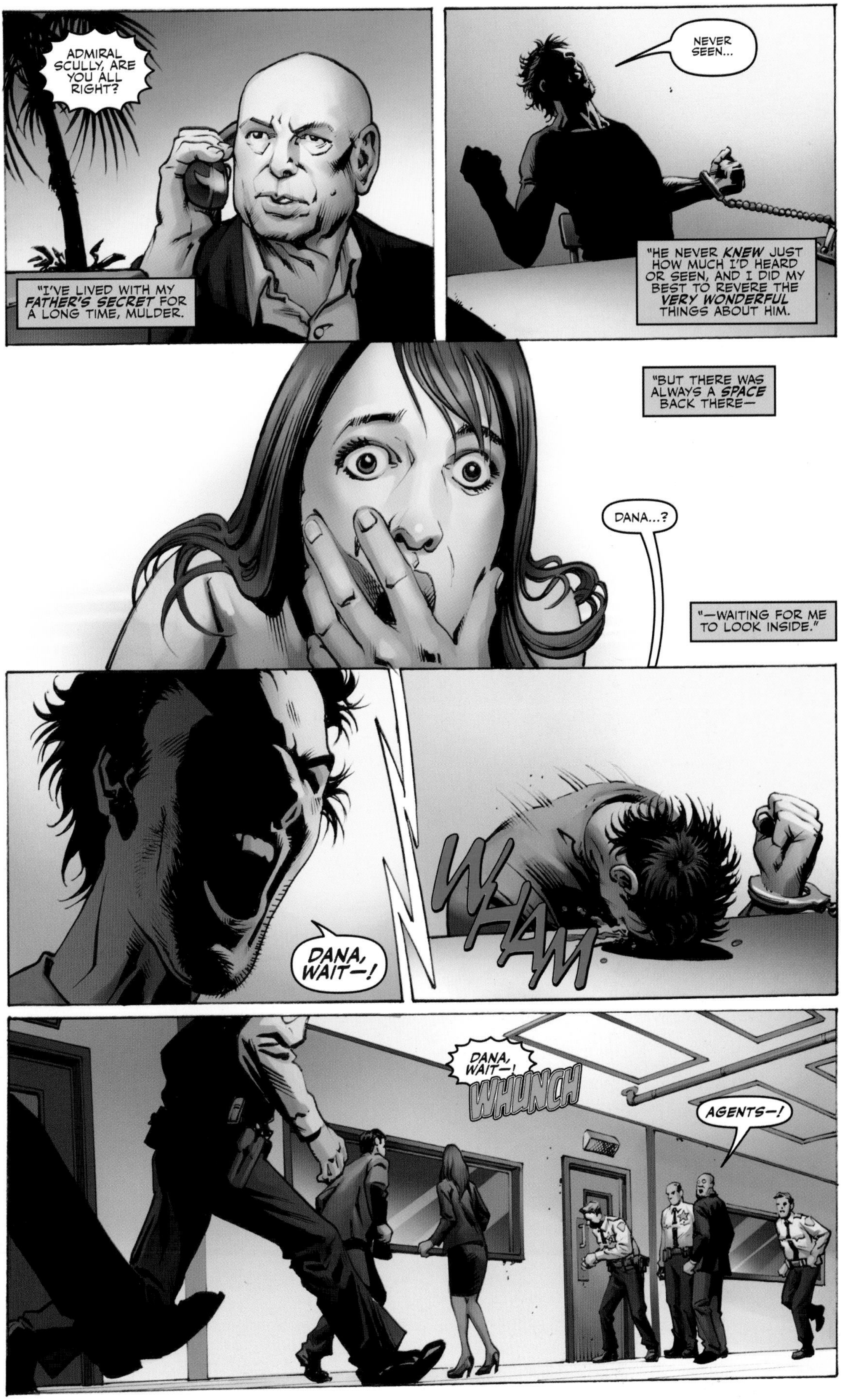

ADMIRAL SCULLY, ARE YOU ALL RIGHT?
"I'VE LIVED WITH MY FATHER'S SECRET FOR A LONG TIME, MULDER.
NEVER SEEN...
"HE NEVER KNEW JUST HOW MUCH I'D HEARD OR SEEN, AND I DID MY BEST TO REVERE THE VERY WONDERFUL THINGS ABOUT HIM.
"BUT THERE WAS ALWAYS A SPACE BACK THERE—
DANA...?
"—WAITING FOR ME TO LOOK INSIDE."
DANA, WAIT—!
WHAM
DANA, WAIT—!
WHUNCH
AGENTS—!

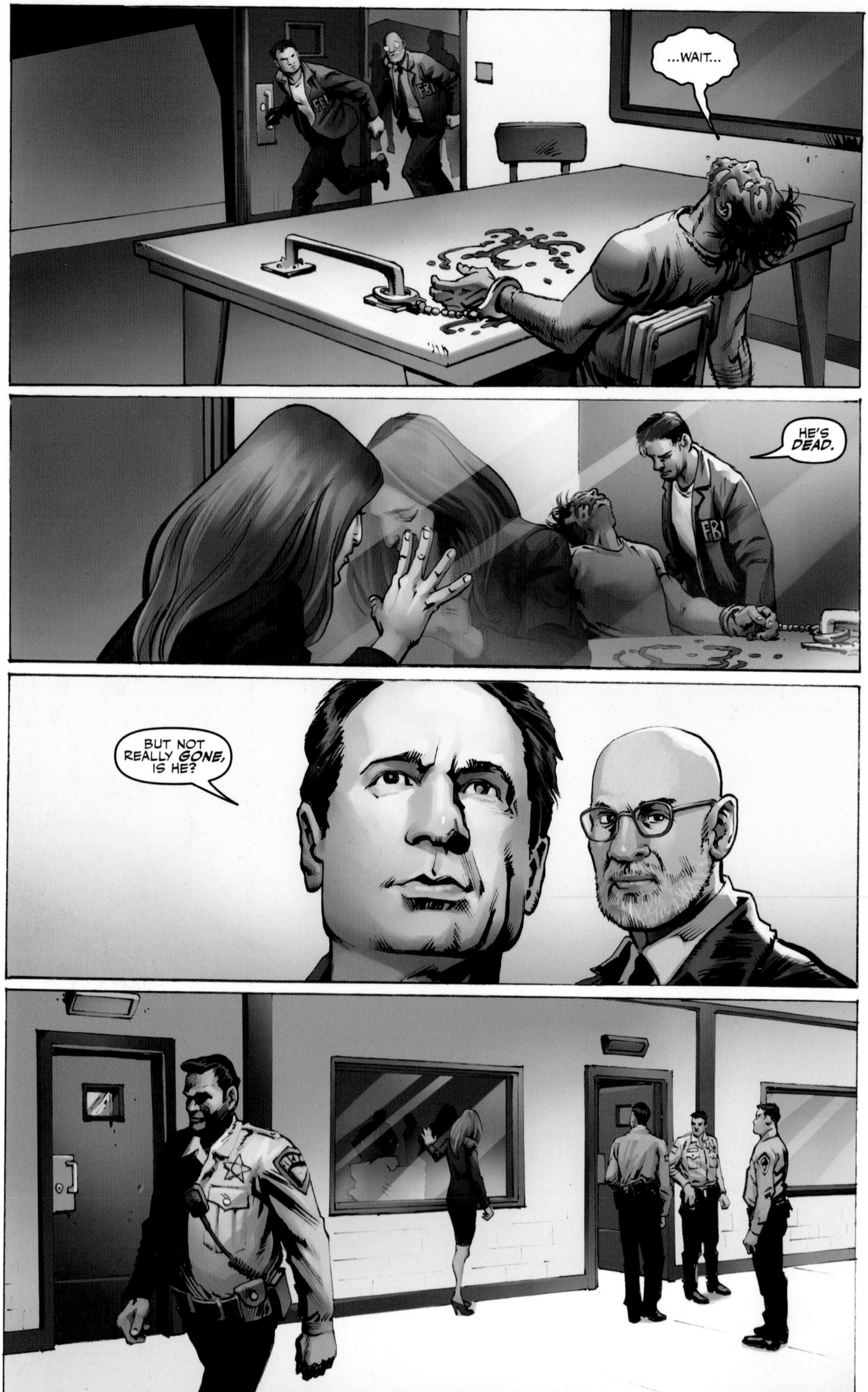

...WAIT...
HE'S DEAD.
BUT NOT REALLY GONE, IS HE?

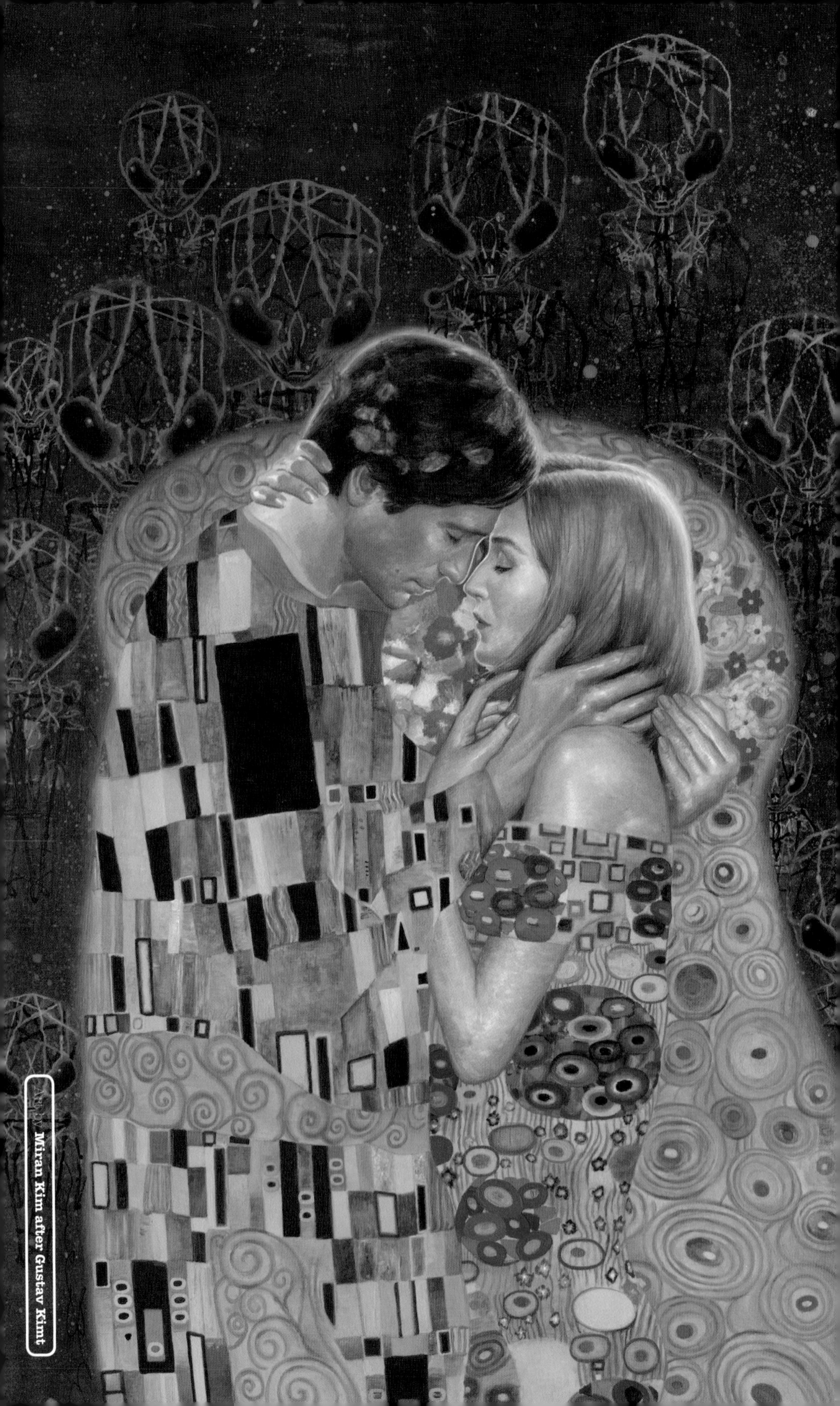

Art by Miran Kim after Gustav Klimt

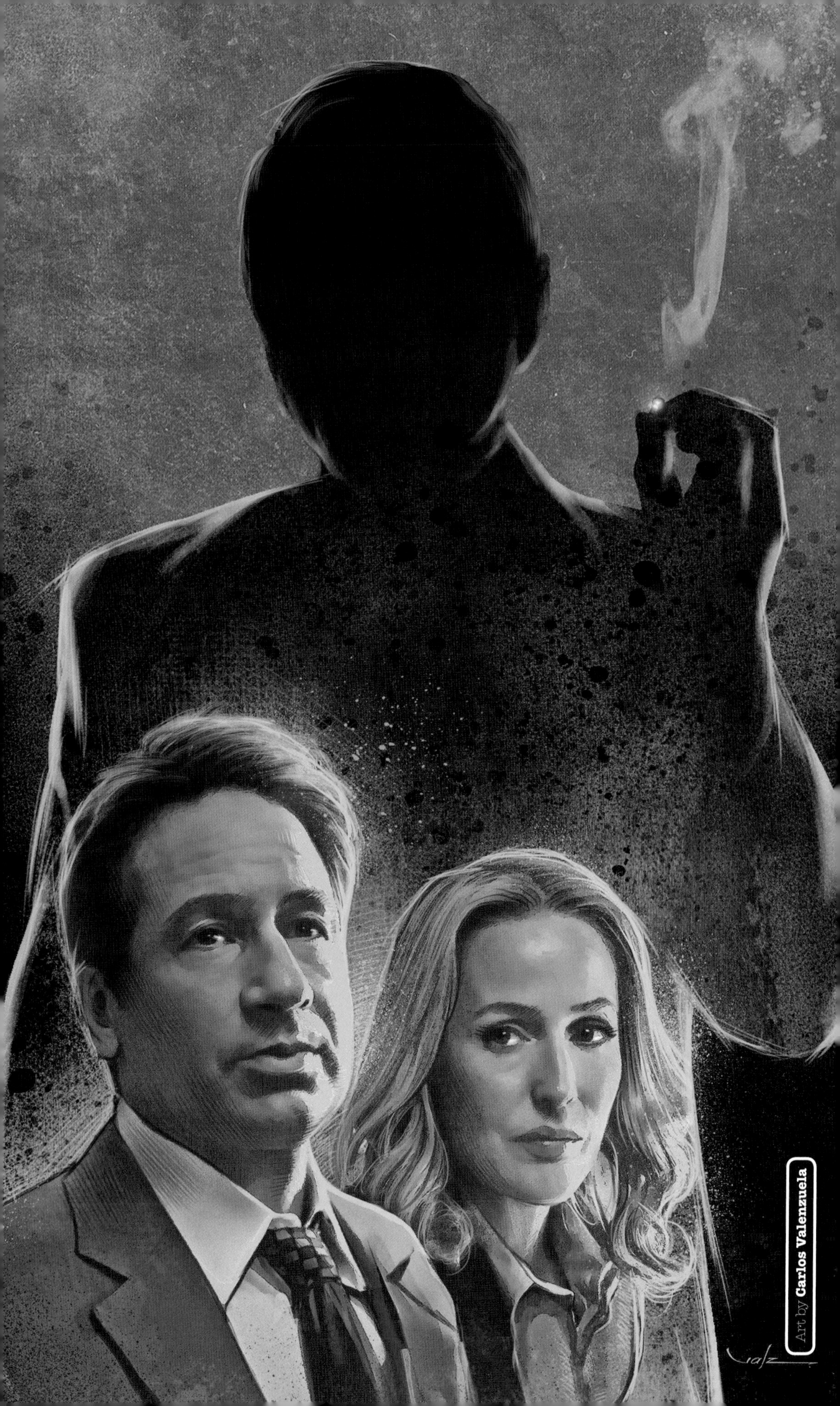
Art by Carlos Valenzuela

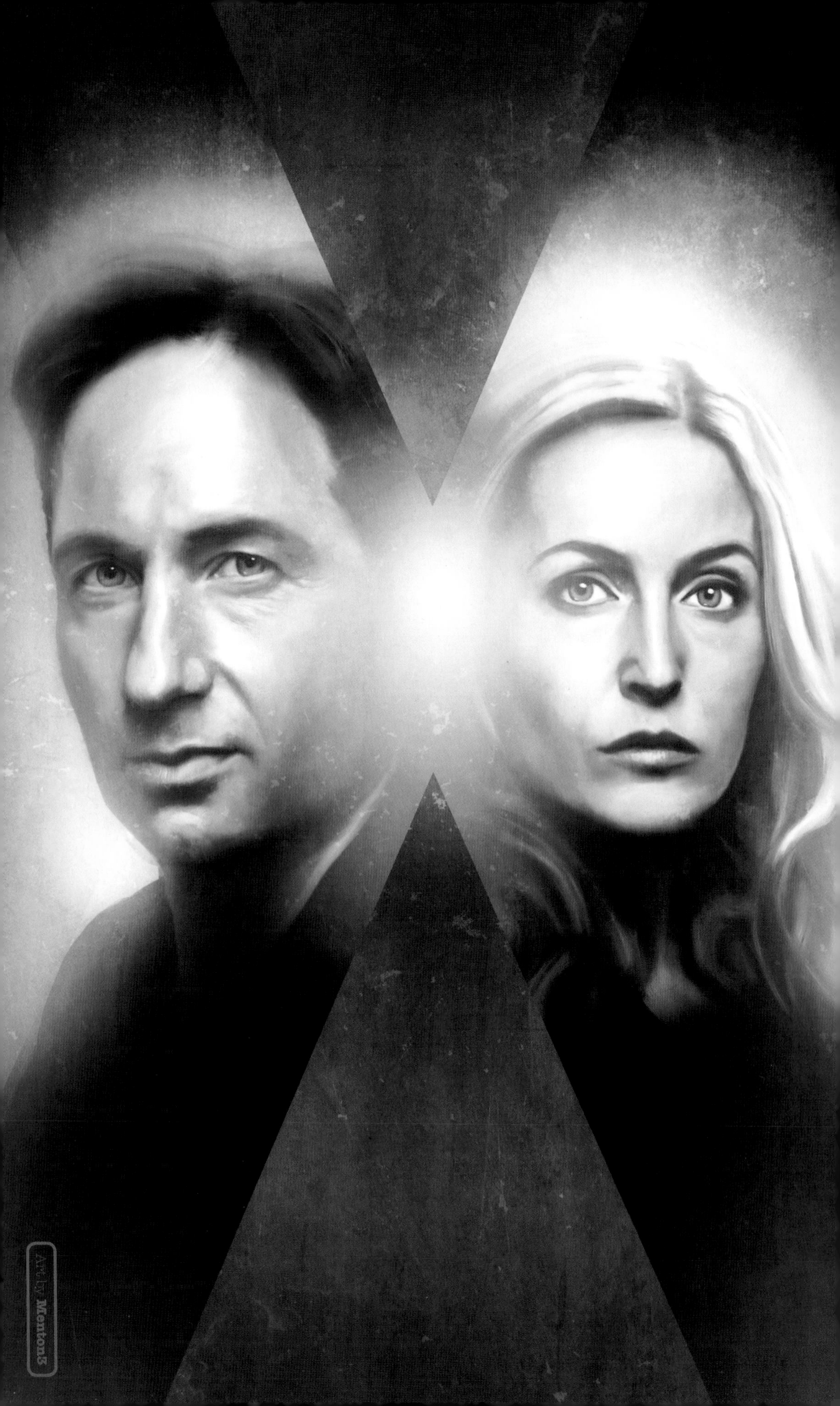
Art by Menton3

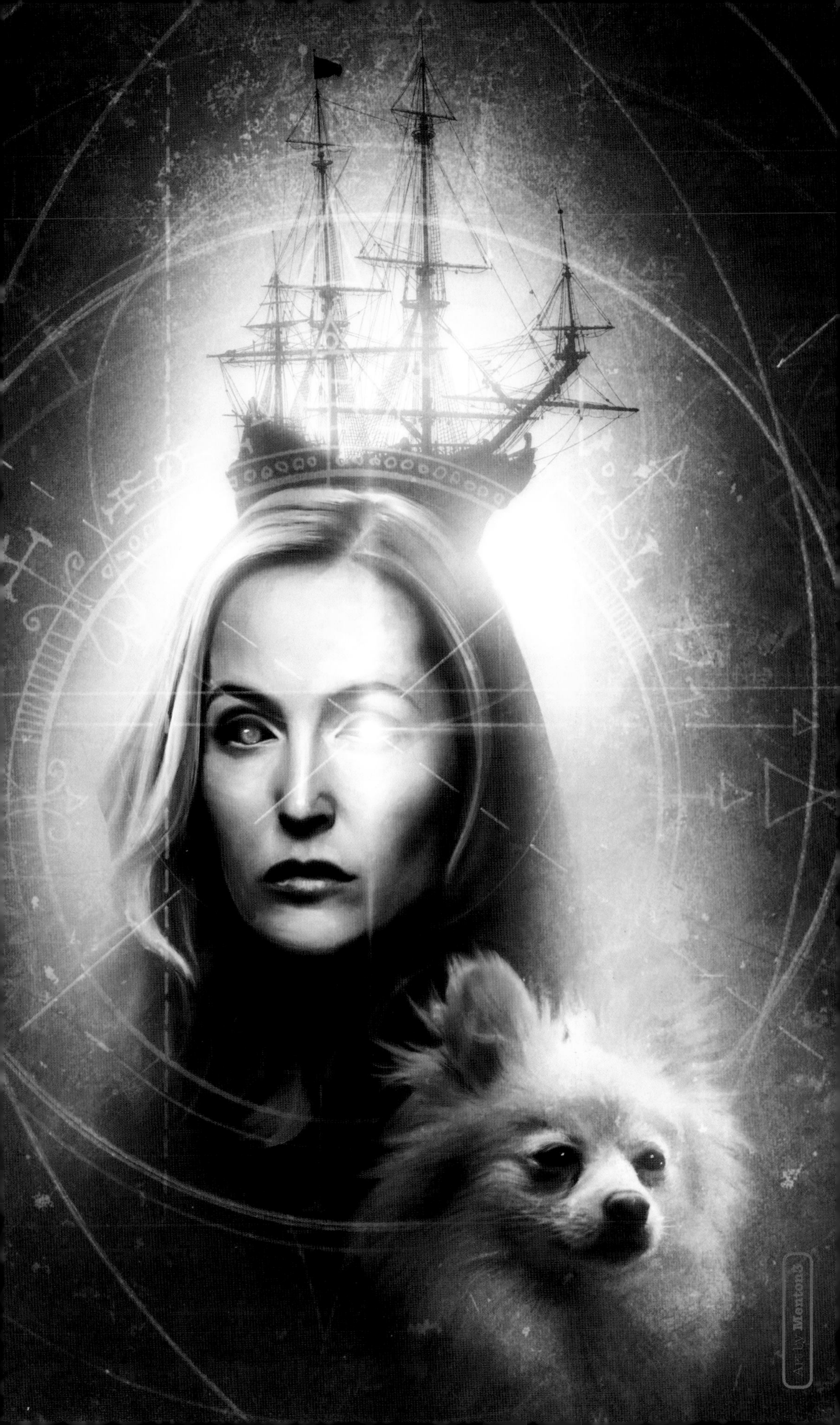
Art by Mentos

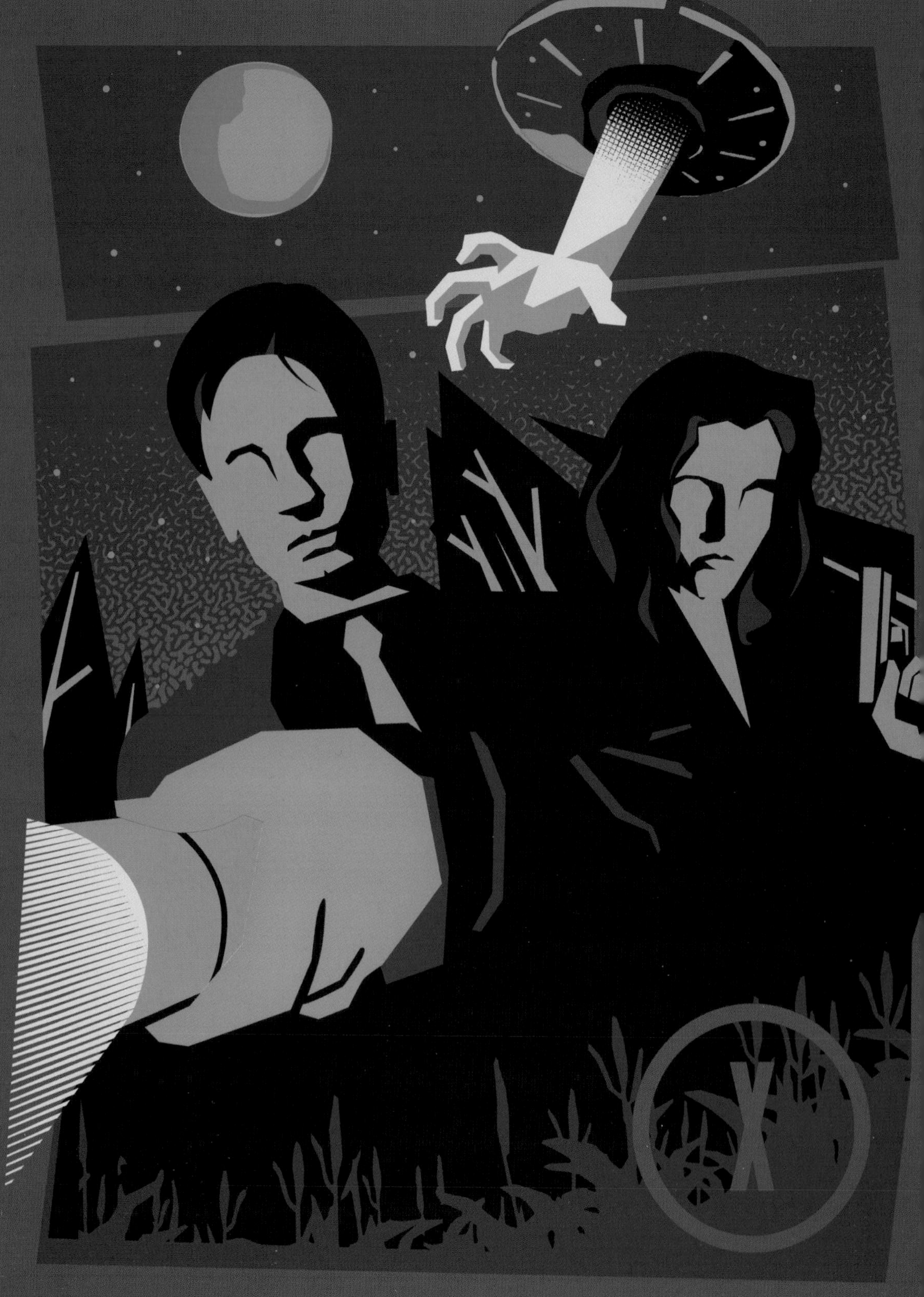

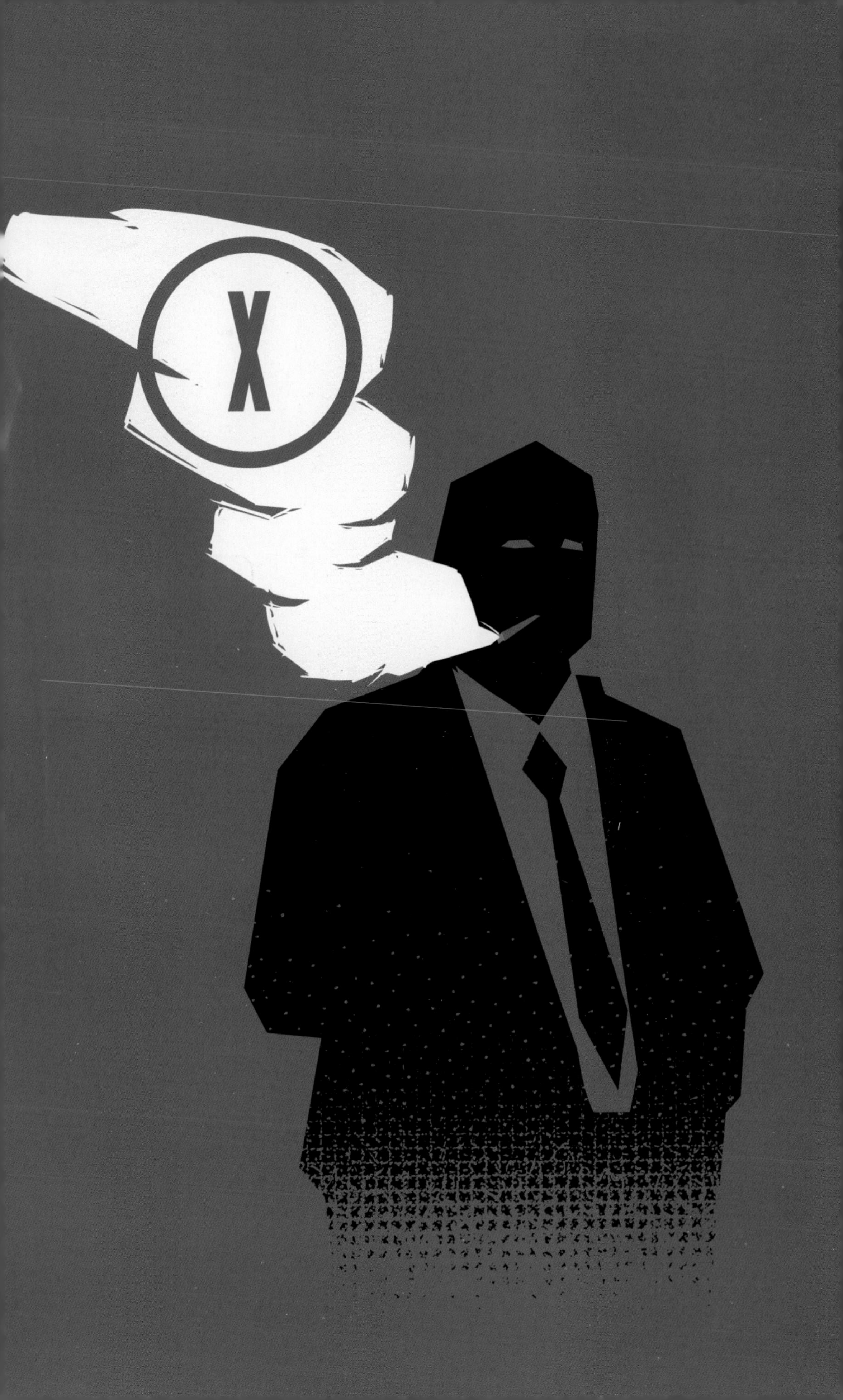

THE SEARCH FOR THE TRUTH CONTINUES

The X-Files: Season 10, Vol. 1
ISBN: 978-1-61377-751-0

The X-Files: Season 11, Vol. 1
ISBN: 978-1-6-3140-527-3

The X-Files: Year Zero
ISBN: 978-1-6-3140-236-4

The X-Files Classics, Vol. 1
ISBN: 978-1-61377-663-6